Praise for *Get the Picture*

A Natalie Portman "Natalie's Book Club" Pick

"Engrossing... Bosker explores the art scene by throwing herself in head first."
—*Time*

"One of the funniest books I've read.... [*Get the Picture* is] a dark comedy of manners... [that] exposes the often-abusive labor practices of art institutions... [and] asks deeper questions about the ways [they] now fetishize political radicalism." —Martin Gelin, *The Washington Post*

"True tales of secrecy, opacity, and outright thievery... like *Liar's Poker*, but for art." —*The Economist*

"The brilliant, hilarious prose stylist Bosker goes undercover behind the scenes of the art world.... Expect to have your perspective blown."
—*Oprah Daily*, "The Most Thought-Provoking Books of 2024"

"A page-turning romp around New York's art world... [that reveals] many of the baffling codes around intangible value, served up through genuine laugh-out-loud moments." —*Financial Times*

"A delightful book on an inspiring topic by a writer who could make dust sparkle... Immersive reporting along the lines of George Plimpton or Barbara Ehrenreich with [Bosker's] own blend of relentless curiosity, bottomless energy, and a gift for clever formulations that recalls Oscar Wilde... It could not be more fun." —*Kirkus Reviews* (starred review)

"Exceptionally accomplished... *Get the Picture* is almost a Biennale in itself, a vivid spin through a kaleidoscope of confounding, maddening, surprising, and sometimes enrapturing artworks." —*The Times Literary Supplement*

PENGUIN BOOKS

GET THE PICTURE

Bianca Bosker is the *New York Times* bestselling author of *Cork Dork* and a contributing writer at *The Atlantic*. Her writing has appeared in *The New Yorker, The New York Times, The Wall Street Journal*, and *The Best American Travel Writing* and has been recognized with awards from the New York Press Club, Society of Professional Journalists, and more.

Also by Bianca Bosker

Cork Dork

GET THE PICTURE

A Mind-Bending Journey

among the Inspired Artists

and Obsessive Art Fiends

Who Taught Me How to See

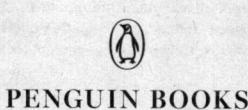

Bianca Bosker

PENGUIN BOOKS

PENGUIN BOOKS
An imprint of Penguin Random House LLC
1745 Broadway, New York, NY 10019
penguinrandomhouse.com

Two-tone image on page 243 by Christoph Teufel

Designed by Amanda Dewey

ISBN 9780525562221 (paperback)

THE LIBRARY OF CONGRESS HAS CATALOGED THE HARDCOVER EDITION AS FOLLOWS:

Names: Bosker, Bianca, author.
Title: Get the picture : a mind-bending journey among the inspired
artists and obsessive art fiends who taught me how to see / Bianca Bosker.
Description: [New York] : Viking, [2024] |
Includes bibliographical references and index.
Identifiers: LCCN 2023049037 (print) | LCCN 2023049038 (ebook) |
ISBN 9780525562207 (hardcover) | ISBN 9780525562214 (ebook)
Subjects: LCSH: Art–Psychology. | Art and society.
Classification: LCC N71 .B675 2024 (print) | LCC N71 (ebook) |
DDC 701/.03–dc23/eng/20231117
LC record available at https://lccn.loc.gov/2023049037
LC ebook record available at https://lccn.loc.gov/2023049038

First published in the United States of America by Viking,
an imprint of Penguin Random House LLC, 2024
Published in Penguin Books 2025

Printed in the United States of America
1st Printing

The authorized representative in the EU for product safety and compliance
is Penguin Random House Ireland, Morrison Chambers, 32 Nassau Street,
Dublin D02 YH68, Ireland, https://eu-contact.penguin.ie.

For my parents

CONTENTS

The Heads

An Introduction

To be fair, everyone warned me it was a bad idea. What I wanted to do was not only impossible but vaguely dangerous, they intimated. They didn't come right out and threaten my safety or anything. My reputation, well-being, and livelihood as a journalist—that, however, was another story.

It's not like I was trying to expose CIA spies or anything. I was dead set on infiltrating what turns out to be a nearly as paranoid group: the art world.

I'd gotten obsessed with understanding why art matters, if it does, and whether quality time with a few smears of colored rock on stretched cloth—a "painting" as it's more commonly known—can really transform our existence.

And how better to find out, I figured, than by handing myself over to the culture fiends who live for art: Artists who hyperventilate around their favorite colors. Up-and-coming gallery owners who max out their credit cards to show hunks of metal they think can change the world. I wanted to study the fanatics who fly their art with them on vacation and see if I could feel fireworks when I looked at art—instead of, as was often my experience, the urge to holler at the artist to *just tell us what you mean.*

Except as practically everyone in the art world saw it, what I wanted—this is where the warnings came in—was to stick my nose where it didn't belong. "You'll make some powerful enemies," warned a seasoned art collector. "It's not worth it for you living in New York." Then an art dealer volunteered that he'd have no qualms trashing my reputation—personal, professional, and psychological—if I wrote anything he disagreed with. *Nice career you've got there—be a shame if something happened to it.*

IN RETROSPECT, I blame my grandmother's carrots. I'd never have gone poking around the art scene if it wasn't for them.

There I was: Early thirties, living in New York, with a nice career in journalism and a flawlessly optimized routine, albeit one that didn't make room for art. And yet once upon a time, art had been my thing. Growing up in Oregon, I was a sun-starved little weirdo who painted obsessively, showed art in local shows, and flirted with applying to art school. I had it all planned out: I'd move to New York to squat in an East Village loft with my painter-lover-muse, who'd feed me cigarettes for breakfast and poetry for lunch.

Then serious Bianca grabbed the wheel. In college I took econ—never art history—with an eye toward the kind of career that would come with a dental plan. I graduated with a vague hope that I'd become an art appreciator if not an art maker, which lasted until I moved to New York and actually started seeing art on a regular basis. Whoa, was I out of my league. My first trip to galleries in Chelsea left me with the distinct impression I'd wandered into a private party by mistake. Pretension hung in the air like an unacknowledged fart, and at each show, I felt two tattoos and a master's degree short of fitting in. I went to museums, which seemed friendlier, yet as I wandered through halls of oil-painted nobles and brooding marble statues, I felt overwhelmed by everything I didn't know—the people, the periods, the -isms. Whatever love of art I'd felt shriveled in comparison to the bewildering feeling that I was woefully uninformed and thus doing it wrong. As the years passed, my visits to art shows became dutiful, and I let friends drag me along while I fidgeted awkwardly in front of exhibits I didn't understand. Bit by bit, art and I became estranged. Eventually, we were no longer on speaking terms.

Then, a few years back, I was home in Oregon purging my mom's basement when I yanked open a drawer of yellowed papers and my breath snagged in surprise. There, with their delicate black commas for feet and green whirling-dervish stems, were my grandmother's dancing carrots.

My grandmother made a point of telling me the carrots' origin story whenever I visited. My grandmother—this is my dad's mom—was a twentysomething Jew in Warsaw when Hitler invaded Poland. By the time she was my age, she'd lost relatives to mass graves, narrowly avoided concentration camps, and been forced to labor in Soviet coal mines. She ended the war in a displaced-persons camp in Austria, where, though she was an economist with no children of her own and no artistic inclination that I know of, she started teaching art to the kids. Once, as a special occasion, she helped them organize a dance show, scrimping paper to make costumes, which had to be cheery but politically innocuous: She rejected apples (red could suggest Soviet sympathies) and birds (which could evoke bombers) in favor of carrots (which still got her interrogated by some overzealous official). She ended up in Illinois, where she worked long hours selling suitcases at a small shop in Chicago and spent her days off at the Art Institute collecting postcards of impressionist paintings she kept in old shoeboxes. In her eighties, after she retired, she picked up painting. One of her most treasured pieces was a watercolor she'd made of three skipping carrots that hung above her kitchen table until she died.

I'd forgotten all about those carrots, but now their prancing feet kicked loose a jumble of memories: afternoons with my grandmother sketching still lifes, our shared love for Seurat, a time when life felt limitless. I remembered sitting for hours in her kitchen studying the graceful swing of the carrots' bodies while she described the art classes she'd taught in the camp, then proudly read aloud letters from her former students, who kept writing to her sixty years on. I never thought to ask her why she'd felt a pull toward art. The way she held forth on the carrots didn't leave room for questions: Art simply wasn't optional, or a luxury, but a necessary part of life. I felt a sharp stab of regret that I didn't know the feeling.

I stuffed the carrots back into the drawer, but those sneaky vegetables followed me back to New York and trailed me around as I settled back into my routine. The carrots stomped their feet when I ate takeout at my desk. They crossed their arms when I texted from the toilet while listening to podcasts at 2x speed. Their wagging orange heads insisted that something was missing, that my life was dull dull dull compared to what I'd once imagined it could be. While I tried to answer emails, they danced my mind round and round the puzzle of why my grandmother had treated art, arguably the *least* essential thing, as essential—what she turned to when life turned itself inside out. I couldn't shake the carrots. Worse, I couldn't shake the sense that my predictable, ruthlessly optimized life had started to feel maddeningly claustrophobic. The carrots stirred up an idea: What if art could stop the walls from closing in?

MODERATION HAS NEVER been my strong point, and once I got the itch for art, I cannonballed in. I thought art might inject beauty into my blah routine—"wash away from the soul the dust of everyday life," as Picasso supposedly said it could.

My awakening was rude.

I know I'm not supposed to admit this, but between you and me, a lot of the art I saw was barely recognizable as art. In the hushed halls of a renowned art museum, I beheld a giant stuffed bear with horns and a nose ring, and felt my heart go out to a mutilated chair. I spent a particularly disorienting evening at Bridget Donahue, a Lower East Side gallery my detective work had revealed to be the womb for all things cool. At the gallery's opening, I squeezed past neckbeards and ironic tube socks to squint at a plasticky black seagull dangling ankle-height on a string. "Alcohol helps," volunteered a guy next to me. (It didn't.) I stayed long enough to catch a performance by the artist—a burly, middle-aged man who padded out into the gallery in a Snow White costume, climbed halfway up a metal ladder, and started mumbling into a microphone about an "animatronic goat trapped in an inflatable bush of cooked pubic hair."

I don't know what else to tell you about the art. It was there. I was there. I knew enough not to utter the two phrases guaranteed to brand

me a lowbrow loser ("But is it art?" and "A five-year-old could do that").
But beyond that—I stared at it and got nothing but the familiar feeling
that everyone got the punch line except me. I mean, was art just whatever people with expensive graduate degrees said it was? What made it
good? Were those stupid questions? What did these geniuses nodding
thoughtfully at the world's worst Snow White impersonator know that
I didn't?

I stalked artists on Instagram, scoured art blogs, subscribed to every newsletter I could find, and forced myself to make small talk with
strangers at art openings. I went to art talks, art shows, art museums,
and art galleries (which is a fancier way of saying art *stores*). I hit up
every remote acquaintance vaguely connected with art to catch up
over coffee, then pelted them with questions. But all over town, the art
refused to speak to me. It sat there, smug and withholding, whispering
an inside joke to everyone but me.

Try a simpler hobby, I encouraged myself. Bake bread. Pickle. And
it was tempting, really it was, only I couldn't stop thinking I had to be
missing out on something major because the art I was seeing inspired
such extremes of devotion—on the part of not only viewers (who'd do
things like hock a car to buy a painting) but also the artists themselves. I knew artists had a centuries-old reputation for being masochistic obsessives who'd sell a kidney for a tube of paint, but that looked
relatively painless compared to what I was witnessing. I met artists
who skipped meals, sleep, surgeries, having kids, seeing dying parents,
and putting a roof over their heads in order to pour every last drop of
themselves into making their work, with no end in sight except the art
itself. "Our relationship ended because he was really concerned about
the future of our finances and I was really concerned about the future
of my paintings," said one painter, who had uprooted her life in

Georgia to move to New York—not for a lover or a job or friends but because, as she put it, she "wanted to be where all the paintings were." Most artists I met were working at least two jobs, and their art lived better than they did, sleeping soundly in the studio while they woke up on a friend's couch covered in cat pee. And for what? Beyond the hand-ful of acquaintances they convinced to come to their studios, their art rarely got seen. They had to do mental math to decide if they could afford a bagel, and the advice they got was to "give up now." Yet they kept giving everything they had to make objects that were supposed to show us something, communicate something, *do* something. And it drove me crazy that, despite a long relationship with art and a very expensive education, I couldn't clearly discern what that was.

I'd never met a group of humans willing to sacrifice so much to create something of so little obvious practical value. With all due re-spect to my grandmother, I'd always thought of art as a luxury—I mean, it can't clothe you, feed you, or be used to kill predators. But when I asked artists why they made art, they made it sound like I'd asked them why they eat food. "There's, like, zero other choice." Or: "It's just natural, like how I have black hair." And: "Because I feel like if I don't pay attention to that, it will kill me." Being an artist wasn't a choice, it seemed. As a sculptor friend-of-a-friend told me over dinner one night, "The people who are canonized—it's not because they're great artists but because it's life or fucking death for them."

You might be thinking that all sounds a bit much, but then you, like me, might be surprised to learn that scientists are right there with artists in insisting art is fundamental to being human. Art is one of our oldest creations (humans invented paint long before the wheel), one of our earliest means of communication (we drew long, long, *long* before we could write), and one of our most universal urges (we all engage with art, whether preschoolers, Parisians, or paleolithic cave dwellers). I began to notice that art—or what scientists dispassionately call "human-made two- or three-dimensional structures that remain unchanged"—was everywhere: hung over the register at the hardware store, spray-painted on a bakery window, cockeyed in a dive-bar bathroom. As humans, we've filled our lives with art since practically forever. The earliest known painting keeps getting older, but the last time I checked, archaeologists had traced the oldest portrait to a cave in Indonesia where, around 45,500 years ago, artists put their finishing touches on a fat figure with purple testicles for a chin. In other words, before Neanderthals went extinct, before mammoths died out, before we figured out how to harvest food or heal bloody wounds, humans applied themselves to painting the portrait of a warty pig. "It is clear that the creation of beautiful and symbolic objects is a characteristic feature of the human way of life," wrote the biologist J. Z. Young. "They are as necessary to us as food or sex." I, for one, didn't feel the necessity of art in the way I felt my stomach growl for a juicy burger. But reading that only made me more curious to experience whatever soul-rattling epiphany supposedly lurked in a sculpture of a dirty mattress.

I kept trekking to art shows, hoping to be moved, and while the art didn't do it for me, the humans around it fascinated me. Like people who join cults or travel to space, art connoisseurs had the peculiar aura of the transformed. They'd *seen* things. Things that would *blow* your *mind*. Whatever it was had to be some heady stuff, because their reality bucked all the usual laws of nature. People held vicious grudges against the color blue or got breast implants and called it artwork. They got really excited about being really uncomfortable and took classes on pretending to be sequins. These artists frowned on my idea of beauty—there was beauty, one insisted, in a grotesque medley of chopped dildos glued to a canvas. More than that, they insisted my search for beauty was pitifully off base. "Beauty is my fucking nemesis," spat a sculptor in one of many lectures I'd get on the evils of the *b*-word. They also had very different ideas about what was a valuable way to spend one's time. "A big part of my practice at home," said one, "is examining the garbage there and both being repulsed and inspired by it."

It was thrilling. Or maybe it was bullshit? Either way, my life looked drained of color by comparison. My days were efficient. Theirs seemed expansive, like they'd accessed a trapdoor in their brains. Should I live that way? *Could* I?

Art connoisseurs insisted I couldn't afford not to. They pitied me: They said I lacked "visual literacy," which they swore was downright dangerous in a world so saturated with pictures. After all, there's probably no time in history when we've been inundated with so many images. In the Middle Ages, we might have stared at the same pained portrait of Jesus on a church altar week after week, year after year, but now images crowd us when we check Instagram, throw themselves in our paths from billboards, and leer at us from packs of frozen peas— all hoping to exert influence. The people I was meeting worshipped the idea of an "Eye," by which they didn't mean the organ, but a painstakingly cultivated outlook that allegedly enables you to see lots that doesn't meet *the* eye, like who'll be the next Picasso or what's transcendent about a middle-aged man climbing up a ladder to lecture about burnt pubes.

I hit the books. I read memoirs, investigations, biographies, and histories. I learned that art museums evolved out of aristocrats' palaces and that Piero Manzoni canned his own shit for a sculpture. But what I didn't learn was why. Why bother with art? Everything I read started from the assumption that Art Was Important, and if I didn't know why, too bad. "One of the best things about art is that it doesn't have to appeal to everyone," said one art critic dismissively in an article that maintained the problem with art isn't that it's too elitist but that it's not elitist enough.

I took some comfort in the fact that I wasn't the only person I knew who could rub two brain cells together and yet was baffled by contemporary art—as in, art made by artists living right *now*. (Though technically the words *modern* and *contemporary* are synonymous, the term "modern art" counterintuitively refers to older art—generally made between the 1860s and 1970s—whereas "contemporary art" refers to everything that follows.) I started to think someone needed to get in there and ask some fundamental questions about how art works, then explain it to the rest of us. And I started to wonder if that someone could be me.

I fired off emails to artists, gallerists, curators, and collectors, hoping to get schooled and then swept up in their passion. I was hungry to learn how to engage more deeply with everything from Rembrandt paintings to *The Ren & Stimpy Show*. Eventually, I'd reach out to a wider cast of characters: conservators, psychologists, neurologists, the lucid-dreaming guide at an artists' retreat I attended. But I was especially curious about the obsessives who control the nerve center of what's called "fine art"—a distinction I'd learn is as solid as mud, but a label that's nonetheless applied to painting, sculpture, and other kinds of visual art of the sort you see celebrated at museums, galleries, auction houses, and universities. These fine-art fiends intrigued me because they play such an outsized role in determining which artworks go from obscurity to the pantheon of illustrious cultural artifacts. These are the people—the "Heads," I'd been told they called themselves—

who shape art history and, while they're at it, shape us: our idea of art, who makes it, and why we should bother to engage. I waited excitedly to hear from them.

The response I got back was unequivocal: Butt out. Lots of people didn't bother to reply at all. There were a couple of gallerists who emailed saying they'd be happy to meet, then ignored all my follow-ups, never to be heard from again. A few brave souls sat down with me, but only on the condition that everything they said was off the record. "Honestly, any little thing could just end me," said the owner of a virtually unknown gallery, who asked me not to mention his name. An artist, barely out of grad school, said she was scared to talk to me—of what, I wasn't sure. I've done reporting in China, where there is a deep distrust of foreign journalists, not least because talking to one could get you thrown in jail. I'd had an easier time sniffing out answers in Chengdu than Chelsea.

Every once in a while, my Deep Throats murmured warnings that I should get out before it was too late. "Things that pass for ethical in the art world would be criminal anywhere else," said one art dealer. People who'd spent their careers in the art world described it as a "big con," "fucking horror," "quagmire of shit," and "the world's biggest high school." Scratch that: A gallerist who'd taught at a high school assured me his colleagues were way worse than high schoolers—"*Their* ignorance is nowhere near as entrenched."

A word to the wise: Nothing gets a journalist's undivided attention like hinting something is rotten to its core, then clamming up. It's like seeing your neighbor whistling "Oh, What a Beautiful Mornin'" while he pats down freshly dug earth and incinerates a pile of clothes. Um, yes, I have a few questions. I realize that talking into a tape recorder while a reporter lobs questions isn't most people's idea of a relaxing afternoon. But I found the fear, the reticence, the cageyness that seemed to pervade the art world bizarre. And tantalizing. Artists broke out in hives if you asked them to explain their work. Gallerists hid the prices, then refused to sell you a piece, even if you could pay for it. Curators turned a sickly green when you mentioned the words "general public," and critics often wrote about the art in code. ("Indexical marks of the artist's body" would be "finger painting" to you and me.) What happened to art being a "characteristic feature of the human way of life"? Why keep people out? Why keep *me* out?

I couldn't stop wondering what secrets lurked behind the gleaming white walls. Were these gatekeepers trying to protect the sanctity of a singular spiritual oasis? Or were they just trying to hide the fact that these turtleneck-wearing culture peddlers were carrying out the world's most audacious con? The more I was told to stay away from the art world, the more determined I was to get inside it.

I began to develop a plan. A pushy, you-can't-be-serious plan.

BEFORE YOU GO any further, I feel obliged to offer my own warnings. I didn't heed the advice to stick to the party line. I didn't discover the joy of impenetrable art theory. I also didn't come around to the argument, which I heard a lot, that explaining art will deprive it of its magic.

What I did do, over a period of several years, is disown my normal life and discover just how messy "fine art" can be. I attached myself to brush nerds, color lovers, Eyes, Heads, and artist groupies, and learned what keeps them up at night. I bled over canvases, lost patches of skin to a sculpture, and let a nearly naked stranger sit on my face in the name of art. I worked as a museum guard protecting a pile of dust and learned why scientists call art a "biologically essential tool." I got drugged, dared, shamed, shushed, and befriended by art obsessives who treat paintings like vital organs and know how to find beauty where we least expect it. In the process I discovered another existence, one where the act of looking is an adventure.

Part I

The Machine

CHAPTER ONE

My plan was this: I wanted to go work at a gallery, the snootier and more influential the better. I know, I know—who did I think I was? "A normie philistine" (my prospective employers' words) can't just show up at an art gallery demanding a job—*especially* not in New York City. But I'd tried cracking open books and quietly lurking in the corners of galleries, and I'd gotten nowhere. I wanted to see art, not just stare in its direction; I wanted to develop an Eye. I knew from past experience that there was no substitute for learning by doing, and the all-consuming passion of the compulsive lookers who signed their souls over to art had me convinced: To get at the truth about art, I also needed to understand the art *world*—the throbbing jumble of genius, money, and love that the artists I spoke with nicknamed "the machine."

By my calculation working at a gallery was the ideal first step since gallerists saw all parts of the machine. They scoped out artists, schmoozed collectors, and buddied up to museums. Best of all, a friend

of mine who knew the international gallery scene assured me I was su-
premely qualified for an entry-level gallery-attendant role. "You have," he
said approvingly, "an excellent resting bitch face." And yet for months I
hit only dead ends. I spent the summer chatting to as many art pros as
would meet with me, and after emailing half the population of Brooklyn—
the epicenter of the city's artsy and avant-garde—I finally managed to
unearth some gallerists who weren't allergic to talking to an unfamiliar
journalist. After peppering them with questions about art, I'd gently
steer the conversation to all the reasons I was desperate to work for them.
I offered to get their coffee, dry cleaning, *anything* to get inside.

It was going about as well as an FBI agent wearing his badge to a
job interview with the mob. The word *spy* came up more than once. I
tried applying to assistant jobs I found online, with the idea that I'd
explain the whole "spy" situation once they met me, but that was before
a gallerist broke the news that even a "no-name artist" looking for an
unpaid studio assistant would get a hundred applications, and any
opening at a gallery would get approximately three times that many.
No wonder no one wrote me back.

Then, a glimmer of hope: A woman who ran a cool gallery in Chinatown *loved* the idea of letting me come shadow her. There was talk
of after-parties and learning to suss out which customers wanted you
to be a little mean to them and how, in the art biz, "you're kinda always
trying to extract information, but, like, with a martini in your hand." I
emailed her about setting up a date. I followed up about setting up a
date. I never heard a peep from her again.

But I did get an email from someone named Jack Barrett, who ran
a gallery called 315 in downtown Brooklyn. The woman who ran the
cool Chinatown gallery had apparently mentioned me to Jack, and
Jack asked if I'd like to speak. I would. Very much.

I'd never heard of 315 Gallery, which says more about me than Jack, but when I mentioned his name, people universally sang his praises. He was a rising star who "saw through the bullshit," had a "cool program," and was not only "really sweet and nice" but also "in it for the long haul." His gallery, an out-of-the-way spot for the in-the-know, focused on "emerging" artists, a polite euphemism for up-and-coming artists who you probably don't know and may never hear of. Jack gave lots of artists their first chance to show in the city, which immediately piqued my interest. I was more curious to witness the convulsions of art history being born than to hear the romanticized myths of the conquering heroes, and Jack was exactly the sort of person who helped the Andys and Jean-Michels of today become the Warhols and Basquiats of tomorrow. Plus, Jack possessed one extremely attractive quality that set him apart from nearly everyone I'd contacted thus far: *He* was interested in meeting *me*.

I WENT TO SEE Jack on the sort of suffocating August afternoon when even the air rubs its sweat on you. His gallery was up a steep flight of stairs on the second floor of a slouching building in downtown Brooklyn that shared a street with Global Praise and Deliverance Ministries, Foye Princess Hair Braiding, Sako Amy African Hair Braiding, Diallo Nene Hair Braiding, Nu-Expressions Hair Salon, Top Nail Design, and—two horsemen of the gentrification apocalypse—a natural wine boutique and an Edison-bulbed café that didn't sell coffee but farm-fresh specialty third-wave Colombian pour-over coffee.

I found Jack at an angular white desk overlooking his one-room gallery, dwarfed behind a giant Mac computer. He had dirty-blond hair, fawn-like features, and, though he was just shy of thirty, I would have carded him before serving him booze. He wore a mock-turtleneck over boxy pink pants and purple sneakers that snaked up his ankle like an orthopedic brace. I'd been told he was *the* most fashionable male art dealer, but to my untrained eye, his look reminded me of a toddler dressed for a moon landing. Clearly I had a lot to learn.

Jack leapt up from his desk to take me on a tour of his current show: five works by three artists, including an animatronic drum set that bashed itself rhythmlessly and a wearable shrine made of antlers, cinderblocks, marshmallows, and soil (not dirt, I noted—*"soil"*). We paused to contemplate a pair of gold-and-black lines that shimmied and swerved along one whole wall. This was, in Jack's words, the artist Guadalupe Maravilla's "wall-based piece."

I stared at the artworks and nodded politely. My mind was a gaping black hole, a blank void of nothingness. It was precisely the type of art I didn't get but wanted to.

Jack settled himself at his desk while I wedged myself behind him on a low gray couch jammed between a filing cabinet and a minifridge. I hadn't figured out how to comfortably balance my notebook on my knee before Jack launched into a primer on navigating the New York art scene. "I really don't like the whole sort of like cold Chelsea vibe," he announced. He'd interned at a Chelsea gallery in college, an experience that must not have sold him on the art world because, after graduating, he'd opted to get a master's degree in psychology and counseling instead. After grad school he'd been in a slash career phase—working in fashion showrooms slash at a friend's start-up slash doing freelance photography—when a friend persuaded him to split the lease on a space and start putting on art shows. The friend immediately bailed for a job at a swanky gallery uptown, and in the four years since, Jack had basically run 315 solo—because, he said, "I don't make enough money to hire someone."

For the next four hours, I scribbled in my notebook while Jack rattled off facts and survival tips. Installation art was harder to sell than photography, which was harder to sell than painting, and abstract painting (which doesn't aim to depict the real world) could be harder to sell than figurative painting (which, like "representational painting," does aim to depict something real). Galleries typically split each sale fifty-fifty with the artist, which still didn't come out to enough that Jack could work at his gallery full time. Like a lot of young gallerists, he juggled a classifieds' section worth of side jobs—hanging other galleries' exhibits, photographing their shows—and his gallery was only open from 12:00 to 5:00 p.m., a holdover from when, until recently, he'd had to jump on his bike and book it to the dinner shift at a South African restaurant nearby. Not that Jack was in it for the money—"If I could turn my space into a nonprofit space and still do what I do, I would," he said. 315 was about community. "That's the meaning of this space: It's able to be a space where people can come and gather. Talk. Converse. Enjoy each other's company. Meet new friends. Be exposed to new ideas." Oh, and—no big deal—Jack thought the art he showed could change the world. "I think art has the ability or power to move culture, which I think actually really changes peoples' lives." He hinted, obliquely, at grand aspirations to shape art history, even as he emphasized that "maybe *one* artist that I work with over the course of forty years will, like, 'make it' kinda thing."

I had the distinct impression that Jack was going places. He spoke about art with a blasé intimacy that suggested he'd mastered the rules, mapped out the hierarchies, and—despite his nonchalance toward fame and fortune—was doing his damnedest to crack into an elite group of gallerists who didn't just push boundaries but leapfrogged them. I was a little surprised someone this cool could be so down to earth, but more than anyone I'd talked to over the past few months, Jack overflowed with practical advice. He also prickled with passionate intensity, like a cattle prod masquerading as a teddy bear. I didn't want to leave. I was convinced I'd found the perfect guide for my journey into the machine.

I was starving, close to peeing my pants, and horrifically late to another meeting by the time I reluctantly cut Jack off, just as he was telling me to make it my job to go to ten openings a week, plus dinners and after-parties and after-after-parties. He pulled out his phone to check that evening's openings. "Out at the party is where things happen," he told me. "So you have to do everything and go see everyone."

I took all this as an invitation to ask, as I was stepping out the door, whether I could maybe join him at some openings sometime. I definitely needed to see him again.

Jack smiled thinly and shook his head. He couldn't be seen coming with "the enemy," he said, sounding a bit bored at having to explain such a known fact. The *writer*, he clarified, in case I was confused. The *pariah*, he added. He waved it away as a joke, but my stomach flopped as his first word kept ricocheting around my skull. *Enemy.* Me. The enemy.

Maybe I should have recognized this as a warning sign. But I was desperate to get inside a gallery, consumed with curiosity over what Jack's Eye might reveal, and out of options. So when Jack emailed me again to suggest, enemy status notwithstanding, that I should come help out at his gallery, I didn't hesitate. When do I start? He texted me instructions to report to 315 in clothes I didn't mind getting dirty: "I'll put you to work."

CHAPTER TWO

I had no idea what "work" I'd be doing, but my plan was to do it so superbly that Jack would ask me back again. One day of assisting was no guarantee of a second, plus there was my reputation to consider. Everyone I met, including Jack, had offered the same pair of contradictory caveats: There are *so* many art worlds, and the art world is *so* small. I took this to mean that the art world was unknowable, but you were not, so you'd better watch yourself. "The art world is built on reputation. It's *all* what people think of you," said a gallerist, a piece of advice that came out sounding more like a threat. My gut told me if I messed things up with Jack, another door was unlikely to open.

The Monday we were set to meet, Jack texted up a storm, live-blogging me updates on his pit-bull rescue and their leisurely afternoon swimming at a pool in Princeton, New Jersey. I took his chattiness to mean he'd put the "enemy" stuff behind us and, later that afternoon, arrived at 315 antsy with excitement.

Jack informed me I'd be helping him prepare the gallery so he could hang a solo show of paintings by the artist Haley Josephs, which was set to open in ten days. Any opening is a big deal, but this was an opening in *September*. I'm sure I stared blankly. "I think of the year as basically September to June, because that's basically when the art world functions," Jack explained.

New York's art scene operated according to a predictable rhythm: An artist represented by a gallery got a solo show every two years, a show lasted four to six weeks, an opening lasted from six to eight in the evening, and the whole shebang ran on Jet-set Standard Time, where business hours are convenient only for the idly rich and the seasons are not summer, fall, winter, and spring, but Hamptons, Chelsea, Palm Beach, and Gala. Come June, said Jack, "everything decamps to the Hamptons"—including collectors' routing numbers—and galleries reacted accordingly. If you aren't an everything that decamps to the Hamptons (a landing strip of compounds at the outer reaches of Long Island, where a dozen eggs can run twenty-four dollars), you'll have noticed galleries' default summer art shows tend to be, well, sleepier: probably a group show, meaning they exhibit a piece or two from a handful of different artists, many of whom the galleries are showing for the first time to test the waters. (A solo show, as the name implies, features a single artist.) Jack's August show, with the drums and shrine, had been a group show. But September! Galleries saved the big names, the big prices, the big splash for September. September was "the first day of school," Jack stressed. "There's an energy. Everyone's checking each other out."

I inspected the gallery to assess how I could help. The room looked drunk: The walls slouched, the floor couldn't follow a straight line, and the wheezy air conditioner looked ready to pass out. Josephs had dropped off five paintings, which leaned against a wall. I'd have said she made bright paintings of glassy-eyed young women, as if Lisa Frank illustrated *Children of the Corn*. Jack said, "She's a figurative painter" who is "taking you into these deep intrapsychic conflicts going on in people's minds." The animatronic drums and the antlered shrine that I'd seen on my first visit to Jack's gallery were gone, though the enormous black-and-gold mural—ahem, the "wall-based piece"—remained.

White walls, check. Art, check. The place looked pretty much ready to go. Sure, the gallery was a little banged up, but then Jack had let on that money was tight. Bigger galleries could divvy up tasks among a cast of characters that included directors (who pick and sell the art), preparators and art handlers (who muscle the art into the gallery), registrars (who track the art's whereabouts), archivists (who file documents for posterity), and artist liaisons (who cater to artists' whims). Jack did all of the above and then some. He picked which artists to show, schlepped work from their studios, bought beer for the openings, sold the art, and photographed his own shows (saving him $150 a pop, easy, he boasted). He also brought home the gallery's garbage to avoid paying for trash hauling (saving $60 a month). "Every little thing adds up," Jack told me. "I do *everything*. That's why I'm *always* doing shit." Rent—$2,200 a month—was one of his bigger expenses, but I wouldn't find anyone paying less, he scoffed, unless it was a shoebox.

Given all that careful budgeting, I figured Jack would take a less-is-more approach to Josephs's show. Prepping the space would take us, what, an hour?

Jack, however, saw nothing but problems. I hadn't been there ninety minutes before he flopped down on the floor, stared up at the ceiling, and ticked through our to-do list as anxiety crept into his voice. One of Josephs's pieces—a painting, nearly eight feet tall and six feet wide, of a woman scooping honey-ish goo out of her vagina—would need to be restretched: The wooden bars that held the canvas taut were cockeyed, so the painting sagged (imperceptibly, to me) on one end. Jack also wanted to spackle one wall, repaint another, and build an entirely new wall from scratch.

What he actually said was, "I want to construct an architectural element in the space." He and Josephs had been "talking about the impression of time," and he wanted a temporary wall that'd divide the room in two so he could hang the paintings of younger-looking figures in the front and older-looking figures in the back. "When you enter the space, it's like a bit of a pocket," Jack said. "Interpret that as a womb, interpret that as nothing." Jack left the gallery and practiced walking in and out a few times, to imagine how the show would look to visitors at first glance. The wall would have the added benefit of blocking the windows: "People love natural light, but it's hard to compete with the stimulus." Also, Josephs wanted to show nine paintings, which Jack worried would look cluttered—the official, rather porny, term was *overhung*. "The only reason I'm willing to have a lot of work in here is because of the wall," he told me. The wall would allow each piece to have "its own plane."

The number of walls I'd built before this was a grand total of zero. Did I understand why Jack asked me to insert myself *inside* the wall, once we'd joined four fiberboard slabs to form a solid, freestanding rectangle in the middle of the gallery? I did not. Did I immediately squeeze my body through a nonexistent opening so that he could properly close up every side of the wall? I did. My status as Jack's assistant was too tenuous to debate the point, so if Jack wanted me in a wall, I'd do my best pancake impression and slide on in. Faster than you can say "OSHA," I was sealed into the architectural element.

From the outside, the wall had looked like an oversized white matchbox. That vision would be my last memory of the outside world,

I realized. My new home had four brown walls that grazed my shoulders and barely enough room to turn around. I could see the ceiling—at least my loved ones could drop food in, I reassured myself—but otherwise, it was a spacious coffin.

Then the drilling started.

A screw shot through the wall, its silver fang nearly piercing my right hand.

"Watch your face. Watch your—everything," Jack yelled from outside, just a few seconds later than would have been helpful and—SKREEEEE!—a new screw shrieked through the wood at my eyeball. The walls around me trembled with the force of the drill. I felt like a cavity being drilled out by a dentist.

Trying to sound nonchalant, I asked Jack if he could please maybe give me a heads-up before drilling again, but, you know, *totally* no big deal if not. By way of response, a screw lunged for my ribs.

"What if this is just a hazing ritual for you, and I wasn't going to put a wall in the show," Jack shouted as I strained to hear if he was loading fresh screw.

"Ha!" I said. I waited for him to clarify that he was joking, then darted sideways as he shot a screw at my thigh.

I involuntarily thought back to my first moments inside the wall. "Alright, Bianca," Jack had called from somewhere above me, "this is where your life ends."

He was right. And I was thrilled.

JACK INVITED ME back after my first day, then again, and before the week was up, I had basically no life outside 315. We'd meet at the gallery at 10:00 a.m. or 1:30 p.m. or 6:00 p.m., depending on whether Jack had a freelance gig that day. Dinner was takeout from the sparkling new mall down the street, which we'd eat on Jack's couch, the garlicky smell of my Chinese food mingling with acetone from the nail salon downstairs and cigarette smoke from Jack's neighbor down the hall—an underground gambling operation, he suspected. Jack tried not to eat mammals and got a pained expression when I took a plastic fork. "This. Is. So. Wasteful," he said, staring me in the eye, after a café put a plastic lid on his smoothie. We'd work through eleven or midnight: spackling, sanding, vacuuming dust, blasting Travis Scott or Erik Satie while Jack cracked open a beer and I scrawled notes in my notebook. I'd given him the standard journalistic Miranda rights—you will be recorded for accuracy; you have the right to go off the record; if you *are* on the record, you may be quoted. "Starting the recording? *Okay!*" Jack would say in the morning, sly smile on his lips, before launching into his diagnosis of an exhibit he'd been to see since I saw him last. He wondered whether my husband minded that I was never home. Beats me. I hadn't had time to ask him.

I blew off writing deadlines to fix Jack's printer and stood up friends to help him restretch Josephs's canvas. "You have to live it and breathe it" was the advice I got from a Whitney Museum curator I'd met through one of the gallerists who wouldn't hire me, and I was determined to go as deep as Jack would let me. Also, a few days at 315 had convinced me that the best way to learn as much as possible was just to put myself at Jack's beck and call, since there was no telling where each day would lead. A trip to Home Depot would turn into a studio visit with a painter would turn into us back at the gallery till 10:00 p.m. while I updated 315's newsletter and Jack dished art gossip, like the artist he knew who would only let people buy her work if they bought two pieces and donated one to a museum. ("Buy one, give one," it's called, or just *BOGO*, and if you're an in-demand artist, you can set those kinds of rules.) I felt like Jack was offering me a crash course in contemporary art and I needed to do whatever I could to stay underfoot. I never knew when he would swerve from railing against puppy mills to dissecting a "masterpiece" by the artist Danh Vo he'd seen at the Guggenheim.

We were futzing around with the architectural element one night when Jack practically dragged me over to his computer to show me Vo's work. I hovered behind him, preparing to have my mind blown, and beheld the masterpiece: a boxy television set balanced on a white minifridge balanced on a washing machine.

"It's one of the best pieces I've seen in a long time," Jack breathed, eyes glued to the computer.

I leaned closer to the screen. I could see how it'd be pretty mindblowing if you were, say, unfamiliar with modern appliances, but as it happened I'd been using washing machines for years now.

I knew better than to say that out loud. What I said was, "Why?"

"Be*cauuuuseee*..." Jack said, struggling to find the right words to capture the magnitude of his experience of the work. "It sums up the most poignant experience of his life! Which is his family leaving their home and relocating to Europe and the experience of cultural assimilation. Like him and his grandmother arrived in—I think it was Denmark? Fleeing Vietnam, following the war. The refugees and the people immigrating there were given these objects—a washer-dryer, a refrigerator, and this TV—as, like, 'You're now a part of this culture.' They were given as gifts to refugees to basically help make their lives easier, but it was simultaneously this way of like—" Jack exhaled deeply. "It's cultural assimilation," he said, a note of sadness in his voice. "Like, moving to the capitalist West and being told, This is what we value, this is how you should live your life."

How were you supposed to get that without a working knowledge of Vo's biography and Danish immigration policy circa 1970? I wondered. I envied the thoughtfulness with which Jack opined on art and how moved he was by the piece. But I was baffled by how I'd ever come close to doing or feeling the same. Looking at the art was apparently a necessary but insufficient condition for "getting" it.

Jack, who genuinely seemed to share my concern that I was an ignorant rube, took a keen interest in my development, and I gratefully handed myself over as a lump of clay to be molded. "I have homework for you," he texted one Saturday evening, followed by a link to the trailer for *The Square,* a satirical movie about contemporary art. Another day, his jaw unhinged and crashed to the floor when he discovered I hadn't read the art critic Clement Greenberg's essay "Avant-Garde and Kitsch." "Oh, you've *got* to read Greenberg," Jack babbled excitedly, with the caveat that "a lot of people hate him now because it seems very last century" and "all the people he wrote about were men" and while there *is* Marxist theory in his work, "it's a bullshit understanding of it." Jack showed up one morning with a stack of art books for me: Clement Greenberg, Calvin Tomkins, Nicolas Bourriaud, *Art Since 1960.* "Do you know what object-oriented ontology is?" Jack asked. Negative. Again: jaw, floor. "If you don't know about object-oriented ontology, I'm not sure you can have a conversation about contemporary art." (Object-oriented ontology: The idea that any animal, vegetable, mineral, or lamppost can have its own private existence, independent of and unknown to humans.) Jack's pleasure reading at that moment was Kenneth Clark's *The Nude: A Study in Ideal Form,* which *The Guardian* had ranked number twenty-seven on its list of the hundred best nonfiction books but Jack dubbed "just an old white guy talking about nude portraits of women by straight white guys." He wouldn't dare read it on the subway or bring it under his arm to a gallery. "I don't want to set that bomb off. You get chastised a lot in the art world."

Hold up—I'd never taken an art-history class? Jack's eyes bulged. "Without education or training, you won't be able to comprehend a lot." I got the sense that to Jack, looking at art without studying art history was like doing surgery with a butter knife: You were dangerously unequipped and someone was going to get hurt. Jack suggested I pick up *Janson's History of Art* (1,200 pages; nine pounds), even though "art history is just the history of the creative white male." Still, he promised that knowing art history would help me judge quality. "There is objectively better work, but you have to place it in the timeline of art history," said Jack, who'd studied both art history and fine art at New York University. "You can't trust your instinct. It's influenced by mass culture. Your gut falls back on the safety of what's accepted by society."

Oh! And memes. Was I familiar with art-world memes? *No?* Jesus. I started getting daily roundups of Jack's favorite memes, and he'd sometimes hijack whatever we were doing to sit on the couch scrolling through memes. "Do you know this meme format?" he asked, holding up his phone to show me a cuddly, smiling Gremlin ("Artist's opinions at the opening") juxtaposed with a fanged Gremlin chewing a glass bottle ("Artist's opinions once they leave"). "Do you know *this* meme format?" He gave a frustrated gurgle. "*Ughhh!* There's so much beauty to memes if you just know how the format works!"

It was a steep learning curve, but Jack was a passionate teacher, and I tried to be a model student. I signed up to audit an art-history class at Barnard and slogged through *Relational Art* on the subway, taking comfort in Jack's confidence that there were concrete steps I could take to develop an Eye.

One afternoon, I'd just arrived at the gallery when Jack crooked his finger at me to indicate I should join him at Guadalupe Maravilla's wall-based piece. I obediently trotted over. The two of us contemplated Maravilla's lines—one black, one gold—that squiggled the length of one whole wall, as far down as the electrical outlet and up nearly to the ceiling. From left to right, the lines zigzagged like spiky shark's teeth, then swooped up into graceful humps, then settled into rectangular notches like the crenellations of a castle wall.

I eagerly waited for him to hold forth on Maravilla's artwork—*Shrine for the Undocumented Children*, I'd seen it was called, and a particularly timely piece given that the Trump administration was in the midst of separating families at the nation's southern border. According to Jack's press release, Maravilla was an immigrant from El Salvador who'd "devoted his artistic practice to raising awareness around the struggles of undocumented immigrants and asylum seekers." The wall-based piece at 315 was similar to one that Maravilla had up right this minute at—long whistle—the Whitney Museum of American Art.

Finally, Jack broke the silence. "I don't know how many coats of paint this needs."

Alarm bells jangled in my brain. Paint? *This?* Nooooo, he couldn't possibly. Maravilla's wall-based piece—hadn't Jack himself written this?—was a "tribute to children who were lost while journeying to this country." It was also, need I remind him, art. Granted, I was new here, but I felt solid on the point that painting over someone else's artwork was frowned upon. Even, I'd go so far as to say, actively discouraged.

Maybe *this* was the hazing ritual. Maybe I was supposed to put up a fight. I tried not to panic. I stalled for time.

"Sooo," I said, as Jack rummaged through his storage closet for a fuzzy purple paint roller and a tub of Ultra Pure White paint, "is that Maravilla piece something that someone could have purchased?" Maybe the idea hadn't occurred to him.

"They could," Jack conceded. Actually, someone *was* interested in buying Maravilla's piece, he clarified. Good thing I checked. I got that Jack wanted to repaint his wall so he'd have a plain white surface on which to hang Josephs's work, but still, he couldn't *possibly* want me to paint over a piece of art that he was in the process of potentially selling.

I had a flicker of doubt: But what would the person be buying, exactly? I'd heard of an auction house selling a Banksy mural on a surgically excised slab of wall, only Jack didn't seem prepared to saw into his gallery's wall.

Eventually, he seemed to grasp my hesitation. A site-specific piece such as this—meaning an artwork made for a specific site—could be sold as a set of instructions so it could be remade without the artist ever touching it, Jack explained. "The whole point is that anyone can execute it." In a museum, in a Miami condo, in a hundred years when the artist is dead. Owning one of the artist Sol Lewitt's site-specific wall paintings means owning a piece of paper, signed by the artist, with directions for how the work should be made to look (i.e., "Straight lines about six inches long, touching and crossing, drawn at random using four colors, uniformly dispersed with maximum density, covering the entire surface of the wall").

Hold up: Meaning the artwork was not, in fact, the swirling lines Jack wanted me to cover with paint? What *was* it, then? I burbled with questions.

"Don't ask so many questions," Jack interrupted, as he thumped down the paint bucket. "There are things it's better you don't know."

That shut me up. I listened as Jack rattled off an endless list of instructions on how to properly paint a white wall white. Then, determined not to violate Jack's so-many-questions ban, I gingerly dipped the roller into the bucket of paint and pressed it against a patch of spiky humps Maravilla had drawn near the center of the wall. White drips rolled down the wall over the artist's lines, like blood from a wound. With each swipe of white, I silently apologized to Maravilla.

While I painted, Jack contrasted his gallery to the deli down the block, where we stocked up on bottled water to avoid drinking the rusty stuff that flowed from his tap. "It's not a traditional business model," Jack said of 315. "You're literally selling an idea. A discussion. It's *so* different."

We weren't screwing together walls and hanging paintings. We were mounting ideas.

"The difference between me and another emerging space? It all comes down to the decisions I make to showcase, display, certain artistic practices," Jack said. "It's an idea. It's also a way of looking at the world. It's a style."

EXCUSE THE STONER SENTIMENT, but have you ever looked at a white wall? Like, really *looked*? That wall and I communed. Ever notice the raised scars of dried paint drips? Or how paint morphs before your eyes, so it's thick and shiny when it goes on (and you think you've finally—*finally*—done your final coat) but then—whoa!—the stuff underneath shows up again? Do not believe what you've heard: Watching paint dry is an adventure.

This could be the paint fumes talking, but as I lost myself in the

expanse of Jack's wall, I started to wonder why nearly every art museum and gallery wore the exact same uniform. It was as though city
code forbade showing art anywhere except in hushed white rooms
with surgical-grade lighting and squeaky floors. Turns out, that formula has a nickname—"the white cube"—and for centuries, it didn't
exist.

Back in the 1800s, New York's galleries and art museums looked
less like operating rooms and more like hoarders' dens. Paintings
weren't hung on white walls, in single rows, at eye level. Paintings
crawled up the walls. They hung at knee height and overhead; in col-
umns of four; on flowery wallpaper below gilded cherubs. For a time,
the go-to wall color in Europe's museums was a grayish olive ("the
most neutral of all the decided colors," per an 1828 decorating guide),
which then gave way to a dark maroon. (The most popular color for
German museums in 1890 was a rich burgundy called "Gallery Red.")
The impressionists baby-stepped toward current conventions by adopt-
ing a fashion of spacing out their art and hanging it in single or double
rows (mimicking the look of their studios), and a few decades later
modernists were pushing white as the new neutral. But it was the Nazis who helped perfect what we now think of as the white cube. The
Nazis' first foray into architecture-as-propaganda was building none
other than an art museum, which opened in 1937 with tall ceilings,
spotless white walls, gleaming floors, sparsely hung art, and bright
overhead lighting—a design ethos that failed artist Adolf Hitler praised
as a brick-and-mortar manifestation of his quest for "cultural purification." From then on, the look became so popular that, historian Charlotte Klonk observes, "one is almost tempted to speak of the white
cube as a Nazi invention."

You'd think with friends like these the white cube would be verboten, and yet for ninety years, it's stuck and spread—and not because the white cube has been scientifically proven to be the optimal way of experiencing art. "The white wall's apparent neutrality is an illusion," writes the art critic Brian O'Doherty, who coined the "white cube" term. "It stands for a community with common ideas and assumptions." O'Doherty argues that the white cube is effectively a mechanism for ensuring art is considered art—one that's so powerful it can cause us to confuse mere stuff for artistic treasures. Case in point, Jack and I were out touring art shows one day when, while thankfully out of Jack's earshot, I complimented a wall-based sculpture of a small metal knob protruding from a square hole. "This is a piece of the wall," the gallery's owner gently corrected. "But I will sell it to you."

I was beginning to pick up on the hidden logic of my new sur-roundings. No detail was too small for Jack to fuss over, and as we spent endless hours trekking to the hardware store for joint compound or mending plates, I reconciled myself to the fact that before I could learn to analyze a painting, there was a lot I needed to decode about the elaborate ritual of presenting art.

For instance: Jack's gallery was not a mess, I gradually saw. It was carefully crafted to embody the aesthetic of the "young fucking Brook-lyn space," as Jack summarized it. Scrappy, yes; sloppy, no. I'd assumed the lights buzzing overhead at 315 were a relic of the bookstore that Jack's gallery had replaced. In fact, they were fluorescent bulbs with a temperature of 4,500 degrees Kelvin—slightly yellower than the noon sun on a cloudless day—that Jack specifically selected because natural daylight flattered art. I'd never met someone with a favorite light-color temperature, but Jack said, "4,000 I think is really nice." He delivered a fire-and-brimstone sermon on the evils of "scalloping," the arc of light certain bulbs cast on a wall: "It's *really* gross," he insisted. "It's *disgusting.*" He spent half a day on his hands and knees trying to re-stretch Josephs's painting with help from a professional preparator—an artist friend whose day job was installing shows at a museum—and another few hours trying to wrestle the canvas into place with me. By then, there were smears of blood on the back of the canvas, but noth-ing less than correct would do. "When you're dealing with a luxury product, things have to be nice," Jack explained. "Don't give them"—by which he meant collectors—"an inch of doubt." When Jack evaluated his performance as a gallerist, there was the look of the exhibition and then everything else. "There's three ways that I measure the success of a show," he told me. "Which is basically: how the show looks—the in-stallation, physically, how it looks, is the artist happy with how the show looks, and, with that, I lump in the opening and the response of the general public in that first instance of people seeing it. And then it's press, and then it's sales."

Around the time I applied the third coat of paint to Jack's wall, I learned the gallery was not the only thing that needed a makeover. "If you worked for me, I'd give you a dress code. Severe haircut. No jew-elry," Jack informed me. He'd noticed that I liked to wear chunky silver bracelets to distract from my extremely boring clothes, which I gath-ered hadn't escaped his scrutiny either. My penchant for all black was evidently quite passé. "It's just so easy," Jack lectured of the all-black uniform. "It's just 'New York City.' It's like, 'Oh, I'm chic, I wear black.' It's like—not really!" he said, his voice clipped with skepticism. If I were—very hypothetically, mind you—to get his permission to come with him to an art fair he was doing in London that October: "It's like—maybe you should change your wardrobe." To be fair, Jack was reevaluating his own look and thinking about growing out his beard, although he acknowledged that in the past, friends had challenged him to consider whether a beard was "just this expression of hyper-masculinity." But it was tempting. "The moment you have one, it's like this feeling of power," he said. "When I have a beard, it's like, no one fucks with me."

My personality needed some work too. Jack let me come along to studio visits, where he checked in on artists whose work he planned to show, and having had the chance to observe me in the wild, Jack let me know that asking so many questions made me seem entitled. "You're like a little kid—always *why why why why*," he said, his voice rising to a nasally whine. Jack, who fretted that he himself was too nice, told me I also had a bad habit of complimenting artists' work. "I would, in the studio, avoid what might seem like superficial enthusiasm. Like, 'Wow! That's so cool!' Just because that feels like empty enthusiasm, you know?" I noticed Jack himself mostly spoke in a low monotone that made him sound as if he were running out of batteries, and I began to pick up on the fact that no self-respecting art connoisseur discussed art without lowering their voice to the affectless murmur of a funeral director welcoming the bereaved.

Nix the word *sold*. "It's just a little tacky," Jack coached. "You say, that piece has been *placed*." As I drafted emails inviting journalists to Josephs's show, I tried to internalize the tortured art-world alter egos of words like *video* ("time-based media") and *website* ("online viewing room"). "The mark-making is all done with organic materials," Jack told a collector eyeing a piece by the artist Quay Quinn Wolf, which in English means *those smears are from flowers*. Rather than "hanging paintings," gallerists *installed a show*, after which they didn't email "sales pitches," but sent out *offers*. Buyers—*collectors*—wouldn't "ask" about a piece they wanted to "buy": They *inquired* about a work they hoped to *acquire*. Like upgrading "cow" to *beef*, all these extra syllables distance art from unappetizing mundanities—which is to say, money. There was one exception: Connoisseurs signaled their intimacy with art by demurely referring to paintings, prints, photos, and various other wall-based masterpieces as mere *pictures*.

If you want people to think you know a lot about art, the trick is to sound like a French academic whose opinions have been mangled by a ham-fisted translation job. Because that's exactly what highbrow art writing may be modeled after, it turns out. On my hunt for a glossary of art terms, I discovered research by an artist and a sociologist who'd analyzed thousands of art-world press releases published over a thirteen-year span to understand the origins and influence of artspeak—or, as they call it, "International Art English." The researchers, Alix Rule and David Levine, contend International Art English has its roots in *October*, a journal launched in 1976 by a band of influential New York critics who tried to beef up the rigor of art writing by publishing essays by prominent French academics like Deleuze, Derrida, Barthes, and a motley crew of other deconstructionists, post-structuralists, and post-modernists. *October*'s contributors translated those essays and wrote their own essays that sound suspiciously like an attempt to imitate the translated essays: These Anglophone art critics imported Franco-phone tics, like heady-sounding abstract terms ("the real," "the politi-cal") and scarcely intelligible nouns ending in *-ity* modeled after the French suffix *-ité* ("criticality," "indexicality"). And thus phrases like "summon forces of indexicality and iconicity from the aspirations, ali-bis and abuses of sovereignty that emerge in the fields of postal poli-tics, imperial infrastructure and magazine diplomacy" were born. While trekking to galleries even before joining 315, I'd noticed that art devotees spoke like they were trapped in dictionaries and being forced to chew their way out: A curator and I bonded over our dislike of a performance-art piece, only while I thought it was "boring" she thought it was "durational." But then again, International Art English is not necessarily for communicating. (To pick just one example: The linguistic analysis of the press releases found that "spatial" and "non-spatial" are used interchangeably.) Really, International Art English is more for showing off. It's an "exclusionary" code, according to Rule and Levine, that distinguishes you as "someone who does or does not get it."

I felt like a foreign correspondent dispatched to a strange new land, and I grasped that I'd wind up with my head on a spike if I failed to master the elaborate code of conduct Jack was patiently, painstakingly trying to teach me. Gushing compliments, saying "sold": All that marked you as an outsider, and if you were an outsider—good luck to you. Being able to afford one of Haley Josephs's $2,500 paintings was, I was learning, only one prerequisite for a shot at being Jack's customer.

Just as Maravilla's lines had disappeared under my eighth coat of paint, Jack told me he'd placed the wall-based piece. It had gone to a "good person."

I asked him what he meant by "good person."

"Very involved with museum collections and other organizations," Jack said. "The ideal collector is someone who has a very extensive network and is involved in the art world so that it, like, takes on a life outside this place."

Jack was kneeling on the floor surrounded by a drill, a saw, a mallet, pliers, two rulers, and an exacto knife trying, yet again, to restretch Josephs's painting of the woman pulling radioactive honey out of her vagina. It lay face down under him like a sick patient.

"The reason the art world is so insular is because you want certain people or players to be involved in what you're doing. You don't just want Joe Schmo—" Jack paused and glanced protectively at the painting. "I mean it sounds awful, but for Haley's sake and for the life of that painting, you don't necessarily want just, like, Joe Schmo to buy it and put it in his one-bedroom Bed-Stuy apartment and it never sees the light of day again and that person doesn't care for it, you know?"

I didn't know. I replayed that conversation over and over. How did Jack know whether Joe Schmo cared for the painting? What if, every morning at breakfast, Joe Schmo stared at that painting and the sight of that woman scooping glowing goo from her hoo-ha made Joe Schmo's spirit soar? Or maybe Jack just didn't care whether Joe Schmo loved the artwork. "I don't care about the person who's going to come in and buy one of Haley's paintings and then I might never see them again," he told me.

While mopping the gallery floor a few days later, I asked Jack about his aversion to Schmos.

The issue, Jack explained, while swiveling on his desk chair, was that outsiders have zero social currency and just can't help anyone— not gallerists, not artists, not collectors. "I mean, honestly, people are only really looking for recognition within the art world. It's a weird thing." I assumed that explained why, when we were going over which journalists to email about Josephs's show, Jack told me his media wishlist was *Artforum*, *Art in America*, *BOMB Magazine*, and *The Brooklyn Rail*. I "*could*" reach out to *The New York Times*, he allowed, but it sounded highly optional. He also had strong opinions on which individual journalists we'd invite to cover the show. I suggested sending the press release to a writer who reviewed painting exhibits for a well-respected art site. Jack's verdict: "I don't know about this guy. He's pretty fucking basic." What mattered, I deduced, were the opinions of a certain handful of Good Persons.

There were various ways to keep out the Schmos, and where you put your gallery was a big one. Like many New York galleries, 315 was designed less like a store than a speakeasy: up a flight of stairs, tucked away in a building that could just as easily have housed apartments, virtually impossible to find unless you knew what you were looking for. Jack, who was more generous than many, at least had the courtesy to put a sign on his door. Lots of galleries opted for finger-sized name-plates that omitted helpful words like "art gallery." It took me four phone calls and half an hour of wandering around Chinatown to find a cool new space that had no website, no Instagram profile, and no sign. "Public stuff is so *corny*," whined the gallery attendant when I complained.

You're probably thinking that New York real estate is hideously expensive and ground-floor storefronts cost extra. It was that, but it wasn't only that. A street-level space was, to Jack, actively undesirable: Having 315 on the second floor was ideal because "I don't have to deal with foot traffic or, like, random-ass people walking in." He recounted a conversation he'd had with a real-estate broker who'd pitched him on a space in a Lower East Side hotel by highlighting all the foot traffic Jack would get. Mistake! He didn't want people "who are visiting New York City and want to stay on the Lower East Side, just like *walking* through my *gallery* space," Jack spat.

I don't know for sure that working at a gallery requires you to swear a blood oath that you'll uphold a mafia-like omertà, but that was my impression, and not just because I was a journalist. "I could tell you, but then I'd have to kill you," said a dealer—a childhood friend of Jack's—after Jack asked an innocuous question about the guy's upcoming travel plans. Where would you find prices for the art, which one generally expects to see in a place where items are offered for sale?

Why, you poor rube: "The surest sign that a gallery is not serious is that it openly posts its prices," declared *ARTnews*. (To find the prices you'll have to ask a gallerist, who'll tell you but possibly only after you take a Schmo-detector test: What else do you own? How did you find the gallery? What do you do for a living?) Lots of galleries didn't even share their names on their job listings, and my heart went out to the applicants with one to two years of gallery or museum experience who were expected to write a cover letter expressing their unwavering passion for "Major Contemporary Art Gallery" or "Name Revealed Upon Interview." Jack fretted over the fact that with the art fair in London less than six weeks away, its organizers still hadn't publicized the list of exhibitors. "Which is like *so* bizarre." He paused a moment and seemed to be reconsidering. "But maybe that's part of the cool factor? I don't know." It was cool to say nothing. Straightforwardness was uncouth.

If there was a silver lining to this, it's that I wasn't nuts. No wonder I'd felt left out of the art world. Galleries were evidently doing anything but rolling out the welcome mat, especially if you were a Schmo. (Or as one journal article summarized it: "[T]he art industry actively suppresses reliable information about its products—a behavior that the governing legal regime reinforces.") I found it a little depressing that even the people who devoted their lives to art didn't trust it to stand on its own without elaborate rituals and a secret language to enhance its mystery. At the same time, I was tickled that Jack was initiating me into the cult.

One night, after a studio visit, a friend of Jack's who ran a gallery out of the basement of his parents' townhouse asked Jack's advice on selling art. Say as little as possible, Jack advised over dinner. Don't send long emails—brief emails, I gathered, make you look busy, and busy looks successful. Don't volunteer extra information. "You throw your balls on the table: 'The price is this.'" Jack wanted to redesign his website to make it completely illegible. His vision: White writing on a white background, "and the only way you can figure out what the fuck is going on is either by hovering or by clicking around." But ... why? Jack shrugged. "I don't want it to be an easy process."

JACK FINALLY STARTED hanging Josephs's paintings on the same early September day when I applied my ninth and final coat of paint. He told me a friend of his who'd started a tech company would be dropping by that afternoon, and even though it was just a quick errand unrelated to art, the friend had bought work before and Jack wanted to have some paintings up when he arrived.

When the friend came, Jack ushered the guy over to Josephs's enormous honey-vagina painting. Jack made the gentlest of sales pitches, so brief I almost missed it: "Perfect for your tall ceilings."

It wasn't till nearly midnight that Jack finally got around to inspecting my wall. I stood next to him, chest puffed, waiting for him to congratulate me. I'd meticulously followed his instructions (*massage the roller brush hard-then-soft against the wall*), and the result, if I do say so myself, was spectacular.

Jack took a deep breath in. Finally, he broke the silence. "This is like dog shit smeared on the wall," he said.

My heart stopped.

"Look at this!" Jack commanded, as if disciplining an unhousebroken dog who'd smeared its shit on the wall. He rubbed a hand over the wall. "This is like sandpaper!"

I'd applied nine coats of paint to a very big wall. I knew how precise

Jack was. I knew the Ultra Pure White cost him $130 a bucket. "I thought the whole thing was like, roll the brush really light to get a dappled texture," I squeaked in a voice belonging to a hamster.

"This is like the surface of *Mars*!"

I darted back and forth between Jack's old walls and my new wall, comparing their textures and babbling apologies.

"Bianca, you're, like, complicating this shit!" Jack said mournfully. "This is sand. On the wall. It's *sand. On.* The *wall*," he repeated. "I mean, this is fucking *sand*..." The sentence puttered out of steam, as though Jack was too exhausted by the magnitude of my fuckup to put it into words. "I mean... New intern... Shit." He sighed. "You tried. You're learning."

He was stroking the wall gently when I left, as though soothing a wounded animal. I found out later that, before Josephs's opening, he'd painted over my work with a tenth coat.

CHAPTER THREE

I spent Labor Day weekend with a group of artists in a charming old house in Hudson, New York, surrounded by tall grass, chubby trees, and melty little ceramic sculptures that tottered around the backyard. "You need to join artists in leisure activities," instructed Jesse Greenberg, an artist-slash-gallerist-slash-curator who invited me after we hit it off at an opening. "Hikes. Drinking. Mushrooms. Nature walks." We did all of the above, as well as some aggressive outdoor karaoke and—ending what for me had been a multidecade dry spell—playing with stuffed animals. Besides mushrooms, there was a considerable amount of pot. After our host mentioned that her cat liked to hide in their stove and that she'd totally spaced on the strudel she put in to bake, I spent a lot of my stay extremely paranoid, periodically checking the oven for baked cat.

Jack texted me throughout the weekend from somewhere in the Hamptons. "Subway reading," he wrote, followed by a link to an article from *Artnet News* titled "The Toxic Legacy of Zombie Formalism" (zombie formalism: the taunting nickname for surprisingly gentle abstract paintings made by artists manhandling their paint, i.e., with fire extinguishers or feet). By then I'd gotten used to Jack following me home. Between texts, calls, emails, DMs, and our days in the gallery, I felt like I was communicating with him more than everyone else in my life. Combined.

It was exhausting trying to keep up, but I loved it. When I'm into something, I'm *all* in. Also, everything I'd seen so far suggested that the art world made no distinctions between the personal and professional, so I'd better get used to it. I took Jack's constant correspondence as an encouraging sign that he was bringing me deeper into the fold. I liked getting real-time updates on the life of a gallerist, which offered me the behind-the-scenes view into Jack's role that I craved. "When you think of an artist's job, it's to make work. When you think of my job, it's to display and sell work," Jack said once. This was only partially true, I was discovering. Depending on the day, he could be a therapist, pharmacist, cruise director, or pageant mom, on hand with advice about whether honey is an archival material and ready to comp a critic's Uber if it'd get him to see a show. Jack texted me to say he was going to an opening at the New Museum, to say he was hungover, to invite me to dinner with some artists, to say he'd just dropped off new canvases for Josephs. I was helping Jack look up shipping quotes one day when he held up his phone to show me one of Haley Josephs's new paintings: a woman with Bozo the Clown pigtails that exploded from her head in a riot of fuzzy rainbows. Jack made a face. "The hair—it's too wild, right?" he said. "I can be like, 'Change it.'"

When I got back to the city, New York had cranked itself up to September mode: gridlocked Escalades on Fifth Avenue, mosh pits on the L train, frantic parades of speedwalkers dodging tourists while chattering into their phones. ("Her apartment is infested, her *dog* is infested . . .") By early September, I'd changed too. Per Jack's suggestions, I'd ditched my jewelry, adopted a stony facade, and quit talking so much. I must have been doing something right, because Jack rewarded me with a key to his gallery and a 315 email address. He made passing references to me as his "assistant" and would now allow me to go with him to openings.

Countries have been invaded with less care than Jack put into plotting our evenings. He spent hours combing through See Saw, an app-based guide to art exhibits, squinting uncertainly at my suggestions and breathlessly describing his favorite "spaces." Jack looked up to people who ran the hippest and, within certain circles, most influential galleries in the city. Bridget Donahue, Gavin Brown, 47 Canal—places "so disgustingly cool it's abrasive," as one artist put it. The reputation of the gallery seemed as much a draw for Jack as whatever art they were showing. "I'll spend more time with the work if I like the space," he told me.

Art galleries theoretically survive by exchanging art for cash, but this being the art market, people have come up with countless complicated permutations on that basic model. There are primary-market galleries (like 315) that act as middlemen between artists and collectors, and there are secondary-market galleries that act as middlemen between collectors and other collectors. (The former tend to work with artists who are alive; the latter tend to deal in artists who are long dead.) Some galleries represent artists—meaning they help manage their careers and commit to regularly showing their work. Some galleries don't. There are galleries that sell pieces of art for $20 and galleries that sell art for $20 million and galleries that don't sell art at all, in which case the owner's having a trust fund is helpful. I'd assumed you couldn't buy artwork from a gallery without taking out a second mortgage, but that wasn't true. The online gallery Drawer, for instance, sold pieces for as little as $175, and Got It for Cheap's pop-up shows had art for $30 apiece.

A "good" gallery wasn't necessarily one that sold lots of art. In Jack's circle, the highest praise was to be "pure," and the pure treated money like diarrhea: a fact of life, but gross—if you got it, you didn't talk about it. "Pure" generally required a high-wire act of accruing cachet, then gradually monetizing it in a way that appeared accidental but was, of course, exceedingly calculated. Gagosian—300 employees, 280 artists, 19 gallery spaces, and a rumored $1 billion each year in sales—was not pure, or even a gallery, but, as one painter sniffed, "a bank." Showing edgy artworks, like Danh Vo's pile of appliances, was also a prerequisite for being pure. "Colorful paintings" was gallerist code for "easy money" and, among a certain crowd, uttered with such dripping contempt that you needed to get out a mop. Jack's shows leaned pure: Maravilla's *Shrine for the Undocumented Children* was not colorful painting, or, synonymously, "couch art," but "market unfriendly"—closer to the end of the spectrum known as "fuck-you art." Still, Jack worried that people would read a mercenary motive into the fact that he was showing Haley Josephs's colorful paintings in September, even though, he stressed, it was purely coincidence because *actually* he'd planned on showing her work in March, but another gallery had insisted on hosting her solo show before 315. "I don't think anyone would say anything, but I'm sure people might be thinking, 'Oh, *September*. You have this solo show of pretty paintings,'" he fretted.

For the first week of September, See Saw listed 15 openings in Berlin, 12 in London, 35 in Paris, and 106 in New York. What about

openings in other cities? you ask. *What other cities?* Per See Saw, any-
place else was a barren cultural wasteland.

Jack didn't put it in quite those words, but he did call New York
"the hub of the art world and the emerging-art world." (A museum curator I spoke with called it "the shining beacon of the art world for over
one hundred years.") Jack had briefly considered opening his gallery
in Los Angeles, which was the only other acceptable American city.
"Once you leave New York City or Los Angeles, I'm like, 'Uhhh, what?'"
he said. "It's a snobby thing to say, but." The post-"but" silence was unequivocal.

New York City is unique, Jack informed me, because it contains
the entire art-world ecosystem. There are artists (to make art), critics
(to discuss it), white-collar workers and the leisure class (to buy it),
plus nonprofits, residencies, and project spaces (to support fuck-you or
market-unfriendly art that might languish in the market). There are
small-tier galleries (like 315), there are mid-tier galleries (which show
artists often poached from small-tier galleries), and there are megagalleries. These sell art for more than the cost of houses in my hometown and show artists, poached from wherever, who get splashy shows
at megamuseums, which New York has lots of too. All these elements
"support and feed into each other," according to Jack. To him, New
York is more than just a city: "It is a ladder that you have to climb."
That's the polite way of putting it, I was learning. New York is also an
air-kissing, designer-clad food chain in which each link can be both
predator and prey.

The farther an artist's work travels up the island of Manhattan, the
more ensconced its place in art history. Like any sweeping statement
about the art world, this is not *entirely* true, and there are many exceptions, but the island's geography is illuminating. Clustered around

Chinatown, Tribeca, and the Lower East Side are galleries that specialize in emerging artists. A few dozen blocks north, Chelsea galleries exhibit artists you may have seen in museums, and the ceilings and prices
are higher. Travel farther uptown, to the Upper East Side, and you'll
find galleries with a high concentration of very expensive art by people who are very famous and very dead. By the time you've hit East
Eighty-Second Street, you've hit—cue angelic choir—the Metropolitan
Museum of Art, which is, well, the Metropolitan Museum of Art. Cara-
vaggio, Rembrandt, Van Gogh, O'Keeffe. Artists big enough to appear
in crossword puzzles, paintings famous enough to be mousepads.

The first Thursday in September is synonymous with openings in
Chelsea, and Jack and I left 315 early so we'd get to Manhattan right as
the starting pistol fired at 6:00 p.m. I was fluttery with excitement
and self-conscious about fitting in. Unfortunately, despite getting tips
on what to wear from an artist I'd met—"You don't want to look like
you're trying too hard, but you don't want to look boring"—I realized
as soon as I saw Jack's outfit that I'd completely overdressed. I was in
black jeans, black boots, and a sleeveless white silk shirt. Jack was
dressed like an avant-garde mechanic in an oversized white T-shirt
over wide-legged lavender pants. He resisted commenting on my outfit, which I appreciated, and instead remarked on what I'd had on a
month back. "That was actually one of the first things I noticed: the
mascara that you were wearing," he told me, apropos nothing, on our
drive to Chelsea. "I was like, 'Oh. She's *trying*.'" It didn't sound like a
good thing.

Jack and I pulled up to Metro Pictures, the first gallery on his list,
and were in the door at exactly 6:05 p.m. And *go*:

Metro: solo show of art by B. Wurtz featuring giant black-and-white
photos of colanders and cheese graters. Jack sniffed disapprovingly at a

photo of a spent toilet paper roll. "Look at those grommets," he hissed, eyeing the silver hardware used to hang the piece. His gaze lingered on what appeared to me to be a smooth patch of wall above the photo. "*That's* what happens when you don't apply enough layers of paint." I felt better about the whole dogshit-wall fiasco: I'd fallen short of Jack's exacting standards, but then so had the pros. We paused in front of an amputated hanger with a string of beige buttons dangling off one end. "I love that his work has a sense of humor," said Jack, his face utterly blank.

That was the first and last time I remember Jack commenting on the art. "I don't like this color, it's muddy," he whispered, as he examined the purply walls at the Toyin Ojih Odutola show across the street. He pronounced another gallery's lighting "harsh," fingered a scrape on someone else's wall, and frowned at a poorly extracted nail. Hi to some collector Jack knew en route to Cheim & Read ("Crime and Greed," someone quipped), which was packed with people but was apparently closing, and wasn't it *obvious* that this Joan Mitchell show was their attempt to slide into the secondary market, and of *course* the director from Almine Rech was there because weren't they about to do a posthumous show of paintings by Vivian Springford. Hanging with art people reliably involved me getting pummeled with unfamiliar names. My go-to strategy was to smile and nod, then quietly google everyone later.

Talking shit was essentially a job requirement. "It's almost impossible to not be a gossip in the art world," Jack insisted. "If you exist in the art world, you have to talk about the art world, and in order to talk about the art world, you have to have an opinion." Gossip for art people was like echolocation for bats: You sent out signals of what you thought was great or derivative or phony, then oriented yourself based on what came back. One gallerist insisted I check out Half Gallery; another wouldn't be caught dead there. The Hole had "a really, really wonderful emerging-art program." The Hole was "terrible." Depending on which statement you agree with, the conversation would end abruptly or continue.

Up an industrial elevator, down a hall, to C R U S H Curatorial to see photos of a guy skulking around the forest in an orange spandex unitard. A friend of Jack's was holding court on how he'd recently become a conscientious objector to art fairs. I kept hearing lots of "Where are you going next?" and "Where are you going tomorrow?" and "So how do you know [insert name]?"

Discussing the art was like complimenting the crown moldings at an orgy. I mean, you *can*—only it's not why everyone's there. Openings were, everyone agreed, while jammed shoulder to shoulder, the absolute worst way to see art, second only to art fairs. Then again, you couldn't ask for a better way to see people. Galleries put out guestbooks and on our way in or out, we scrawled our names—"to let others know you were there, like dogs peeing," a gallerist explained. People chatted with each other while their eyes whirled around the room searching for a more important face. Everyone was looking to see if anyone was someone.

Quick: It's 7:30 p.m. To Gagosian ("Gago") or downtown? We took the C train to the B to hit a pair of galleries that shared a space on the Lower East Side. "They have two women. Hashtag September show, hashtag MeToo, hashtag move the needle. You're so woke," muttered the Conscientious Objector, who'd glommed on to our group.

The two downtown galleries were packed and foggy with sweat, their windowsills lined with empty bottles of beer. I squeezed past a woman dressed like a condom to catch a glimpse of art—squiggly bits of metal welded to look like angsty wingdings—before the crowd closed up around me again.

Over to some pop-up galleries on Canal Street, followed by karaoke for Jack, who got home God knows when. The next night we went to Midtown. Or maybe it was the next week. It was a blur: Every night for however many days, a timer started at 6:00 p.m., and for two hours it was a mad dash from Pace to Clearing to American Medium to a different Clearing. At each place, I tried to feel something, *anything*, for the art. The pieces washed over me in a messy deluge of colors and scattered images. A video of an erect penis stabbing a cream pie, a painting of bouncy black circles cradled by orange hot dog–ish blobs. At Anton Kern Gallery, I wandered back and forth in front of paintings of witchy women shouting at tiny cartoon birds, and all I could think was *why this?* My mind kept returning to a question that had started dogging me long before September: Why did *these* particular paintings get picked, out of all the art being made in the world? What made them special?

Even though my Eye was still crap, I took heart in the fact that, socially, I was settling into a groove. Starting over the summer, I'd gotten to know a few artists by introducing myself to anyone standing alone at an opening, and amid the September frenzy, I joined a painter to check out an opening in Bushwick, after which we migrated to a bar to catch a Noise concert where—*What!* Hey!—I bumped into the crew I'd hung out with over Labor Day, and we all squished together to listen to the opening set, which began with a single, piercing scream and progressed to rhythmic static. Hairbone was coming on soon, but Jack, who'd been texting me all night, insisted I hustle back to Manhattan to meet him and his girlfriend, and, feeling manic, I did. We hurried from a natural-wine bar to a basement club in SoHo, where on the stairs I bumped into an artist I'd met at an opening a few nights back—"Where are you going next? Where are you going tomorrow?" I asked, before getting swept downstairs into a plush womb, scarlet and throbbing with techno.

I'm doing it! I thought, squeezing onto the dance floor to bop with Jack and his entourage. I'd even nailed my outfit, I thought proudly— black jeans with my favorite shirt, a black-and-white button-down I save for special occasions, since I always stain things. Jack grinned at me while we danced, and I savored the sense that he approved, feeling flush with the warm hug of belonging. Jack tapped me on the shoulder, then cupped his hand around my ear. "You look like you work for a catering company!" he shouted.

CHAPTER FOUR

I kept getting contradictory advice on how to develop my Eye. The "it can't be done" camp regretfully informed me that an Eye was something you were born with, like the privilege of wearing a family crest on your pinky. "I was always taught you either have the Eye or you don't. I don't know that it's necessarily something you can learn," declared an art advisor, with the posh accent of minor royalty, whose job was to tell the Eye-less what to buy. On the opposite side was the "no wrong answer" camp, which assured me that, with art, there are no rules.

Both extremes were fishy to me. The first stank of elitism, and the second seemed like an outright lie. My friend Teresa told me over dinner one night how she'd recently decided to take the plunge and buy her first piece of original contemporary art from a gallery, so she connected with an art advisor (purportedly a "no wrong answer" partisan), who emailed Teresa a few paintings to consider. Teresa wrote back to say she thought the work was "blah" and "low craftsmanship."

The art advisor—intending to forward Teresa's answer to someone else—accidentally replied to Teresa instead: "This is a lost cause," wrote the advisor. "I can't help this person." That email, like a lot of conversations I'd been privy to, suggested there *were* rules when it came to having an Eye. Only I didn't know them.

Fortunately, there was a third camp, which promised I could hone my Eye the same way I'd build muscle. The best workout, I heard over and over, was to go see art, the more of it and the more unexpected the better. "Go to as adventurous of shows as you can, even if you don't think it's for you" was the advice I got from the gallerist Jack Hanley—and how I wound up outside a loading dock in East Williamsburg watching a grown woman with a fuzzy pink tail screech into a glitchy microphone while rolling on her back like a dying insect. I'd cram in a few art exhibits before meeting up with Jack, then, after a shift at the gallery, dash out to an open-studios event—special days often organized by schools or neighborhoods when artists welcome strangers to their workspaces.

As the fall got under way, I spent more and more time meeting artists for studio visits one-on-one in the hope of mining our conversations for tips on understanding and appreciating art. Names unlocked access, and it became easier to convince people to speak with me once I could drop that so-and-so had met with me already. I gravitated toward up-and-coming artists at the vanguard of the "new," and I met them at night or on weekends, before or after their shifts as nannies, teachers, farmers, servers, bartenders, caterers, art handlers, web designers, construction workers, yoga instructors, photo retouchers, jewelry makers, gallery assistants, figure-drawing models, backdrop painters, crafters of Mongolian horse-hair tassels, and studio assistants to more established artists. I went all over Queens, Brooklyn, and the Bronx, to warrens of rooms above auto body shops and metal yards. Studios were on long hallways set with rat traps, inside buildings that fluttered with ads for saw sharpening, "therapy for creatives," and the chance to rent the corner of a sub-subdivided studio already being split between a group of artists (a space slightly roomier than a Starbucks bathroom could be yours for $435 a month). Mysterious liquids dripped from the ceilings onto my notebook and the dominant studio aesthetic was no one can hear you scream. Windows were an expensive and thus rare commodity, but any space at all was a luxury. A studio could be the extra square footage of a bedroom revealed by tipping the mattress against the wall, or the twenty-four square inches of floor space between a bookshelf, bed, and closet door. To save room, painters painted over finished paintings, downsized to printer-paper-sized canvases, or abandoned painting for video art, which they could more efficiently store on a hard drive. When I asked artists about their wildest hopes and dreams for the future, they didn't talk about seeing their names on banners outside the Met or getting into subsequent editions of *Janson's History of Art*. They talked about affording health care and if really pushed—a "pipe dream," one painter called it—making enough money from selling their art to do it full time.

Between the shows and studio visits, I was looking at tons of art, only I didn't feel like I was *seeing* all that much more. I still clung to Jack's interpretations, and I wanted to hear more of them—all the more so since I'd determined that Jack's Eye was extremely well-regarded by his peers. An artist he'd shown early in her career, Molly Soda, was about to have a piece up at the Smithsonian's National Portrait Gallery in Washington, DC, and while adding email addresses to Jack's newsletter, I'd noticed that quite a few museum curators—the equivalent of art-world royalty—had made pilgrimages to 315. I felt

lucky to have him as a coach. During the workday, Jack regularly
swerved from lessons on Photoshop to lengthy detours on the art that
moved him, and I totally encouraged his digressions, which felt like
precious tutorials that could help me train my Eye.

I was following Jack's orders to draft a Facebook post about Josephs's show when he happened to glance at my screen. "Speaking of
Michael Blake," he said, spotting Blake's name somewhere on the page.
"Michael Blake's art is something that has changed the way I move
through the world on a daily basis."

Jack nudged me out of my chair, clicked onto his gallery's website,
and pulled up a sculpture by Blake that Jack had shown a few months
before. The piece consisted of two bathroom stalls the dull blue of old
Greyhound bus seats. One stall door was closed and the other slightly
ajar, and it looked to me as if Jack had installed a bathroom in the corner of his gallery.

Blake's sculpture was the sort of thing that, previously, I'd have
glanced at for two impatient seconds before giving up in frustration.
Now, I forced myself to wallow in its bewildering vagueness. *What
does it mean?*, I wondered. *Isn't this just ... a ... bathroom? What am I
supposed to feel?* My brain started to turn on itself—*YES INDEEDY,
YOU'RE AN IDIOT!!!*—and my body crawled with a hot, itchy feeling
of confusion I'd come to associate with looking at contemporary art. I
found the whole experience agonizing. I tried to remind myself that
the artists I'd talked with had said feeling repulsed by art was a good
thing, but I doubted this was the kind of discomfort they meant.

Contemporary art, they'd insisted during our studio visits, was not
about beauty. They raved about being disturbed by art and endorsed
feeling uncomfortable, lost, or confused as though these were terrific
new lifestyle choices—way better for you than, say, yoga. They told me

they did everything they could to throw the people staring at their work off-kilter. While I spent hours tweaking sentences to make them clearer, they painstakingly revised their pieces to make them more ambiguous. "I want to find a way to be less direct, less clear," stressed the painter Maggie Goldstone, while I stared at a painting of a purple figure curled up on herself in some sort of bath. Well, good for them that they liked feeling uncomfortable, I thought. Personally, I felt as if thousands of years of human evolution had hardwired me to try to avoid discomfort. I was still searching for the epiphany that supposedly came from feeling unsettled and unmoored.

I squirmed with impatience while I stared at Blake's sculpture, hoping Jack would share his interpretation and just put me out of my misery.

"Every time I use a public restroom, I think of Michael Blake," he began, his voice quiet with gravity. "His piece is in large part about being a gay man and thinking of a public restroom as both a place where you can find love—like a safe haven where you can have a romantic relationship, where you can be yourself... But it's also a place where you can get the shit beat out of you and you can fear for your life." Where someone else might see two bathroom doors, Jack saw life through Blake's eyes, along with the bliss and cruelty of being human. "I understand him better, I understand his life better, and ultimately, I understand other people's lives better. And then you understand the experience of life better. You have a sense of its scope. Its grandness."

To Jack, the value of art wasn't in making your dining room look pretty. Art was where culture touched down first—you'd see it in a painting before it showed up in a music video—and art could be moral homework. "This is giving voice to a marginalized community," Jack said, when I asked why he'd decided to show Blake's sculptures. "And I think it's important to think in terms of moving the needle on how society understands and incorporates those ideas, those lifestyles, and that diversity into its big picture."

I loved staring at an artwork and watching it transform before my eyes as Jack explained what drew him to it. It was moving to hear him speak, even magical. Blake's bathroom suddenly looked depressing and claustrophobic in a way it hadn't moments earlier. Where before there'd just been two stalls, now there was a story. But like Jack's monologue about Danh Vo, I wasn't sure I'd have gotten any of that unless I'd known Blake's background.

Up to this point, my default approach to art had just been to plant myself in front of a piece and wait for the epiphany to wash over me. (When inevitably it didn't, I'd scramble to the safety of the written word and glance at whatever press release had been put out to be helpful, which, to me, it rarely was.) But I was beginning to think I'd been going about it all wrong. Maybe art wasn't like a Big Mac, hardwired to tickle our taste receptors. Maybe it was more like chess, and you first needed to learn the rules.

I craved more chances to see Jack's Eye in action. And then it came: Jack announced he was taking a field trip. A few artists in Yale University's MFA program who'd be graduating next year had invited him to New Haven, Connecticut, to see their work. They were already jockeying to get shows in New York, and a gallery like Jack's would be an ideal next step.

Jack offered to let me tag along, and I jumped at the opportunity. Nothing would be more revealing, I thought, than seeing how he scoped out potential new artists to show. What did he value? What did he weigh? I showed up the morning of our visit practically wagging my tail with excitement. Jack less so. "Please," he pleaded outside the car, "don't embarrass me."

A STUDIO "VISIT" sounds nice and casual, but don't be fooled. For artists, a studio visit with a gallerist can be an adrenaline-fueled cross between a blind date, job interview, and prime-time debate. Gallerists do studio visits with artists they already show to check on new work, or—this is the stressful kind—with artists they *might* show to decide if they should. Curators, same. Artists do studio visits with other artists—to learn, make friends, commiserate. Collectors do studio visits, too—to investigate artists they admire and/or relish the frisson of being near feral creativity. (A gallerist told me her wealthy clients got a "contact high" from "that brush with dereliction.") By virtue of his running a gallery, Jack's meetings at Yale would have a very different tone from the ones I'd done on my own, yet the pilgrimage to the inner sanctum of an artist's workplace—a "sacred space," Jack called it—is a fundamental ritual and never low-key. Those allowed into the inner sanctum often bring offerings—beer, tequila, chocolate-covered brownies—and Jack assigned himself a reading regimen that included, at a minimum, an artist's CV.

An elaborate code of etiquette dictates when and how artists can ask gallerists for studio visits, which, as it was explained to me, essentially boils down to don't speak unless spoken to. "I've definitely had people tell me, 'NO. Don't *ever* ask someone for a studio visit,'" said Liz Ainslie, a painter I got to know at one of Jack's openings. "Don't do this. Just don't, don't, *don't*. Don't do anything. Just wait around for your *whole life* for somebody to come around and say, 'You're chosen.'" I was eager to see Jack evaluate art he could potentially show because the process by which artists got picked still stumped me, and I wasn't the only one. During my studio visits, it became clear that artists had no clue how it happened either, even though they had way more experience and much more at stake. "How does an artist get represented by a gallery?" I'd ask. "That's something I can't figure out," said an artist who'd spent twelve years trying to do just that. Simpler still: "How does an artist get a show?" "It's just, like, a mystery," said a sculptor, who really should have known, given that he ran his own gallery. The words "No unsolicited submissions" come standard issue on gallery websites, and asking a gallerist before you send in your work is no good either. "That's the *easiest* way to just be placed on a blacklist," I overheard a Lower East Side gallerist warn a group of terrified art students. Then again, the artists at Yale had just up and asked Jack to come see them—a reminder, I thought, to be wary of art-world generalizations.

The morning of our trip to Yale, Jack had me meet him at a stately prewar townhouse on what had to be the most charming block in Brooklyn's Cobble Hill. He and his girlfriend lived on one of its floors, in a gracious one-bedroom apartment that caught me by surprise: Its tall ceilings, polished wood floors, and sun-drenched moldings looked more upscale than what I'd anticipated for a guy who schlepped home trash to save on garbage fees. Most twentysomething guys I knew decorated with old dorm furniture, but Jack had tasteful white modern couches and an art collection that included pieces by artists he'd shown, as well as what appeared to be a signed print by Francis

Bacon—a British artist who briefly held the record for most-expensive artwork ever sold. I couldn't help but wonder how Jack made the math work to live there.

Jack drove us up to New Haven in his mom's Audi, and as we crawled along the Brooklyn-Queens Expressway, he filled me in on the hierarchy of MFA programs. Bard had the reputation of "go wild, do something new." Yale was known as a place that "makes you very market ready." According to the *U.S. News & World Report* ranking I googled somewhere along I-95, Yale, which carries a six-figure price tag if you don't get financial aid, was ranked one of the top five best art schools in the country. "People pay attention to it," Jack said, and those people included him. Haley Josephs had an MFA from Yale.

Jack found the artists he showed in all sorts of different ways—he'd met Josephs at an art fair—but he had a soft spot for card-carrying MFAs. The way he saw it, if he was going to invest money and time in building an artist's career, he wanted someone who'd stick with it for the long haul, and the masochism of grad school was apparently a good indicator of seriousness. Collectors also liked seeing the letters "MFA" on a CV: With an MFA, "you know what you're getting," Jack said.

Did Jack pick artists because he thought their work would sell well? "Not at *all*." He sounded offended I'd ask. Jack prided himself on not limiting his program to paintings, which were "steeped in a long history as this luxury good." Painting's rap sheet was long and varied, according to the Jacks of the world: "It's the colonizer... It's commodified so easily... The history of it is super Western," a painter had told me during a studio visit. At the most basic level, painting relied on highly problematic materials: "Like *cotton* canvas and *oil* paint," the painter said. Artists who weren't painters rolled their eyes at painting—"Especially now with global warming, the political climate . . . It just feels very indulgent," said a sculptor—and at certain Brooklyn openings, you could reliably revive a stalled-out conversation by shitting on Gagosian, capitalism, or painting, all of which were roughly synonymous.

Jack was especially wary of paintings by old white men. He and I once crossed paths with a large painting of a naked, reclining woman by Tom Wesselmann (American pop artist, big deal in the 1960s), and Jack waited until the gallerist was out of earshot, then flipped out. "I couldn't stand in that space and try to sell a painting of a nude woman by a white male artist from the last century," he sputtered. "If I'm doing that, I'm literally endorsing, 'This is how women should be viewed. This is what a male can get away with.'" Jack also found the prices for paintings like Wesselmann's deeply problematic. "Let's put a price tag of two-point-five *million* dollars, which is *so* ridiculous." He spat out the numbers as though they tasted bad. "Ninety-nine percent of the world will never have access to that sort of money. Donate that money to a charity." He looked pained. "I couldn't go home and be happy with myself."

Jack preferred to show artists he wanted to hang out with, although someone too social or social-*itey* (such that the first thing you see when you google them is their face, not their art) was also no good. The minute he didn't want to hang out with an artist was the minute his job felt like work, and then it wasn't as fun. Artists' morals and political leanings were also up for scrutiny. One of Jack's mottoes was "All work is self-portraiture." Another was "Everything is political." During studio visits, said Jack, "a question that I go to almost all the time is, 'What are some of your underlying world beliefs that dictate your artistic practice?'" He got heated at the mere thought of "giving a voice or platform to stuff I don't necessarily agree with."

We pulled into New Haven around noon and parked outside Yale's painting studios, a glass-and-brick building with the pizzazz of a Rite Aid. The artist who'd invited Jack met us in the lobby and immediately reviewed the day's schedule: seven artists, forty minutes each, with one coffee break, and dinner with her before we drove back to the city.

The art building felt claustrophobic, but whether it was the low beige ceiling tiles or the off-gassing of grad-student anxiety, I couldn't say. Artwork spilled out of studios into the hallways. We passed a life-sized doll in a black leotard impaled on the wall like a warning to mimes, and the whole place smelled like oil paint—a little fishy, a little plasticky, a lot like something terrible for your lungs.

The first studio we visited, like all the studios we visited, was a mini white cube. In one studio I spotted a calendar with another gallery's name written on a date and a note taped to the wall: *ontology— the branch of metaphysics that studies the nature of existence or being as such.* By way of greeting, artists told us where to park ourselves to avoid wet paint, then recited a thesis statement about their work, rehearsed to not sound practiced: "I'm so interested in malls as spaces," "I like using the body as a design element," "I've been thinking about labor a lot and unseen labor and how time can live in an object." On our sixth visit, the artist went off script. "It's like a reality TV show here. Everyone's performing," she sighed. I could see the resemblance. Cue voiceover: *Artists from every genre imaginable, from every corner of the planet, assemble at an elite Ivy League school where they must not only impress their esteemed faculty but outfox each other to gain the support of experts from every corner of the art industry. Surprise challenges include crippling debt, toiling in obscurity, and inconsistent access to health care—and only one will ultimately be crowned best living artist of their generation.*

The artists seemed—how to put this—fragile. One was burning

sticks of Palo Santo in an effort to cleanse the energy in her studio. Even after a summer off, she seemed to be teetering on a breaking point. "Yale offers free mental-health services, and it's like half the people there are from the art school," she said listlessly.

Down the hall, Jack and I met with the artist who'd organized Jack's visit. She had paintings hanging on the walls, blanketing the floor, and stacked four deep in piles against a wall.

"I've always used sex and humor to explore power dynamics," she began, pulling out even more pieces. Most of her paintings featured buck-naked humans with Kool-Aid-colored skin and rippling muscles, like Marvel superheroes whose superpowers consisted of pummeling enemies with their genitals.

Jack contemplated a painting of three Incredible Hulk–types surrounding a canvas on an easel. One flopped droopy magenta boobs over the easel's canvas, another squished it with balloon-animal breasts, and a third squirted it with supersoaker quantities of blue breast milk. "The images these evoke—what am I trying to say—are more mythical. The idea being expressed transcends narrative and becomes grander," said Jack, as I scrambled to see the same. Mythical wasn't the first word that came to my mind. The first word was *boobs*.

Jack kicked off the conversation with a few questions about her process. Do you prime your canvases? Is there pressure to use oil paint? Where'd the color palette come from?

From there, his questions quickly spiraled away from the paintings. What are you thinking of doing after school? Who are your professors here? Do you sleep with men or only women? The artist flinched at that one. She didn't see what her personal life had to do with it, but Jack pressed the point: *Wasn't* her sex life relevant? Whether or not she slept with men *obviously* informed her work, Jack insisted. "To get really into it—why is this entering his mouth?" he asked, apropos a painting of a steroidal blue man fellating himself.

Not for the first time, I felt Jack sliding my focus off the physical art piece itself: Look past the object till you catch sight of the idea, then gaze upon the identity of the artist, he seemed to be encouraging. That, apparently, was where to look for meaning.

Jack had a keen eye for the most minute details of an artwork—I couldn't see Josephs's paintings without thinking of Jack's observation that she used colors that only existed in the age of iPhone screens—and yet I was gradually grasping that the art world I'd arrived in had a complicated relationship with technical skill. Yale's great-great-great-great-grandfather was the Accademia di San Luca, an Italian art school founded in 1593 in Rome that became the prototype for modern art academies worldwide. The Accademia required aspiring artists to devote four years to perfecting the mechanics of their craft. Students spent their first year copying other artists' drawings of body parts, the following year drawing body parts based on three-dimensional models (humans, cadavers, or plaster casts), and then a year copying paintings by more established artists. Only in their fourth and final year did they earn the privilege of creating original artworks. Four hundred years later, Yale's art school was offering graduate-level classes on cryptocurrency and gender dialectics, but not drawing—a skill that an administrator at another art school called "woefully outdated."

What happened? People like Marcel Duchamp happened. Duchamp is so influential that there may be a law requiring me to mention him, so here goes: In 1917, Duchamp blew minds when he took a porcelain urinal, turned it on its side, and declared it a sculpture. (He dubbed art made from existing things "readymades.") Besides *Foun-*

tain (the sculpture of the urinal), Duchamp made pieces such as *Bottlerack* (literally, a bottle rack) and *In Advance of the Broken Arm* (just a snow shovel, albeit one with a sense of humor). Duchamp believed art needed to evolve beyond the so-called "retinal art" he saw his peers making—paintings of reclining nudes and impressionistic water lilies that, Duchamp sniffed dismissively, were "pleasing" and "attractive" objects that tickled the eye without stimulating the mind. "I was interested in ideas—not merely in visual products," Duchamp wrote. Duchamp didn't single-handedly shift the Zeitgeist, but generations of artists and connoisseurs have followed Duchamp's lead in arguing that what *really* matters about a piece of art these days is, as Jack had emphasized, the idea behind it. The thought trumps the thing. Pretty was suspect, and polish wasn't to be trusted. While I was painting my now infamous wall, Jack had mentioned that he used to love the meticulous black-and-white photographs made by the artist Hiroshi Sugimoto. Now, however, Jack considered them—kiss of death—"decorative." His key criticism of the work: "It's just very technically skilled."

WE WERE MORE THAN halfway through dinner before the painter, the one who'd organized our visit to Yale, backed into asking Jack's advice on how to make it as a professional artist.

First the good news: "Having an MFA from Yale helps," Jack said. "Painter? Helps. Paintings and photographs existing in a digital space?"—translation: art that looks good on Instagram—"Helps."

Now the bad news: Being a woman hurts. Jack knew a collector who'd nixed buying a piece by a female artist because he assumed "she's going to have a child soon." Big paintings are risky. Jack dropped

the art-dealer truism that no one buys art bigger than the size of a
Manhattan coop elevator, which is just small enough to make you
doubt it'll fit your sofa. Also, beware of art people. "All weird human
dynamics are magnified in the art world," Jack said, as he poured us
some red wine. "There's a lot of people who are borderline alcoholics,
who have mental-health issues, who are out late together drinking. It's
a bad cocktail."

Jack's pep talk got more disheartening by the minute. "Your work
might be good, but it doesn't really speak for itself," he said. "People
who navigate this world best are really good networkers and good at
personal relationships." Make friends, but not just any friends. "Consider *who* you hang out with and associate with." Don't assume any
chance to show is a good one. "Consider *where* you show," Jack stressed,
vaguely alluding to some spaces he'd avoid.

Jack sketched out a plan for the next two semesters: "Find five
Brooklyn spaces you want to show at and ten Lower East Side spaces
you want to show in. Reach out to all of them. Tell them about your
practice. If you can reach out to twenty people and three come up, that
would be successful."

But maybe none of them come to New Haven, he conceded. Now
you're in New York. Was she moving to New York? The question had
come up earlier.

"Probably New Jersey because I can't afford New York," the artist
said.

Jack inhaled sharply. "I don't know many artists in Jersey," he said.
"Go upstate. Go to LA. Go to Philly."

"Do people travel to Philly for studio visits?"

"I mean, the moment you leave the city—" Jack grimaced. "It's
tough."

Say you end up in New York. "Make the most of it," Jack advised. "Your job should be going to every single art thing possible." Openings were key. "Go to openings every single night. Make that your job: to network like crazy." Again, *openings*. "Show up to openings," he repeated. "Talk to the artist. If you can get in with the artist, maybe you can get in with the gallery. Maybe you make friends."

The summer after you graduate, try to get into a group show. Maybe a three-person show. Work toward a solo show if you like the gallery. If you don't, start over. "You don't want someone to show your work and talk about it in a weird way." How do you know if a gallerist is reputable? "You have to ask people." Maybe you seek gallery representation. "You want someone that you trust. You like how they present and talk about your work." After showing with a gallery for a while, "you start angling to put your work in an institutional show." Institution as in *museum*—only in the art world is being institutionalized a good thing.

Jack leaned back against the booth with finality. "That'd be my advice," he concluded. "*If* you want to make a go at that world."

"I'm interested," the artist insisted.

"It's a long journey," Jack warned.

"I'm ready," the artist said.

Jack looked at her skeptically, sighed deeply, and crumpled into the booth, as though physically flattened by the magnitude of what she had ahead of her. "Very few people achieve that dream of good gallery representation and living off your work," he told her. "*Very* few."

Jack broke down the odds for me later—in retrospect, an act of mercy for the artist. "It's like, you're *never* good enough in New York City. Like, you're *never* going to get there," he said. "Most artists just slave away their entire life, and what comes from it? Like, you get a couple solo shows and then—" He shook his head sadly. "I mean, you're *never* going to make it in New York. Like, *no one* enters the canon of art history. It's like point zero zero zero zero zero zero zero zero zero zero zero one percent… Have you looked at the numbers? I don't know how artists do it. Wow. No one. *No* one."

It wasn't until the car ride home that I realized what Jack hadn't said. His advice had nothing to do with the work itself.

A FEW WEEKS LATER, partway through Haley Josephs's show, Jack texted me to say he had exciting news. He was getting kicked out of his space.

Jack's lease was supposed to go till the end of March, but he'd need to be out a month early. The building had sold to a real-estate developer who'd be tearing it down to make way for condos, because it is an immutable rule of New York that anything interesting must, eventually, make way for condos.

The first order of business was to tell all the artists Jack showed that his gallery was going to move. No, totally kidding. The first order of business was a vow of silence. "My plan is basically to not tell anyone," Jack said. He didn't want anyone speculating he was closing his gallery. "Part of my business is performing, in a way, that my business is doing well," he told me. "That's why I'm always saying, fake it till you make it. Don't ever let 'em see you sweat." He'd extend his next show into December, close the gallery over the holidays, then reopen in January and just say, "New show, new space."

I could see why Jack would be wary. Practically every week I read an obituary for an art space—often small and emerging art–focused like 315—that had closed down. There were lots of explanations for the extinction event: Collectors only wanted to buy trophies, megagalleries kept swooping in to represent artists as soon as their careers took off, art fairs were too frequent and expensive, foot traffic had dropped off a cliff. I could count on one hand the number of visitors who trickled into 315 during the week while I was there, though I wondered whether that would have been different if the place didn't close at 5:00 p.m., before Joe and Joanne Schmo get off work.

Jack quickly narrowed down the acceptable geography for his new space to a half-mile by half-mile square in lower Manhattan that crisscrossed the Lower East Side and brushed Chinatown, which, pro, had affordable rents, but, con, was already being gentrified by an influx of galleries. "Do I really want to be that white gallerist who comes in and whitewashes everything?" Jack said. Perhaps not for the first time, I resisted pointing out, as we sat in 315, a space previously occupied by a business that, per its website, had been "the largest African American bookstore." (Jack said he'd felt guilty about taking over its lease—"But my landlord said, 'It's you or a tech company.'") Jack's other criteria: No ground floor, no high rise, not more than $5,000 a month, and it had to have character. He was drawn to a now shuttered Fujianese temple covered in roaches, with a hole in the ceiling caused either by a persistent leak or persistent rats.

These struck me as a staggering number of conditions, but to Jack, the borough he picked, the block he settled on, the space's distance from the sidewalk, the texture of his white walls—all of it communicated his philosophy on both art and life. "Everything I do reflects my business," he told me.

By "everything," what Jack meant was *everything*. I drafted an Instagram post promoting Josephs's show, and Jack agonized over whether or not to punctuate the phrase "come on by." "I don't know about the period," he perseverated. "People don't like periods. So definitive." Nix the period, he finally decided

Which collectors Jack took money from and how they'd made it—that weighed on him too. He practically trembled with rage at the idea of even associating with anyone in industries he considered immoral. "There are certain things like arms dealing and trading of a commodity that I think is *THE* worst thing in the world that I cannot—I really can't—I don't even know if I can be friends with people. I don't know how I can exist with someone like that. It's disgusting to me."

Jack's own finances, however, were totally irrelevant—that is, according to Jack, who got cagey when I asked about his family. One side was über-WASP, seventh-generation American—"Pre-Rev," said Jack, which is WASPese for *pre-Revolutionary War*. The other side of his family was "nuh-uh." He refused to go into it, just as he refused to get specific about where he attended high school. (It was, I eventually deduced, a private school in Princeton, New Jersey, where annual high-school tuition currently starts at $50,300.) Jack didn't strike me as a stranger to money—besides the Audi and the apartment, he spent August weekends in the Hamptons, and I assume his $560 Acne sneakers didn't just sprint out of the store and find him. Certainly a privileged background wouldn't make him the exception among New York gallery owners, who, like me and Jack, often had private schools on their résumés and a constellation of stamps in their passports. Both of his parents had MFAs in fine art; Jack's mom cofounded a nonprofit arts space based in Brooklyn (and owned the townhouse where Jack lived), and his dad was an executive at the jewelry goliath David Yurman. But never mind his family. "To me, that's not interesting."

Jack also sought to surround himself with a specific type of person, which, he increasingly made clear, wasn't me. Here I thought I'd been helping Jack by looking up shipping quotes and mopping his floors, but in fact, I was hurting his business, Jack informed me one afternoon.

"I hate to break it to you," he said as we stepped out to get lunch, "but you're not the coolest cat in the art world, so having you around, is like—it's just, like, lowering my coolness."

That physically stopped me in my tracks. It was such a snarky *Mean Girls* thing to say. "Are you being serious?" I asked.

"I'm totally serious," he said. And he looked it.

The hours I spent away from 315, unsupervised by Jack, *really* concerned him. Naïvely, I'd assumed he was just being polite whenever he asked about my week and who else I'd been to see. "You haven't realized that I'm sort of keeping tabs of who you talk to?" he asked, incredulous, as though monitoring an adult colleague's off-duty whereabouts was the most natural thing in the world. He said he wanted to know who else I might write about, because he thought it would be detrimental to be mentioned on the same page as certain galleries. "My life or my business in a way boils down to, like, in what conversation is the work that I do brought up in."

I tried to shrug off the feeling I was being tailed, just like I'd shrugged off Jack's quips about my clothes and coolness as merely ham-fisted attempts at constructive criticism. I didn't mind the tough love from someone who knew his way around a world I was determined to get inside—the more time I spent with Jack, the more I recognized just how savvy he was—and I appreciated his willingness to tell it to me straight. His comments stung, sure, but that didn't mean the guy was *wrong*. Every day at 315 delivered fresh insights into art and the machine, and I wasn't about to leave over a few bruises to my ego. *Especially* not when Jack kept dangling the prospect of letting me get even more involved: joining him to sell work at upcoming art fairs, helping him find a new space, and even—I salivated at the idea— partnering to curate a show.

Then, three weeks after telling me that he'd been keeping a close watch on my comings and goings, Jack announced he'd had a change of heart. He'd decided that relying on me to voluntarily share, here and there, the names of other people I'd talked with was insufficient. He now demanded that I text him the name of anybody in the art world I went to meet (sorry, no can do) and allowed I was welcome to solicit his opinion on the individual. Of course, he clarified, he didn't want to tell me what to do or be "this manipulative, controlling…" Jack trailed off, shaking his head grimly at the thought. "I think that'd be pretty gross and disgusting." But still—he needed to know who I was talking to. "Everything is something," he told me.

FULL DISCLOSURE: I thought Jack's microscopic level of scrutiny was bonkers. Who was even paying attention to his uncool assistant or his philosophy on punctuation?

Everyone, it turns out. And it all formed a part of something I'd been bumping into again and again: "context."

The first dozen times people brought up context, I brushed it off as a vague filler word. It took me awhile to realize I'd underestimated those two small syllables: Context, in the context of the art world, was something so real, so concrete, so precious that you could practically hold it in your hand or deposit it in a bank.

Where an artist went to school, who showed her work, who re- viewed her show, who bought her work, who'd inspired her, who followed her on Instagram, whether she slept with men or women, and whether Jack would want to hang out with her: All of it was context, and all of it influenced whether someone like Jack would champion her work—hence his advice to the artist at Yale. Context was the cloud of names that followed an artist around, and context was, according to the art lovers I was getting to know, inseparable from the art itself. All the details I'd thought were extraneous noise that shouldn't influence my judgment of an artwork were, I was being made to understand, actually crucial to comprehending the artwork. "If you don't know the context," Jack told me, after we had returned from Yale, "you can't understand what the fuck you're looking at."

It's theoretically easier to say what doesn't factor into someone's context than what does, but truly I'm not sure you could find anything to cross off the list. People were constantly wanding each other with context Geiger counters, and everything really *was* something. An ex-Gagosian employee said the gallery had such stringent guidelines on answering the phone that her boss made her record herself rehearsing the one-word greeting ("Gagosian."), then practice till she aced the intonation: curt with a downward inflection, because "you do *not* want to sound happy." A gallerist confessed he'd just advertised a job opening at his gallery—not with the goal of hiring someone, but to make people think he was busy enough to need more help. Artists' prices could skyrocket if their names were in the right mouths, hence galleries paying huge fees to have prominent art historians write essays about their artists' work. At studio visits, I commiserated with artists who said they'd felt pressure to change their demeanor and adopt a carefully honed "artist personality"—to be "flamboyant or strange or eccentric or highly individual." In other words, Jack was not at all paranoid, at least by the standards of the art professionals

I came to meet. He was an astute gallery owner who understood his community.

Having not been born yesterday, I do realize that context sways our judgment all the time. (Exhibit #1,471: Commuters ignoring the Grammy-winning violin virtuoso Joshua Bell that time he went busking in the DC subway.) But when it comes to contemporary art, context has become so powerful that it can affect the fundamental issue of what is and isn't art. Consider Duchamp's *Fountain*. It's a urinal. How do you know whether you're supposed to pee in it or nod at it contemplatively? Aha—*context*. If the urinal is in a white cube, was made by a famous artist, and is getting the thumbs-up from someone like Jack, it's art. "To see something as art requires something the eye cannot descry—an atmosphere of artistic theory, a knowledge of the history of art: an artworld," wrote the philosopher Arthur Danto. You can stick a stroller in a garage and get a few mechanics to claim it's a car, but that does not mean the stroller can do sixty miles an hour on the freeway. But put a urinal in a gallery and get critics to extol its artistic essence, and the urinal becomes a sculpture. There are many schools of thought on looking at art, including isolationists who will wave away context and tell you that anything beyond the artifact itself is irrelevant. But I didn't know any isolationists. The mood in the room was that fine art was what influential insiders said it was, hence the importance of attaching the right names (the right *context*) to whatever you were doing.

I got breakfast one morning with Bridget Donahue, who ran Jack's beloved Bridget Donahue gallery and was from all appearances a context savant. Over my plate of Huevo Kathmandu at Dimes, a stressfully hip restaurant-hangout in a corner of the Lower East Side known as Dimes Square, Bridget explained that art could be context for other art: showing fuck-you art that was hard to sell elevated the other work she exhibited. "That's building trust with my audience," she said. "They get that I'm not just after a buck." Having "huge" artists and "*major*" curators show up to her openings' after-parties—context. Selling an artist's work to museums was *great* context: Tell a collector the artist Martine Syms is having a show at MoMA, "and that's, like, all you need to say." Bridget argued the key difference between what *she* saw when she looked at an artwork and what I saw was a genealogy of names— a.k.a. context. "I can't now divorce myself from walking through the SculptureCenter and thinking to myself, 'Oh, I know the people who are on the board of this . . . So there's Sasha, there's Eleanor, there's Mary Ceruti, who runs this place . . . This is Ruba's show . . . Oh yeah, Lawrence Abu Hamdan, I remember when I sat next to him at a Triple Canopy benefit, and he was cool . . . Everyone told me he's a big deal . . . MoMA acquired a piece of his . . . Now, I cannot take away the analytical charting of all this other information that I have." Having an Eye, it was beginning to seem, meant having an eye for context.

It wasn't the answer I wanted.

CHAPTER FIVE

Like it or not, context was, Blob-like, taking over and devouring everything in my path. I'd be standing with Jack at an opening, trying to analyze a sculpture, and context would ooze into my field of view. First the artist's graduate school would bleed into my peripheral vision, then the names of her friends, then Jack's whispered opinion of the gallery would descend like a goopy, sticky soup. I was touring an exhibit when I overheard the gallery's salesperson nod in the direction of a piece and murmur to her client, "That's on loan from SFMOMA." I got so fixated on dissecting the context clues crammed into those five words—*this gallery is so rich they can afford to show work they can't sell, so respected they can borrow pieces from a museum, so discerning they sell art on par with what's at museums*—that I couldn't for the life of me tell you what art I saw. The more I kept trying to bring the art into focus, the more other things around the art came into focus instead. This, I learned, meant my Eye was maturing nicely.

That didn't sit well with me. Relying on context felt lazy, like I was outsourcing my opinions to the hive mind. I also couldn't shake the sense that all the fuss over context was one more way to keep out the Schmos. Someone like Jack becomes a lot more important if you need an art-history degree, years of going to art fairs, and fluency with Clement Greenberg to commune with a painting.

Which isn't to say I wasn't pleased with how far I'd come. After a few months with Jack, I could join in on the name-dropping at openings, recognize who'd made an artwork without glancing at the label, and use *faux-naïf* in a sentence (as in, *Those stick-figure sharks painted by the Yale MFA grad are* totally *faux-naïf*). But still, I worried that I was losing sight of the art.

I wanted a new perspective. I craved a glimpse at the nitty-gritty process of actually *creating* an artwork and a chance to ask the questions I'd been surprised not to find on the agenda at Yale: How'd you decide to paint *that*? Why *this* green? All the little moves that art critics bloodlessly call the *formal* aspects of a work fascinated me. Artists got this wide-eyed, faraway look when they described how making art both stripped away the magic of art and made you appreciate a piece even more. "Knowing something in theory is a different thing to knowing it in your body. There's a physical thing," the artist Julie Curtiss had told me during a studio visit over the summer. "You just understand from the inside. And you can read art *way* differently than other people."

That was exactly what I hoped to do. I wrote Julie with a highly voyeuristic request: Could I watch her paint?

PRETTY MUCH ALL the gallerists I talked with would, at some point, lower their voices as if imparting a trade secret and confide that their favorite way to find talented artists was by talking to other artists. That advice had led me to Julie.

The first time I stepped foot in her studio, I immediately locked eyes with a cigarette. It was a flimsy little sculpture, barely life-sized, that stuck out from the wall with a thin tail of gray hair flowing out the ash end, like a hairy little waterfall. I couldn't decide if it was beautiful or disgusting. And I couldn't get it out of my head.

Julie's experience as an emerging artist echoed what I heard during lots of studio visits. She'd moved to New York eight years before—virtually sight unseen—after growing up in a suburb outside Paris called Montreuil. In New York, she squeezed art into her off-hours as she cycled through a series of jobs: selling clothes, selling shoes, selling macarons, which required her to wear a French maid uniform and frilly hat. Via a classifieds site specializing in art jobs (and with a warm introduction from a friend), Julie eventually got hired as a studio assistant for Jeff Koons (whom you might know for his mirrored, lobby-sized balloon animals), then for the artist KAWS (whom you might know for his Day-Glo riffs on beloved cartoon characters with Xs for eyes). But Julie couldn't say much about that because they'd made her sign NDAs. It was only in the past year, around her thirty-fifth birthday, that Julie had started earning enough from selling her own paintings to quit her day job. She still got a little pale when she thought about it. Leaving KAWS's studio had been "very scary." She could practically name the day and hour she gave notice.

But Julie also stuck out among the artists I'd met. She had a quiet confidence that gave me the sense, without it seeming rude or standoffish, that she didn't really care if I was there, because her art was all the company she needed. She kept glancing itchily at her paintings while we spoke and talked about them with a casual frankness that suggested she saw plainly the value of her work without needing to dress it up in theory or International Art English. The first time we spoke, I asked her one of those soul-searchy questions that journalists hope will lead to Oprah-worthy moments of self-reflection: How does being an artist change your perspective on the world? Julie wrinkled her nose as if at a bad smell: "I find that a little pretentious." She struck me as someone who'd cut through the crap—and the context.

Julie agreed to let me sit in while she worked, and at 10:30 a.m. sharp on a sparkling October day, I met her on the sidewalk outside her studio. She had a coffee in one hand, a croissant in the other, and I can't tell you what she was wearing, because, after a lecture from Jack on why it was wrong to focus on female artists' appearances (complete with a live reading from a problematic *New Yorker* article to illustrate his point), I didn't write it down. That Jack spent so much time analyzing my own clothes, makeup, and jewelry didn't detract from the conviction with which he made his point.

Julie hustled us inside, eager to get to work. Her current studio was at an artist's residency in DUMBO that she'd gotten into after applying unsuccessfully for six years. They'd assigned her a sunlit room with three windows—by studio standards, the equivalent of a house with a pool, guest house, and tennis court. I complimented her view, which spanned two bridges and a chunk of brick towers in the lower-Manhattan skyline. Julie saw more. "It's like Mondrian or something," she said, glancing out the window. As in Piet Mondrian, an artist born in 1872 who painted abstract paintings of colored grids, as if Excel docs had gotten gussied up in red, yellow, and blue formal wear. "There's something modern about it. Lots of verticals and horizontals. I don't know how it'll inform my work, if it does."

Julie wasn't even halfway through her croissant before she started worrying about all the canvases she needed stretched. Her process was sl-o-o-o-o-w, she groaned—"like a nightmare a bit, when you want to get somewhere but you can't walk and so you miss your plane." She tore off a bite of the croissant and made a strangled gurgling noise of frustration. "It's like giving birth *over* and *over*." Julie had a shoulders-back poise, a long mane of black hair she wore knotted into a bun with a paintbrush, and no poker face whatsoever. Her dark eyes twinkled mischievously when she looked out the window and roiled when she thought about all those canvases. She'd bought twenty preassembled stretchers for around $1,200, but balked at the extra grand it'd cost to hire someone to put canvas on them—"a luxury," she said. She'd asked her new intern, an art student, to do it instead. "These I would have stretched in two days with someone else," she grumbled. "He stretched three canvases, and every one of them, he fucked it up."

I saw an in.

"I know how to stretch canvas," I volunteered, hoping that was true. I mean, Jack and I had spent at least two hours sweating over Josephs's paintings. He was a thorough, patient teacher. I'd absorbed something, probably.

Julie stopped mid-bite. "Really?" She perked up. "Can you help me?"

We both hoped so. Julie grabbed a wooden stretcher from a stack against the wall and rounded up a gleaming staple gun along with a pair of wide pliers that looked like a sadistic dentist's prized possession. She kneeled on the floor gripping the naked stretcher—four skinny pieces of plywood joined at the corners to form a rectangle—and confidently, a little too quickly, showed me how she wanted her canvas stretched. "Usually you start with three staples." She *thwack-thwack-thwack*ed the staple gun, and I *flinch-flinch-flinch*ed at what I remembered too late was a menacing recoil. Julie rotated the stretcher and used the pliers to yank the raw edge of the canvas over the opposite plywood bar. The fabric strained angrily against the three staples. "And I put my thumb flush; it won't go anywhere"—the canvas looked desperate to go somewhere—"and I staple." *THWACK.* "Here." *THWACK.* "Nice tension." *THWACK.* "Then obviously you go opposite." Obviously. "We don't want it to be loose. I don't like working on a loose canvas." She tapped the surface of the canvas, which shivered but didn't slouch. Tight.

Julie passed me the staple gun and pliers, then abandoned me to roll a stool over to a table stacked with spiralbound sketchbooks. She flipped through one. She was trying to decide which painting to start next and tilted the notebook toward me to show me how each piece started as a pencil drawing. "The way I start painting is I have a vision of something. A vision or a feel for a painting, something I *want* to happen." Only a fraction of her sketches ever matured into a piece. She flipped past a drawing of a pasta strainer with hair flowing through its holes. "Didn't work. It looked like shit." There were aborted drawings that devolved into exasperated scribbles and occasional notes in English or French. I glimpsed a scrawled *"chapeau chou"*—cabbage hat— as Julie flipped past it. "The hardest part is to figure out which one I want to do, because I make so many sketches of ideas," she said to the drawings, as if she were apologizing in advance for having to play favorites. She lingered on a still life of a meal arranged on a table. A wine glass, baguette, and fruit bowl flanked a plump croissant made of hair, which lounged seductively on a plate. Bingo: her next painting, Julie decided. She'd trace different versions of the croissant sketch onto little cut-up squares of tracing paper—erasing, adding, shifting parts "until it feels like something." Then she'd trace her favorite iteration onto a plastic transparency, project *that* onto a prepped canvas, and trace it with diluted acrylic paint.

The hairy croissant would make the third or fourth unfinished painting in the studio. Working on one piece at a time wasn't good for either Julie or the art, she said. "It's a lot of pressure on one work. And sometimes, the works don't like that." Julie talked about her pieces as if they were temperamental children. Several in-progress paintings were in time out. They'd been "very noisy," Julie said admonishingly. "And to not have noise, I need to not look at them." She'd made them face the wall. Occasionally, her paintings cooperated. Most were stubborn. Many were complete assholes. "It's frustrating when there's a painting and you never clicked. That painting was just pure *suffering* from beginning to end. It becomes a fight. And then you're not even happy with the result! And you fought so, *so* much." She glared at one painting out of the corner of her eye. "This painting is resisting. It's not complying. It's not collaborating." The painting appeared unmoved by these allegations. You couldn't reason with such an uncooperative jerk. Julie would just have to try to listen to its needs. "It's almost this autonomous entity, and I have to be patient. It's not just me in control." She'd attempt to talk it out. "'What do *you* want? What do *you* need?' Okay. I'll try that.' It's this weird kind of relationship," Julie said. "It's like a couple. You try to avoid the fighting."

A few hours in, the new painting of the hairy croissant, which Julie had only just traced onto a canvas, was already being a total pain. From my squat on the floor, I watched Julie step back and squint at it. "Hmmmmmm . . . Okay . . . The composition is problematic." She pointed to a blank expanse behind the croissant, in between a fruit bowl and a wine glass. "I think there's too much empty space here, which didn't seem bad on the sketch, but sometimes when you blow things up, suddenly scale really matters." She wondered if a vase of tulips could fix the problem. She'd try that, then steel herself for whatever new problem she'd notice at that point.

"Everything is like that. It's going to be touching up a bit of this, touching up a bit of that. It's all decision-making," Julie said. "Painting is *constant* decision-making."

It took until after lunch for Julie to work up the courage to confront another painting she'd been feuding with. While they faced off, I put down the staple gun and contemplated the painting: A pair of woman's legs, elegantly outfitted in black high heels, were stretched out on the grass, her toes pointed up at a dazzling blue sky. The background was cheerful, but the scene didn't add up—who naps on the grass in heels? My mind immediately went to a homicidal maniac who'd gotten bored halfway through hiding a corpse.

"Something is not working there," Julie told the painting. She and the painting faced off in silence.

"I think I'll have to repaint the sky," she announced, with the grim finality of a surgeon telling a patient she'll have to operate. "I have to repaint a bunch of things. It's kind of frustrating." Every now and then, a deeper French accent bubbled to the surface. I *f*ink. Frus*trayt*ing. "Maybe I'm just picknitting," Julie said later, after scrutinizing an *eemaj* of a sculpture she thought was a little *sheety*.

The problem was the sky's color. "Too vivid or artificial." She wheeled over a plastic cart heaving with old coffee cans filled with brushes, scissors, rags, paint, and latex gloves.

"The hue is too crazy," Julie said. I sensed she was trying to talk herself into the unpleasant chore of repainting the sky. "The sky is going to be a *pain* in the *ass* behind those plants," she whined. She repeated herself again: "I'm *going* to redo the sky." She said it the way

shaky swimmers dared onto the high dive announce, *On three I'm* going *to jump.* She commanded herself to start. "You *have* to redo it." She
didn't want to. "I spent *three hours* on that stupid sky." She told the
painting to look on the bright side: "Lucky for us, today is a blue sky."
Julie blamed the sky's current "artificial" color on the fact that it'd been
overcast the day she painted it. And then there'd also been that irre-
sistible new shade of blue. She fumbled in her cart and whipped out a
mangled tube of blue oil paint, her eyes sparkling as if she'd won a
prize. "I wanted to try this new paint. A cyan color."

I sat on the floor behind Julie and kept one eye on her as she
painted while trying not to maim myself with the staple gun. Stretching a canvas is like trying to put formalwear on a rabid monkey using
only chopsticks. The wood will bite. The staple gun will *really* bite.
The pliers aren't the dream tool for the job, but I was happy to have
them because by the time I was *thwack*ing the opposite side of my second stretcher as Julie had showed me, the canvas was biting, the blisters on my thumbs were swelling, my arms were shaking, and the
staple gun was increasingly baring its teeth in my direction. Canvas
has about as much give as a kitchen chair and loathes stretching, pre-
ferring to twist and pucker. It lumps in weird places if you don't pull
enough but tears or warps if you pull too hard.

All the hushed murmuring about historicity and post-postmodernism
that goes on in galleries hadn't quite prepared me for the blistery business of making art. The emphasis on ideas glossed over the blood,
sweat, and tears, as though being an artist meant lounging around
the studio daydreaming while swirling a snifter of brandy in the air.
But making art was practically athletic: Julie was alternately yanking
out my errant staples, furiously swishing blue paint, and struggling
to muscle fake hair into the shape of a fish. She had the sculpture's

herring-sized carcass on her work table and couldn't look at it without going off on how the stray hairs were driving her crazy—she'd refined her wig-sculpting technique by taking a class on Victorian hair art, but the hair *still* wasn't lying as smooth as fish scales. Gravity frequently got in her way, and practically every work was an engineering challenge. For each one of her pieces, Julie had to translate a thought into a thing, then make it stick, lie, stay.

Something clicked in me as I sat there on Julie's floor. It sounds ridiculous to say I realized I needed to look at art. I'd *been* looking at art. Only I hadn't known what to pay attention to in the work itself. Seeing Julie paint offered clues for how to look at a painting like an artist. I needed to slow down, examine its physical form, and consider the artist's decisions. Because painting is *constant* decision-making.

How you prep your canvas, whether you prep your canvas, whether you use canvas: All of it matters. There is cotton canvas (which has an even blond nub) and linen canvas (which has a bumpy flaxen weave), and then there's ditching canvas altogether for paper, parchment, wood, copper, tree bark, fridge doors, you name it. (Canvas is everywhere these days, but until the Venetians embraced it in the 1400s, it had a lowly reputation among European painters, who used canvas for temporary backdrops and parade banners. Back then, if a painting was important, you'd do it on wood.) Your choice of surface will change how the light reflects off the painting, what if any texture shows through the paint, how the paint goes on, and how the brush glides, which Julie's wasn't doing at all. "If there's too much absorption, it's hard to blend," she muttered, as she swept her brush over the too-vivid sky.

You could paint with paint, or you could use berries, bleach, rabbit blood, anything, really, to make a painting. Each medium had its own personality, I was learning. Julie was painting with oils that day, but on another day it could be gouache, acrylic, or Flashe. She often used multiple different kinds of paints on the same piece and was constantly wrestling with the foibles and eccentricities of each. Oil paint, which Julie was using on her blue sky, was good for gradients and blending and getting something "a little richer in color," plus it had a haughty air of historical importance—it's been "the dominant paint medium for well over five hundred years," according to one conservator. (The Early Renaissance painter Jan van Eyck, who made the famous *Arnolfini Portrait* of a wealthy couple standing in front of an enigmatic mirror, gets credited as the medium's pioneer, but the earliest known oil paintings are seventh-century cave murals in Afghanistan that illustrate the life of Buddha.) Acrylics—which are water-soluble, made of teensy plastic acrylic resin particles suspended in water, and got popular in the 1950s despite owing their start to a company owned by the firm that made nerve gas for Nazi death camps—are a reliable workhorse that dries fast and dries matte. Julie used acrylic for her base coats and for sketching the outline of the hairy croissant. Flashe, a vinyl-based paint developed in 1954 for scenery painters that comes in candy-bright colors so appealing I wanted to lick them, dries flat and opaque and easily hides brushstrokes. "It creates something more velvety, more blended," Julie said. It also reminded her of gouache, a paint she adored because it "reflects the light in such an intense way." Each paint had its own reputation: Spray paint was the ripped jeans to oil paint's pressed khakis. Egg tempera—an egg-yolk-based paint that was the go-to for millennia—was a papal robe.

So you've picked paint to make your piece. How will you apply it? There's no wrong answer—artists have smushed painted breasts on canvas, pooped paint on canvas, kicked paint on canvas—but if you,

like Julie, choose to paint with brushes, your choices are just beginning: What size? Whose fur? There are brushes made of horsehair,
squirrel hair, goat hair, badger hair, wolf fur, weasel tail, a pig's neck
beard, and nylon, and that's not the half of it. "I'm not a big brush
nerd," said Julie, before proceeding to wax poetic about the special
subset of brushes she reserved for painting strands of hair. She held up
a brush most artists would have thrown out long, long ago: Its tip was
skinny as a pencil's and, once upon a time, had probably been just as
sleek, but now its ends frizzed as if the brush had jammed a fork into
an electric socket. "I really like when they're fucked up, because that's
when I do this kind of stuff—you see the little strands here?" Julie and
I stuck our faces up to a painting so she could show me how each hair
ended with forked split ends. "It does the feathering thing that I like to
keep. That's more, like, my trademark."

You could paint a thin line or a thick line, a line that bleeds, wad-
dles, stands at attention, or retreats. Letting a stroke look sloppy
was often a carefully calibrated decision. "You can either have a really
clean delineation or you can let it be messy, and, in that case, it stays
more light and airy and open in a way," the painter Liz Ainslie told me
later. Like footprints, each mark held the memory of a specific action.
Staring at Julie's brushstrokes made me think of how different they
were from Haley Josephs's. Like muddy tire tracks on a clean road,
Josephs left a record of how her brush moved: The paint was gloopy
where the brush touched down, striated where it slid, and thin where it
pulled away. Julie's marks hugged the canvas as tightly as shadows on
a wall, and she blended her brushstrokes to hide her hand—to the
point that I could barely make out a brush had been there at all. I was
beginning to appreciate that different marks carried the emotional
oomph of sound effects in a comic strip. Julie's feathery strands of hair

were a *thwip*! Jackson Pollock's layered splatters of paint hit you with a GA-SHPLUCT! "When I went to the new MoMA the other day and I stayed in front of a Pollock, the energy was amazing," Julie said, an excited smile spreading across her face. "I was *in* the moment. I was looking at the painting, but really I was *watching* it rather than looking at it. You know what I mean? It's like, stuff was in *motion*."

I could see motion now when I looked at Julie's work. Her hand had moved *there*, in that way. She'd chosen this blue over that one. Seeing the act of creation—the way a work doesn't come out fully formed but grows by fits and starts—made me aware of how delicate and fragile an artwork was. How improbable it was that it existed. Someone had agonized over this square inch. They'd poured themselves into that *flink* of a line. I thought of the bewildering piles of supplies I'd seen in studios: Vaseline, turpentine, wax, Q-tips, chopsticks, marble dust, masturbators. It's not magic that makes a piece. All the Hollywood visions of possessed artists throwing pieces together in a trance-like state overlooked the fact that this was work. Each piece may have started with an idea, but there was more to it than that. "An idea is not a painting," Julie said, as she worked, her nose practically grazing the canvas. She was already thinking ahead to how she'd fix the brushyness of the tights, maybe go over the shoes again. The soul of the artwork needed a body, and she belabored every hair of that body. Seeing Julie work gave me a path to follow into the piece.

By the late afternoon, half of Julie's sky had turned a pale baby blue. She'd replaced the cyan with a cobalt, a warmer blue that reminded me of waves and ship hulls and a sea captain's faded cap. (Warmer colors lean yellow, while cooler colors lean blue. You may think all blue leans blue, but not exactly: The so-called temperature of a color is relative, and the cobalt was cooler than, say, ultramarine, a hypnotic blue that puts the eye of a peacock feather to shame.) Julie's original sky had looked fine to me, but as Julie painted over it, I could see now that the cyan version had had a greenish tint, as if the sky had gotten carsick.

Julie already missed her paintings, which would eventually leave for a show. "It's like babies: I enjoy living with them, spending time with them." I already missed Julie. She'd coaxed her paintings to open up to me, and I wondered what else they might say if I stuck around. I wanted to ask if I could come back, maybe work regularly, but Jack's voice drowned out the idea. The art world considered me the enemy, he regularly reminded me—"because you're a journalist."

When I left a little before dinnertime to meet Jack at 315, Julie was just getting into her groove. She might work another three hours. Maybe four. In the evening, everything quieted down, and she liked that. That's when she could hear the art best.

AT THE END of October, Jack and I took down Josephs's paintings, destroyed the architectural element, spackled walls, and, once again, made a lot of trips to the hardware store. For his next show—the one he'd be extending in advance of losing his space—Jack planned to pair sculptures by Michael Blake with paintings by Caitlin MacBride. He asked if I'd like to take a stab at writing the press release for the show.

The job felt like a suicide mission. Every now and then, when I did something dumb at the gallery, Jack would shake his head at me and say *"Fired!"* as if I'd been voted off a reality TV show of one.

In this addled frame of mind, I sat down to write the thing.

I spent a very, very long time watching the cursor blink on an empty white page. It was hard to hear myself think over my imagined soundtrack of Jack's voice—*Fired!*—calling out as he read whatever it was I might write.

Finally, I pulled up some pictures. MacBride planned to show meticulous, colorful paintings of mystifying Shaker contraptions, including a laundry rack that looked like a wiry TV antenna. Blake planned to show a spandex gimp mask stretched over a balloon and various skinny black pipes assembled into upside-down *U*'s like bent pull-up bars.

This should be easy, I chided myself. Gallery press releases, which get stuck out on a desk at nearly every art show, typically follow a formula. They start with a sentence declaring the gallery's pleasure to be showing so-and-so's work, have a few lines about what the artist makes and how, then wrap up with a paragraph about the broader significance of it all. The dirty secret of contemporary-art press releases, one gallerist told me, was that there are only two possible punch lines: "Every fucking artist allegedly transforms the familiar into the unfamiliar, or vice versa."

I was a professional writer. I could do this.

I got as far as "315 Gallery is pleased to present," then hit a wall. What did the work *say*? I read over my notes from Jack's musings: *Circles as infinite space*. Huh? I couldn't do anything with that.

Next I turned to a traditional writing exercise: procrastination. I read every interview Blake and MacBride had ever given and made a seven-page outline.

I opened a new Word document. *Just say what you see in the work*, my brain screamed at itself.

Which was…?

I eventually gave up on finding an answer key and went back to staring at photos of the art, willing the words to come. Inspired by my day with Julie, I thought about the materials. Blake had said he'd made his sculptures using black pipes from a hardware store. I thought of Jack, who I'd listened free-associate his way to an interpretation. Pipes led me to plumbing, plumbing to poop, poop to digestion, digestion to bodies. Some of Blake's pipes wore tube socks on them, which made me think of gyms, and were also encircled by silver hoops, which got me going on cock rings. Well, hello: Suddenly Blake's twisted black shapes morphed into little bodies that had been choked, cuffed, and squeezed. In the language of gallery press releases, that became, "Blake's floor-based sculptures recall bodily organs and, in their placement relative to one another, evoke figures, uniformed and poised for action, that are constricted and controlled." I thought about the hours it must have taken MacBride to render those Shaker forms so exactly and her decision to make them so realistic. An obsession— fetishization?—seemed to infuse her process, and next to Blake's sculptures, her Shaker accessories looked like... like... bondage gear from a dominatrix's dungeon? I went with it. I wrote that MacBride's forms were imbued with "desire and longing" and "erotic meaning."

It took me a week to string together eleven sentences that said Michael Blake and Caitlin MacBride transform the familiar into the unfamiliar. But I'd done it: I'd forced myself to wallow in art's ambiguity and discomfort. I'd survived. I didn't feel my spirit doing somersaults, but I'd grappled my way to an understanding that I could stand behind.

"It was very good," Jack told me after he read the draft, sounding a little surprised. "Reading it put a lot more faith in you than I'd had."

So I wasn't fired. But increasingly, I wasn't sure whether I should stay.

CHAPTER SIX

I thought I'd been behaving myself. Fewer questions, less makeup, more mute nodding. While out perusing art, Jack hissed at me not to stare so much, so now I darted my eyes around rooms like a spooked horse, terrified he'd catch my pupils lingering.

But Jack only seemed more frustrated with me as time went on. He was shushing me more when I ventured questions—"My business is my personal life," he told me when I asked if he'd sold any of Josephs's pieces—and he'd started dropping "off the record" with what felt like every other heartbeat. I respected his wishes and volunteered that if he was uncomfortable having me around, I could back off working at the gallery. Even though we'd laid down the ground rules early on and discussed them frequently, I sensed he viewed my presence as a journalist with mounting suspicion and was beginning to have deep misgivings about how little he could control what I might go on to write. "Nuh-uh," he instructed me one afternoon, wagging his finger back and forth. "Don't write that down." (I didn't.) He'd lately supplemented calling me "the enemy" with questioning my ethics as a reporter.

One night, Jack and I were shoveling down dinner after openings when I asked what he'd thought of the shows we'd seen.

Huge. Mistake.

"My taste is my business," he snapped. "If I share what I think is important, I give away everything. And I can be critiqued. It puts me in too vulnerable a position."

It wasn't a friendly conversation, and at some point I tried to diffuse the storm clouds by joking about what a shit job I'd done repainting his wall, since dissecting my flaws usually seemed to put Jack in a good mood. "I could probably have used another demonstration on how to use the paint roller," I said.

"You don't think I showed you a certain way so I could then come back and say you did it wrong?" Jack shot back.

I froze. "Did you do that?"

Jack mumbled a reply I couldn't hear.

"Did you do that?" I repeated.

He said something under his breath I still couldn't make out.

"Did you deliberately show me the wrong way to do it?" I pressed.

Jack never answered the question. "I feel sorry for your husband," he told me, as we were getting up to leave. "I feel like I'm shouting into the void."

Being around Jack was giving me whiplash, but by then I'd learned enough to see that the art world was one big melting pot of hypocrisies and contradictions. Museums made a fuss about welcoming the public, but a curator told me his measure of success was whether a tight-knit crew of artists liked his show. Jack was wary of foot traffic, but he hoped the art he showed could change the world. He wanted an inclusive program, yet wanted to show artists he'd like to hang out with. He was thinking of renaming the gallery after himself, only "I don't like any sort of spotlight or attention or anything," he told me, the journalist he'd invited to trail him around. One day he'd encourage me to stay with 315 another few months so I could *really* learn the ropes. Another day he'd threaten to kick me out.

Several weeks before, we'd been saying our goodbyes after a studio visit one night when Jack asked if I'd ride along with him to a bar. He was running late to meet an artist for a drink but wanted to talk.

Jack parked directly in front of the bar and sat rigidly in the driver's seat staring at a bodega's flashing neon sign. He said he was having second thoughts about letting me trail him around.

"There's sort of some mystery to the way the art world operates, and I don't know if pulling back that curtain is such a good idea," he said quietly. "Like, it's weird, but the art world is the way it is because not everyone has access to it. And not everyone understands it. And that's sort of what creates interest and intrigue."

I attempted a reply, but Jack held up a finger to signal he wasn't through.

"Information is power. And the more you know about how to move through a world, the more power you have in that world," he continued. "If you're selling a commodity or something, you *do* sort of want to wield a certain amount of power in that situation. And giving that to people—" He struggled for a moment, as if he couldn't bear to imagine the consequences. "Is that even a good idea?"

I mean, I thought so. I started in on a rebuttal, but Jack pulled out his phone to text the artist he was meeting, so I waited until he put down his phone and then tried to speak again.

"I don't want to cut you off," said Jack, cutting me off. "This goes back to the art world as this exclusive 'You have to be in the know'... There's whole conversations about collectors that you want to work with, why you want to work with them." When it came to the sort of people who read the things I write—Jack paused: "I don't know if I have any interest in them."

BY NOW, I'd internalized what should have been patently obvious for some time: Jack and I did not have the world's healthiest working relationship. But since Jack's urge to rid himself of me seemed to come and go, I told myself to buck up and stick it out. I was fine—*fine!* Jack was teaching me so much, and anyway, I kept hoping things would get better. There were glimmers of positivity. "I respect how dedicated you are," he told me, apropos why he'd invited me to work with him. "If I value what I do and if I value my life and my interests, then to be able to share that with someone closely is a meaningful experience." Everyone I mentioned Jack's name to gushed about how great he was to work with, and I wanted to think we were just going through an extended rough patch. Truth be told, I couldn't imagine what I'd do if things *didn't* get better. I worried that if I ever did leave, Jack would waste no time trashing whatever I had in the way of a reputation. He told me he'd been talking about me with artists at 315, and what he recounted wasn't all that complimentary.

That conversation we'd had in the car haunted me, and not just because it made me second-guess my future at 315. It so perfectly captured a mood I'd encountered over the past few months: Even among those in the New York art world who professed to champion inclusivity, the vibe could be very much *thanks but no, there are too many people already, check if the modern-dance folks are taking applications.* I said, "Make art more accessible," and many artists heard, "Dumb art down," which seemed like a dim view to take of one's fellow humans. In the Clement Greenberg essay Jack had assigned me, Greenberg argues that the "peasant"—presumably his generation's term for *Schmo*— can't appreciate art without intense effort and "conditioning," and only the elite have time for that. "Superior culture is one of the most artificial of all human creations," Greenberg writes, "and the peasant finds no 'natural' urgency within himself that will drive him toward Picasso in spite of all difficulties." Yes, well, but: It certainly doesn't help that the handmaidens of "superior culture" hide the art, discuss it in a made-up language, and call people "Schmos."

This corner of the emerging-art world, which I'd thought would be at least a smidge more open, was starting to feel like one of the most exclusive parts of the art scene. While megagalleries all but advertised that they discriminated on the basis of money, the pure excluded on the basis of murkier standards. It was the type of exclusion I associated with stodgy old country clubs, not the hip downtown arts scene. Do you believe what I believe? Would I want to sit next to you at a meal? *Are you our type of person?*

I kept thinking about this in the days after Blake and MacBride's opening. The night their show opened, a parade of people, all dressed differently in the same way, had filtered through Jack's space. Uptown, the crowd was as sparkly and smooth as baby dolphins. In Brooklyn, the uniform was dress to transgress, and the more you looked as if you'd gotten hazed by a theater troupe, the better. One guy showed up to Jack's opening in a neon orange crossing-guard vest.

An hour in, a woman in her early twenties—let's call her Meihua—approached me nervously to ask whether I knew Bianca. I'm Bianca, I told her. Meihua, who'd exchanged Instagram DMs with Jack, had just gotten her MFA from an art school in the Midwest and had decided to take a chance on moving to New York instead of back to her hometown in Taiwan. I asked about her work, and she pulled up her Instagram so I could scroll through paintings on her phone—dark, mushy worlds full of lonely little people with big sad eyes.

I admired her pluck. It's not easy showing up to an opening and trying to meet people, but, just as Jack had advised the student at Yale, she was out doing exactly that.

I brought her up to Jack a few days later while he was reviewing the gallery's exhibition plans for the spring. Had he had a chance to look at Meihua's work? I asked. You know, Meihua—the artist who'd introduced herself at the opening.

"Did you embarrass us?" Jack asked. "What was she like?"

"What do you mean, 'What was she like?'"

Jack chuckled. "I mean, you met her. What was she like?"

I rehashed our conversation: recent grad, showed me her art, seemed friendly.

"Is this someone you'd want to hang out with?" Jack asked. "Like, if you had a conversation and she just like started talking about herself and her work and like trying to like sell herself, I'd be like"—he inhaled sharply—"that seems inappropriate. Like, you're at *someone else's* opening," he chided. "This isn't the place for you to start talking about yourself kinda thing. So that's why I'm like: 'What was she like?'"

Jack didn't wait for a reply. "If she did something like that, I'd be like, 'Well'—" He frowned. "I don't know if that's someone I'd want to work with kinda thing." He paraphrased the sort of conversation he'd approve of an artist having. "'Oh, this is a really cool space, I like this show, so nice to talk to you'... Someone who seems nice and enthusiastic and interested. Versus someone who's just, I don't know, completely socially awkward and can't form a sentence.

"I hate to say it, but like, that matters too. You have a public-facing persona as an artist. If you can't even manage a conversation—there are people that are like that—it's like, I hate to say it: You might have the best work in the world, but if you can't exist in a public space and articulate yourself, like, how far are you going to get at that?" He paused, then added in a stage whisper, *"Everything matters."*

I stewed over Jack's response. Go to openings and schmooze, but actually don't go to openings and schmooze. What were artists supposed to do? And did *anyone* look at the work? While Jack himself made an effort to show a diverse range of artists, I couldn't stop thinking that there was something nefarious about the art world's emphasis on context and the Heads' squishy selection criteria—even though art's gatekeepers insisted that the process by which unknown artists become celebrated geniuses works just fine. "You might think there are thousands of great artists desperate for representation, overlooked by a cruel art world. Not at all," writes the art advisor Barbara Guggenheim—whose last name is chiseled on museums around the world—in her book *Art World*. "Gallerists and collectors are quick to snap up quality artists, leaving few good ones, if any, languishing in obscurity." So it's pure coincidence, then, that the artists languishing in obscurity tend to be overwhelmingly women and people of color, while the "quality artists" in major American museums are 85 percent white and 87 percent male.

JACK'S INTERPRETATIONS OF ART, when he'd share them, still made my brain crackle with excitement, although as the weeks went on, those moments felt fewer and further between. More and more I sensed him turning his critical eye on me rather than the artwork. While we were photographing Blake's sculptures, I mentioned I hadn't been to a gym in years. "It shows," Jack quipped. Without my asking, he treated me to a blunt critique of my last book ("I see the wine world as a sort of hedonistic, superficial, luxury good, and there's no content behind it"), my reading of the audiobook (not as good as I'd thought, apparently), and my past articles for *The Atlantic*. "Le Corbusier is *not* a brutalist. He's a modernist," Jack lectured, pulling up an old story of mine to review line-by-line. "I don't want you to feel like you're being criticized," he told me. "Unless it's helpful."

And you can imagine how hard having me around was on *him*. Jack lifted up his shirt one day to show me an angry constellation of welts on his stomach: shingles. "This," he said, pointing to his belly, "is totally you."

As the weeks went on, I was noticing something funny. No—*funny* is the wrong word. Sad. When I first started hanging around people in the New York art world, I was shocked by how paranoid they were: constantly checking over their shoulders, hedging opinions, going off-the-record to share anodyne platitudes.

But now, after a few months at 315, I'd become terrified too. Of having the wrong context, wearing the wrong outfit, liking the wrong thing. I couldn't even form an opinion without consulting a chaperone.

One afternoon, as Jack's lecture on the life choices of mine he found gravely disturbing entered its second hour, I started wondering: Was it something specific about me that kept setting him off? Was it Jack? Was this just standard operating procedure in the art industry?

I started to poke around, curious to hear what assistant-interns at other galleries had been through. They said they'd endured far worse: gallerists who were door-rattling screamers; who threw staplers, shoes, books, and punches; who threatened homicide while holding a letter opener—maybe for dramatic effect, but maybe not. It wouldn't fly with an HR department, but what I'd experienced of Jack's managerial style was penny-ante stuff compared to what went on elsewhere. I also had the luxury of having a career outside 315, one that didn't make me wholly reliant on being in Jack's good graces. I came to see that the art world's strict omertà veiled something more sinister than I'd initially realized: behavior that was at best morally dubious, very frequently discriminatory, and at worst potentially criminal.

The experience shared with me by two former gallery employees over coffee one afternoon stood out even among all the horror stories I heard. The two of them—I'll call them James and Simone—had met each other while working at a gallery in Brooklyn. Simone had started an unpaid internship there while she was in art school and a couple months away from becoming homeless, and she sometimes had to invent excuses to dodge lunch with her coworkers so she could sneak away to a nearby pharmacy and shoplift food. Eventually, Simone left school and got hired to work at the gallery full time—though, in Simone's telling of it, "full-time just became 24/7." She said she and her boss both lived out of rooms adjoining the gallery's massive warehouse space, which meant Simone played where she worked, worked where she lived, and lived with her coworkers. Especially at night, business and pleasure blurred. She'd be hanging out with her boss and the artists who showed at the gallery, "and we would all be smoking a lot of weed so it wouldn't feel like work. But what I'm *actually* doing is free labor for this man. But because I'm high, I don't mind doing it until 3:00 a.m. And then waking up and doing my work at noon," said Simone. James, who joined the gallery after Simone, also recalled his boss plying his staff with LSD-infused water to give them the energy to work longer and said he often had to beg for his paycheck—to the point that, during a stretch when James worked eighteen hours a day, thirty-seven days straight doing "literal slave labor," he had to scrounge through the gallery's change jar to afford a packet of ramen noodles. Another time, after flying to Miami at the gallery's request to work on a show, James told me he was essentially held hostage in Florida, living out of the gallery's space there while being told he just needed to do *one more thing* before he'd get paid—money without which he couldn't afford to return to New York.

James quit not long after that, but Simone had tried to stick it out. It was a job at a gallery, which allowed her to connect with other artists. "My goal was just to be a living creative. Anything that put me in a creative setting, I did." She felt "fucking dedicated" to the gallery. "My plan A, B, and C was always to work through it, never to leave." She got promoted. She kept discovering what a small world it was. She'd mention she was going to an artist's lecture, then learn her boss knew the guy from way back when. Did it feel as if quitting would mean giving up her whole network? "He"—her boss—"never said outright, 'If you quit, you're going to lose access to all these people,'" Simone said. "But of course you already know that." Eventually, burnt out and fed up, she left anyway.

I DIDN'T FEEL BETTER learning that my situation wasn't unique, or that it wasn't even particularly bad by the standards of the art world. Candidly, by late November, I was a wreck. Jack's negs were small, but they added up, and looking back at it now, I was constantly sick with stress. (My incessant supply of snotty tissues—another thing about me that irked him.)

The discomfort I was experiencing with Jack no longer felt like the productive kind, if it ever was, and it was dismaying to admit that so far, immersing myself in art hadn't made my life more expansive or beautiful. I'd left Julie's studio feeling primed for a big epiphany, but as that day receded into the rearview, I felt further away than ever from developing my Eye. No matter how talented Jack was or how great of a guy everyone found him to be, I worried I was going down a path where soon I'd be the one warning would-be art lovers to stay away from the art world because—as I'd been told months before—it's "a fucking horror." I thought about taking the coward's way out and slinking away from art again. I'd glimpsed other ways of existing in the art world (*there are so many art worlds*), only I wasn't sure how to make my way to them.

Except then, as December neared, I started to hear more about Miami.

"Where are you going tomorrow?" became "Are you doing Miami?" "Miami" was short for Miami Art Week, which was short for a weeklong bacchanal of eye candy, nose candy, beats, bites, and pills held in the name of shopping for art. The first week of December marked the kickoff to Miami, which featured two or maybe three dozen different art fairs, at any rate too many to count. The poshest of the bunch was

Art Basel Miami Beach, an art fair (pronounced "*Bahhh*-zil," like bay-ing sheep, not "*Bay*-zil," like the herb) that started in Switzerland in 1970 and expanded to Miami in 2002.

Depending on who I asked, Miami was either an unmissable art pilgrimage or more tasteless than a Señor Frog's wet T-shirt contest. There were more votes for the latter. "If I had to choose between going to Art Basel Miami and dying in a plane crash, I'd pick going down in flames," said one veteran. It was fun. It was gross. It was "the bourgeois indulgence that comes before a Communist revolution." I read that the year before, the galleries participating in Art Basel Miami had brought $3.5 billion worth of art to sell, and that was just one fair. Is there any other gathering where people spend so much money in so little time? Only defense expos came to mind.

From all accounts, Miami during the first week of December was like nothing I'd seen before and tantalizingly different from life with Jack, who wasn't "doing" Miami. I'd experienced the pure. Miami beckoned with the puerile. I wondered whether, before giving up on art, I should at least take a peek.

Something Julie had said kept rattling around my brain too. That day at her studio, our conversation had meandered to what Julie most wished *she* understood about the art world. Her answer was a question: "What is it you buy when you buy art?" It got me wondering what compelled someone to pay through the nose to bring home an artwork and wake up to it day after day. Maybe the answer would help me understand art in a new way, or at the very least glimpse it from a new angle. In short, I decided I needed to "do" Miami.

Only this late in the game I couldn't nail down a hotel room in Miami, let alone an invitation to tag along with someone who was going. Go to Miami alone? Are you crazy? At this point it took me four pep

talks and a fifteen-minute breathing exercise to work up the courage
to show up alone to an opening ten blocks from the safety of my bedroom, so no, I was not about to roll up to Miami solo, announce I was
down for whatever's groovy, and hope for the best. I come from a long
line of neurotic Eastern European refugees. We are not a hope-for-
the-best people.

I'd almost given up on Miami when I bumped into an acquaintance I knew from college. I mentioned I'd been helping out at a gallery
in Brooklyn. She mentioned that she'd just had a very strange experience at a gallery on the Lower East Side. She'd been touring the neighborhood with an art group when the co-owner of this Denny Dimin
Gallery bustled out to bare his soul by delivering a fervent manifesto
about the artists he showed. She didn't go into detail about his speech,
but the guy, Rob Dimin, seemed unguarded in a way Jack had long
since stopped being. He also sounded, if not unhinged, then extremely
passionate.

Rob and I got breakfast one morning at Soho House, his favorite
place on the planet, and that turned into an invitation to join him at
an art fundraiser a few days later. We met that evening at a bar across
the street from Denny Dimin, a five-year-old gallery founded by Rob's
business partner, Elizabeth Denny.

Denny Dimin was a few doors down from the natural-wine bar I'd
been to with Jack (memories cling to New York buildings like cigarette
smoke to a scarf) and surrounded on all sides by art galleries (wander
off in any direction, and you'd hit at least one white cube within a
block). The gallery had a huge glass window—right at street level,
where any Schmo could just wander on in. I could see the current show
from the bar. Big, colorful paintings of reclining women in cheery
grade-school-mural hues. Rob told me he and his partner believed his

peers were too closed off and needed to open up to survive. "We want to see people love art."

We ordered drinks, and Rob, clearly hyped up by the day's work, proceeded to vomit information. He and Elizabeth had just received final payment ($25,000) for work that a client had had since July, co-ordinated a studio visit with curators from the Whitney, and sold a painting to a regional museum for a higher-than-usual discount (20 percent max for institutions, usually). They were getting ready to drop an artist from their roster, open a branch of Denny Dimin in Hong Kong, and make an offer on a new space in Tribeca. Rob's gallery was only a year older than 315, but Denny Dimin had progressed a bit further along the food chain. The gallery represented fifteen emerging artists who were a few more years removed from grad school, and it sold art with an additional zero on its price tag.

Rob drained his cocktail, then leaned forward across the bar's low wooden table. Did I really want to know what the hell was going on in the art world? Well then, he had a proposal for me: "Like, the only way you'll know is if you're absolutely pushed into the deep end," he said. "And there's no bigger push than working on the floor during Art Basel Miami."

I ENDED THINGS with Jack. "Okay. Alright. I can check back in at a later date" was all he said, his face stony, when I told him I wouldn't be able to keep helping at 315. A sense of peace washed over me that vanished three seconds after I left the gallery as I imagined all the ways Jack might tank my career, art-related and otherwise, with a couple taps on his iPhone.

But I couldn't dwell on that. Rob had asked me to start spending a few days each week at Denny Dimin before we headed to Miami—to "learn our system and our eccentricities," he said over the phone, but I could tell it was more about Rob studying me than the other way around. I didn't know why he and Elizabeth were so open to welcoming the "enemy," and I didn't care. I was getting thrown into the deep end.

Part II

The Dance,
Dance, Dance

CHAPTER SEVEN

There was a manic nerviness at Denny Dimin in the lead-up to Miami for the simple reason that if it didn't go well, they'd be screwed. I found my new bosses tucked into their office in a windowless nook at the back of the gallery, which reeked of brussels sprouts from the brunch spot next door. A full two weeks before the fair opened, Elizabeth and Rob were already locked at their computers, mashing the keys emailing clients to try to sell the art they'd be bringing to Miami. "In Miami you'll see," Rob said, breathy with excitement, "it's *all* about the fucking deals."

Elizabeth had started the gallery after getting her master's in art history, then getting traumatized working at other galleries ("*so* toxic," she said). Rob joined the gallery after dropping in and out of various educational institutions, then getting a master's in fine art, which culminated in a performance-art piece exploring athletics and masculinity: "I was told I was a male privileged artist and I couldn't make art, and so I said I'll do the most white male thing I can do and just play squash," he said, giggling, still tickled to death by the idea.

You don't need to spend more than a few minutes with Rob and Elizabeth to see they're an extremely odd pair. I'd have bet my life that seating them together at a dinner party would guarantee blood on the walls before dessert, and yet here they were, several years into running a business together, still on speaking terms and free of visible flesh wounds.

Elizabeth was a jack-of-all-trades with a knack for charming academics into writing about the gallery's shows and a predator's instinct for hunting rats in the basement. Hanging out with Rob was like rubbing your gums with whatever white powder you found on the sink at a nightclub, then watching *Gossip Girl* at 2x speed: He'd hold forth on the "least desirable Hamptons" (West Hampton), the absurdity of someone who lived near the World Trade Center claiming to live in Tribeca when it was so *obviously* the Financial District, and the indignity of Manhattan doormen making him take the service elevator instead of the main elevator. Elizabeth, roused from a deep sleep at 2:00 a.m., could immediately rattle off the current balance in the gallery's checking account. Rob, ditto, for his childhood friend's rich dad. Elizabeth was in her early thirties, with red hair bobbed short, a penchant for jewel-toned silk blouses, and a quiet spunk that reminded me of hale heroines from childhood fairy tales. Rob—late thirties, dark hair scrabbling at his shoulders, ferrety beard, and a closetful of gray cardigans—always looked like he'd been out all night the night before, and odds were he had. Elizabeth and Rob bickered constantly, finished each other's sentences, and cracked each other up with a glance.

"We're very different people," said Rob.

"*Very*," said Elizabeth.

"I kind of think we share the same soul," said Rob.

"I disagree," said Elizabeth.

After applying to various Art Basel fairs and getting rejected, Elizabeth and Rob had decided against applying to this year's Art Basel Miami Beach, which, if you're in the know, is simply called "the main fair"—which tells you everything you need to know about its place in the pecking order. The $550 application would have required images of the art Denny Dimin planned to show, as well as a rundown of their context: past art fairs they'd done, artists they represented, links to their social-media accounts. The Art Basel Miami Beach selection committee included six gallerists whose galleries all—would you believe it—got into the fair. What criteria do they use to decide who gets in? According to Art Basel, the selection committee relies on "criteria." That's all I could scrounge up on the website—*criteria*. Instead of the main fair, Elizabeth and Rob would be bringing abstract photographs by Erin O'Keefe to an art fair called Untitled, which, among the approximately 235 individuals who decide such things, was considered one of only two acceptable alternatives to Art Basel Miami. (The NADA—New Art Dealers Alliance—art fair being the other.)

Art fairs were, depending on how you looked at it, either a necessary evil or just evil. True, they offered exposure. Forty thousand people, including museum curators and big-time collectors, had visited Untitled the year before—thousands more than set foot in Denny Dimin each year. On the other hand, fairs "*do* destroy galleries," Rob conceded. "If you have two bad fairs in a row—people can't dig themselves out from them." Thick plumes of anxiety poured out of the office each day—it didn't help that Denny Dimin's recent show in New York had sold barely to not-at-all—and Elizabeth, keeper of bills and invoices, finally pulled up a spreadsheet to show me her budget. Her openness took me by surprise after Jack, but Elizabeth said: "I don't care if you know what a shit show this industry is. I kind of *want* people to know." Doing Untitled would cost about $39,000, which was on the high end of what it cost to run the gallery for a month. I scanned the line items: $20,000 for the booth, $5,000 for hotels, $500 for flights. The column of numbers snaked down the page and swam in front of my eyes. "We had to take out a whole new credit card to deal with the framing," Elizabeth said, white-knuckling the Mac's mouse.

To the uninitiated, it must have looked like business suicide: Elizabeth and Rob were betting $39,000, cobbled together on credit cards, that they could fly to a different state, hang twenty-one pieces of colorful paper onto a glorified elementary-school science-fair booth, and over the course of five days, convince strangers to fork over tens of thousands of dollars for said paper. Oh, and Elizabeth and Rob had the harebrained idea of bringing me along to help them pull it off. Me. Someone who was such a chickenshit at sales that she'd "lost" her gift-wrap samples to avoid participating in her elementary school's fundraising drive. To be clear, I had better help Elizabeth and Rob pull it off. Even though they knew I was a writer and even though I was paying my own way, Miami was too important to support dead weight. I was expected to get in there and contribute, plus, the invitation to Florida came with the condition that if I messed up any sales, my tenure at Denny Dimin would come to an abrupt, ignominious end. "I don't *think* you'll fuck it up," Rob volunteered, sounding less confident than I would have liked.

Denny Dimin was a three-ring circus compared to 315. We needed to deinstall the current show, install a new show, ship art to Miami, ship art to a fair in San Francisco in January, and yell at Rob for announcing the Hong Kong gallery on Instagram before checking with

Elizabeth. Jack always had a spare moment to show me something on YouTube, but with Miami to attend to, Elizabeth and Rob immediately pawned me off on Dylan Lilla, an artist with shaved temples and a flowing crown of green hair. Dylan had moved to New York from Nebraska a few months before and quickly made themself indispensable to Denny Dimin. (Dylan uses "they" pronouns.) Depending on who Rob was talking to or trying to impress, he alternately referred to Dylan as the gallery's "preparator," "shipping manager," or "exhibitions manager." Rob called me his "intern" to my face and his "assistant" when talking with anyone else. I was just pleased to have a semidefined title.

Dylan's to-do list ran longer than anyone's, and I got sweaty, dusty, and blistered helping them maneuver art on and off walls, in and out of cardboard boxes, and up and down from the storage crypt in the basement. Dylan, like lots of artists who work second jobs, belonged to the city's army of art handlers. These are the roadies of the art world, who help billionaires hang their second Rothko in their third home, quietly shuffle artwork in and out of low-tax states, and resist throwing things when a museum curator asks them to lower all the paintings in a gallery by one-quarter inch. "Dealing with the gallerists and the artists, if you can be patient and realize it *is* all about them—" Dylan chuckled. "That'll get you far."

The art Denny Dimin showed was, by the standards of the world at large, virtually indistinguishable from what you'd see at Jack's gallery and, by the standards of the New York art world, just completely different, no question, how could you even put them in the same sentence? Like Jack, Elizabeth and Rob worked with emerging artists who ranged from painters to performance artists. For Denny Dimin's December exhibit, a solo show of Paula Wilson's work, Dylan and I had to mount flat-screen TVs that would play videos of Wilson dancing on a former Confederate monument and gliding through the surf holding a giant paintbrush. But there were subtle differences that nudged Denny Dimin toward colorful-painting territory. Jack's show on abortion had featured a creepy sculpture of Garfield seated across from a carving knife, as well as a press release that vowed to donate a portion of sales to a pro-choice clinic. Denny Dimin's show on abortion featured lush photos of abortifacient flowers in elegant ikebana arrangements, as well as a press release that made no such promises. Wilson, who'd just flown in from New Mexico to help us install her show, made work that Elizabeth described as "totally in line with what we show." Which was? "Formally beautiful and having a great concept behind it."

That probably doesn't sound revolutionary, but for Denny Dimin's niche of the art industry, and in a neighborhood where lots of galleries showed art that looked brutalized, leaning into formal beauty was a questionable career move. Fumbling for words early on, I had occasionally—and very regrettably, I now saw—praised artists' work as "beautiful." Since then, I'd had it drilled into me that *beautiful* meant "decorative" and *decorative* meant "dumb," and the only graver insult was "accessible," which beautiful art was assumed to be.

Elizabeth, however, rejected the notion that art has to be abrasive to be deep, which was the message she thought museums reinforced by consistently promoting artwork that's "performing this idea of the art world being an infeasible, incomprehensible bundle of conceptualism," she said one morning in between juggling phone calls from the landlord. "And that just doesn't help our mission in the world."

Which was?

"Getting the broader world excited about what's going on with young contemporary artists."

Elizabeth didn't say "broader world" as if it was a bad thing.

I could imagine Jack's whisper, the whisper of pure kids everywhere, that beautiful art was couch art—a cop-out commodity that was easy to sell. Well, of course Elizabeth wanted to sell art. That's how the gallery stayed in business and supported artists so they could keep making work. "I just want the art to exist," Elizabeth said. "I don't need to own the work. I just want to be around art and artists. And I guess that led me to having a gallery." You don't open a gallery to become rich—"This is like the *worst* business idea ever," Elizabeth grumbled. You do it because "you *need* to," she stressed. "We're doing it to show the stuff. I've never been interested in like, 'Oh yeah, let's just have some remote cheap place in Brooklyn,' or 'Let's just do art fairs.'" Running the gallery, said Elizabeth, "means that there are artists and things that people wouldn't have seen, that the artist wouldn't have put together, if it weren't for this place." When Elizabeth talked about art, her eyes widened, her voice melted, and she glowed as though someone had lit a bonfire inside her ribs. "The show looks *fantastic*, you guys," she gushed, when Wilson's work was on the walls. "I'm really excited to have video *and* paintings *and* prints... *So* beautiful." She said the word *beautiful* like no one I'd ever heard: crisp, clear, ringing with such joy that it made me worry that if others didn't share her love for the work, it'd break her heart.

LIKE A COACH rallying players for a big game, Elizabeth gathered us shortly before leaving for Miami to announce that the gallery needed to sell around $70,000 worth of art, or about thirteen photographs, to break even. Really, we needed to sell a lot more, both to avoid Elizabeth going into cardiac arrest and to afford their ambitious expansion plans: the Tribeca space, the gallery in Hong Kong, more art fairs. Elizabeth and Rob hoped spending money would ensure the gallery grew in lockstep with their artists, who were "emerging" now, but asking for more as their careers swelled. More prestigious fairs. More help paying to produce expensive pieces. "If they're doing their job well, they're demanding," Elizabeth said. It was grow or be out-grown, and they worried artists would ditch them for bigger galleries that would provide. The finish line was the museum door. "I can't wait for the day an artist of mine has a show at the Whitney," gushed Rob, who considered MoMA "the ultimate canonization."

I was filing invoices one afternoon when Elizabeth suddenly shoved her chair back from her desk and dropped her head into her hands. Rob and I stared in silence.

"I just want you to know that I need you to pick," she mumbled, her face still buried in her hands. "Do you want to do five art fairs next year, do you want a new space, or do you want to do Hong Kong? We can do *maybe* two of the three."

"Hong Kong and the new space and three art fairs," Rob counterof-fered.

Elizabeth peeked out from between her fingers, her face ashen. "We are *still* not caught up in cash," she whispered. "I can't do this. I *cannot* do this." Her voice got higher and more panicked as she spoke: "I cannot do a renovation. I cannot do a lease signing… I *can't* do this right now… I seriously, like—I'm going to have a *mental breakdown* if you try to make me sign a lease right now." She ticked off expenses for the new Tribeca space: new lights, new basement storage, new plywood-backed walls. "If we try to do it now—I *will* lose my mind."

Elizabeth's tone of voice put the fear of God in me to sell, *sell*,

SELL. "Ultimately, we need to crush Miami and make a shit ton of money" were Rob's marching orders. "Because in a place like Miami, we *cannot* afford to lose money."

Even with so much at stake, sobriety was optional. Perhaps even a liability. "A very prolific art dealer, who's a friend of mine, said to me five years ago that the only way to have a successful Miami is to either be drunk, high, or hungover during fair days, and so two years ago, I tested his philosophy," Rob announced one day. "It was our best Miami. And I was literally drunk, high, or hungover the entire time." Getting shitfaced was Rob's first advice. The other: "RSVP to everything. Literally, like, *literally*—RSVP to *everything.*"

CHAPTER EIGHT

I RSVPed to *everything*. At least I tried. No mortal could. Rob forwarded me more than a dozen invitations and a friend shared a molar-grinding list of parties that ran seven single-spaced pages yet opened with the disclaimer that this included only evening events—"daytime art touring plans elsewhere." From the Monday before the fairs opened until the following Monday, from cocktail hour through breakfast, I could, if on the guest list and immune to sleep, bowl with Swizz Beatz, pay seventy dollars to celebrate a billionaire real-estate developer's birthday, watch a photographer's live photo shoot of a live Brazilian supermodel, and get down to beats beats beats while a DJ and artist held space for a "collective catharsis" from commercial activities at a bash sponsored by Facebook. Every party was a "bash," music was "tunes," food was "culinary cuisine." The invitations, which had guzzled tequila shots, leaned in close to yell with hot, spittled breath to "COME TO THIS GLITZY BASH FEATURING

'N SYNC'S LANCE BASS." There was a festival feel twinged with a corporate kiss of death, like a coke-y Carnival cruise.

I quickly realized that RSVPing was a competitive sport, and I was losing. Everyone would be hanging out without me, I worried, then confirmed when a gallerist flashed me his schedule—a mess of bashes I hadn't known existed. I bartered naming rights to my firstborn for a VIP pass to the main fair, which allowed me to RSVP for even more events and enjoy the satisfaction of leveling up in a video game. This must be the feeling Art Basel Miami's ex-director had in mind when he congratulated his fair for having "fine-tuned the idea of contemporary art as a lifestyle choice."

Two weeks after starting with Denny Dimin and two days before Untitled officially opened, I flew to Miami on a plane packed with tote bags pledging allegiance to Hockney, Warhol, and the Whitney. On the taxi ride to my hotel, I passed sprawling art fairs I hadn't known existed, billboards advertising fairs I'd never heard of, and three art museums. (Four if you count Lock & Load Miami, home of South Florida's "premier Machine Gun Experience, Museum, and Art Gallery.") There were two art fairs on the beach across from my hotel and a plane over the ocean dragging a banner by the artist Mister E: "MONEY ISN'T REAL."

I checked in to my hotel—"if you're looking for a state of the art hotel... this is NOT it," read a TripAdvisor review—and discovered I'd be bunking with the Scarface of immune supplements. My roommate, a Miami veteran who was letting me share her queen bed, knew this week's manic pace better than I and, within hours of landing, had cornered South Beach's zinc and vitamin C supply. She eyed me territorially over her mountain range of vitamins. You *cannot* afford to get sick this week, she warned, with no indication she'd share her stash.

I beelined to the Untitled fair, which hulked over a stretch of beach in an aggressively white tent, and met Elizabeth at Denny Dimin's booth, a three-walled stall in a long row of three-walled stalls. Elizabeth fretted over the photographs as we unpacked them. "The most dangerous thing about doing an art fair is people thinking that things are trash," Elizabeth warned as she cordoned off the booth with tape. "The first year I did Untitled, I had someone throw away an artwork. And it was a piece that had sold!" I hoped my *No!* sounded sufficiently outraged, though between you and me, I'd gleaned this happens a lot. Hang around enough art people and you'll find almost everyone has a story—recounted with a surprising dose of pride—about the time someone confused their art for trash. Dylan, who makes work using strands of hair they collect during showers, once lost a piece to a cleaning crew. An artist's installation of cardboard boxes went the same way. Ditto the bag of garbage that got mistaken for an actual bag of garbage.

While I unpacked the art, Elizabeth plotted its placement. O'Keefe made photographs, which I'd initially mistaken for paintings, of hovering geometric shapes in a mixture of beach-umbrella hues. Should the earth-toned photos get the prime real estate on the booth's outside wall, or better to put the really colorful photos there? "I'm going to try putting the really colorful pieces on the outer wall," Elizabeth decided. "What we really want to do with the outer wall is get people in the booth."

Out of the corner of my eye, I watched as gallerists all around us lugged painting after painting out of cardboard boxes marked FRAGILE. I'd meticulously plotted my schedule for the coming week so I could carve out time to dash over to other fairs, but between the commotion around us and what I'd seen on my drive from the airport, I started to feel overwhelmed by all the art I'd be seeing in the days ahead. I waited until Elizabeth seemed satisfied that I was properly stacking each framed photo front-to-front and back-to-back while wearing clean white cotton gloves, then asked her advice on how to thoughtfully experience the deluge. In other words, how to work on refining my Eye.

"First of all, I'm never going to tell you to read anything I read when I was studying art history, because according to every single one of them, there was never a woman artist," she said. "What *was* critical was spending all those years looking at art and thinking, 'What does this mean? Where does this come from? What do I think? How do I write about it? How do I use words when I talk about it?'" Memorizing slides had taught her less than being forced to articulate what she noticed in an artwork.

The artist Gina Malek had made a similar suggestion when I'd visited her studio in her apartment in the Bronx. "Just walk up to a piece and try to think of five things that it brings up," she suggested. Not five things that the art is about. The observations don't need to be grandiose, like *this probes masculinity in the postinternet age*. Just, what are five things you notice, either in the work or in how it makes you feel. "Like, that red is very cool or very warm... That shape really dominates the canvas... I love how that paint is gushy and then it thins out," Gina said, ticking through formal features. "All those things are important, and they're intentional." I thought of Julie wrestling with her blue sky. *Painting is constant decision-making.*

I called my husband that night to say I'd landed. I told him I was woefully unprepared for Miami's intensity, desperately needed to get some rest, and would call him in the morning. That last bit was a lie. I basically didn't sleep, eat anything not speared with a toothpick, or acknowledge my loved ones' existence for the next seven days.

———

I HAVEN'T MENTIONED IT till now because I'd failed so utterly in all my efforts, but by this point I'd spent a good six months trying to weasel into art collectors' homes. I'd naïvely thought collectors were just mall rats with a bigger budget, but New York's artists and gallerists discussed collectors with a mix of fear, reverence, and occasional disdain that made me think of civilizations forced to sacrifice virgins to placate vengeful gods. Collectors sounded so powerful, so otherworldly, that I'd gotten fixated by the idea of studying these deities up close for myself, preferably surrounded by their spoils. But how? Everyone was too scared of pissing them off to introduce me, and even though I'd been studiously collecting collectors' names by reading every "here's how I spend my millions" interview I could find, I couldn't very well just show up at a billionaire's door, ring the doorbell, and ask to see the joint.

In fact, I discovered less than twenty-four hours after getting to Miami, that's exactly what you do. Like kids passing around their baseball-card collections, there is a pre-art-fair ritual of South Florida's biggest art collectors flinging open their doors to let perfect strangers gawk at what they've bought. As was my God-given right as the proud holder of an Art Basel VIP pass, I joined the poreless and exquisitely orthodontiaed in touring these art demigods' sprawling homes. Uniformed valets relieved visitors of their Maseratis, rented baristas fed us espresso shots, and pretty young women handed out maps in case we'd failed to recognize that the painting over the couch was a priceless Anselm Kiefer, which, feeling smug, I did recognize. You see, one doesn't just show up in South Beach and start shopping.

We're not *animals*. One needs a little foreplay, a little friendly competition, to get in the mood.

Having not been born yesterday, I realized that rich people could
buy lots of art, only I hadn't realized until now that my definitions of
rich and *lots* were off by many orders of magnitude. "Clients ask me,
are we collectors? And I say, 'Has the word *warehouse* entered your
vocabulary?'" said an art advisor, an old hand on the Miami circuit.
Collectors' houses were merely a warmup for tours of what my online
VIP guide demurely referred to as their "collections," which I would
call private museums. You see, when people love art very, very much,
they requisition a gigantic windowless warehouse, move in their art
arsenal, and put their names over the door. The "Miami Model," it's
called, and I direct your attention to Florida's balmy winters and tax
code. Residents pay a grand total of zero dollars in income, estate, in-
heritance, and capital gains taxes—a nice perk for many high rollers,
who naturally bring their art with them.

One collector, Beth Rudin DeWoody, had taken over a former mu-
nitions depot to show all the art she couldn't fit in her art-filled apartment in New York, her three art-filled apartments in Los Angeles, or
her three art-filled homes in Palm Beach. Wandering through her
invitation-only bunker The Bunker, I passed art on the ground and art
in a mound. I abandoned all hope of savoring each work—I'd be here
for days, possibly weeks—and videoed the rooms like everyone else,
vowing to review the footage later.

Curious to know what fueled her apparently insatiable passion
for art, I managed to claim a few minutes with Beth, flanked by her
two curators. Beth, whose support for emerging artists has made her
something of a patron saint to gallerists, was legendary for purchasing

art omnivorously, without putting too much stock in context, and I asked how she decided what art to buy. "How do I decide?" she repeated, as though the question had never crossed her mind. "I decide because I see something I like and I want to have it." She was working with a budget that, I gathered, allowed for *all of the above*. I'd hoped her enthusiasm would be like poison ivy—one brush and I'd catch the itch—but my soul was not yet itching. I tried again: Why had she surrounded herself with art and not—I pulled from thin air—posters? "Well, I have posters too." Okay, but why collect art as opposed to, let's say, stamps. "Well, I do," she corrected me. "I just went up and got some Ellsworth Kelly postal stamps. When you're a collector, you're a collector." Beth defined a collector as someone who "buys beyond their walls," and it'd gotten so she had trouble keeping track of what she'd bought. She'd gone to a show by the artist Theresa Chromati and raved to the gallerist about how much she loved Chromati's work. "He said, 'Oh, you know you own one of these,'" recalled Beth. Beth's response was: "I do?"

Per the email I received, the art collection I went to see on Monday afternoon was at a "home," but I've been to smaller airports. In one living room (I counted three), a crowd had gathered around the matriarchal owner. *Speech! Speech!*, they practically begged, and I thought they were going to break out in applause when she granted them a few words about what an honor it was to be such a generous person who shared her art by inviting us here today and opening her own museum. I'd done it, I thought: I was finally face-to-face with the sort of art champion who might meet Jack's criteria of a "Good Person."

Maybe my blisters were making me cranky, but as I circled a wing of the house that was the spitting image of a museum, my mind drifted to Pierre Bourdieu, a sociologist famous for raining on rich peoples' parades. Bourdieu theorized that we like what we like—cold-brew coffee, Harley-Davidson hogs, Anselm Kiefer paintings—not because those things are inherently superior but because filling our lives with them signals us as members of a certain class. And no object broadcasts social cachet as does a work of art. According to Bourdieu, collecting art simultaneously demonstrates you have the wherewithal to hone an appreciation for an acquired taste *and* are rich enough to light money on fire. Acquiring art, he wrote, is perfectly analogous to "the ostentatious destruction of wealth." Not that I planned on telling Denny Dimin's clients that.

I began to imagine this whole scene through Bourdieu's eyes. These collectors obviously had oodles of what Bourdieu calls economic capital (a.k.a. cash money), which they'd used to buy art that in turn got them cultural capital (an aura of cool) as well as social capital (access to a clubby in-crowd of Heads and their wealthy patrons). I could picture Bourdieu circling the rooms of this mansion while muttering archly that art offers a way to invest economic capital in cultural capital that can be turned into even more economic capital—all while racking up social capital along the way. Or as David Walsh, a professional gambler turned art collector, bluntly described his rationale for opening his own art museum: "Turns out it ain't so great getting rich… What to do? Better build a museum; make myself famous. That will get the chicks."

Doubling back into one of the living rooms, I attempted to silence Bourdieu's party-pooping by concentrating on a painting of fuzzy red, black, and blue stripes by the artist Sterling Ruby, which hung over a porch door. Funny: I'd just come from a house that had a green Sterling Ruby next to the fireplace. Near the front door, I passed an explosion of mirrored shards by the artist Jim Hodges, which caught my eye because I'd just seen his work in someone else's living room earlier that day. What do you know: These people had one of Mark Grotjahn's fireworksy abstractions, too, just like the collectors I'd visited in Key Biscayne.

The same artists kept showing up in different collectors' homes, and Bourdieu butted back into my thoughts to insist he could explain that too. Per him, we all try to distinguish ourselves by embracing the same things as the people we want to impress, and art collecting, like hairstyles and pant legs, follows trends. In the late 1800s, as Americans were suffering from an acute European inferiority complex and racing to open art museums, rich collectors plundered the continent for Old Master treasures. That had a good run, then the collectors were on to nineteenth-century French painting, and through the 1940s, if it wasn't French, they wouldn't touch it. And yet in Miami, I passed no Virgin Marys or stretching ballerinas. Given what was on the walls, you'd think art wasn't invented until after the Walkman. But it wasn't until the 1960s that American collectors got seriously interested in work by living, breathing Americans. Gallerists of the day attributed this only partially to the art itself: "A great change has taken place in the art world with two new classifications among collectors—THE IN-VESTOR and THE RICH MAN WHO IS BORED," wrote the gallerist Edith Halpert in a letter circa 1965.

It was frustrating to feel as if my attempts to develop my Eye were once again getting hijacked by the social machinations of the art world. Only I couldn't deny that, even if it wasn't romantic, I was getting a crucial answer to my question of why we engage with art. For the collectors around me—and for many of us, if we're being honest—art's value doesn't exclusively reside in the private experience we share with a piece. Engaging with art is also social: a way to make friends, to be admired, to become the person we dream of being. And when people surround themselves with art, what rubs off on them is much more than status, artists insisted. "People often scoff at their work ending up above someone's couch, but I think that's a damn beautiful thing," the artist Deirdre Sargent would tell me later. "When you're living with something, it seeps into your consciousness. That's a really big deal."

I was getting ready to leave when I glimpsed an area off the kitchen that, given the total absence of paintings on the walls, I took for another room-sized art installation. (I'd toured two already.) A woman standing in the kitchen waved me in, and I followed Elizabeth and Gina's advice to observe five things about the piece. The room was small, head-to-toe white, and perfectly symmetrical: Two matching metal chairs stood beside two identical twin beds arranged foot to foot, as though to make the sleepers watch each other while at rest. It felt institutional and claustrophobic, with a creepy whiff of surveillance, and I wanted to get out of there. As I turned to go, I glimpsed, behind a partially open closet door, a nightgown, purse, and laundry basket of clothes.

This wasn't art, I realized. The art luxuriated in cavernous rooms overlooking the ocean. The humans who served the art's owners were crammed together here.

TUESDAY MORNING. I woke up late and hungover, thanks to Rob, and was a sweaty mess by the time I hustled to Untitled shortly after noon. At 1:00 p.m. on the dot, the fair would officially throw open its doors—to those VIPs who'd snagged an invitation, that is. Collectors, curators, museum patrons, and journalists were Very Important.

Untitled's organizers and exhibitors gave them free passes to the fair. The Schmos could come starting tomorrow, at thirty-five dollars a head.

At 12:40 p.m., Elizabeth buzzed around the booth dusting frames and checking, for at least the third time, that the photos were level. Rob was the capitalism fluffer. "We need to *sell*!" he urged. "This is like, late capitalism at its highest." His emotional state was car dealership inflatable flailing tube man.

At 12:58 p.m., disaster: Elizabeth discovered a mysterious goo on one frame. "Call Dylan!" she yelled to Rob. She rubbed the goo with paper towel. "It's like, scratching," she said frantically. "It's literally scratching." At 1:01 p.m., she was greeting a VIP. "I'm going to get a little bit of glass cleaner—hi! Let me know if you have any questions." The VIP had questions. The VIP said he, too, was from New York. "Oooooh, very nice," Elizabeth said. "No, I mean, that's typical of Miami, right? We see everyone from New York."

At 1:15 p.m., I was talking to my first VIP. I'd spent days reading everything I could find on O'Keefe, then memorizing two pages of talking points. "So the artist paints wooden blocks," I told the VIP. That didn't sound right. I tried: "She cuts out painted pieces of cardboard." *Fuck.* I was making her sound like a preschooler.

At 1:19 p.m., Rob made the day's first sale. "This gentleman would like to acquire edition one," he announced. Rob's assistant Bianca would take down the client's information.

There was a peristaltic flow of air-kissers who left spicy trails of Le Labo perfume. A man in a dark blazer was explaining how to set up and structure trusts. A middle-aged woman with a soft blowout reviewed her daughter's headshots, occasionally pinching-and-zooming to scrutinize invisible flaws. The men, in pastel linen button-downs over pressed khakis, were delicious little sorbets plopped on cones, while the women—gold pants, metallic jackets—glittered like disco balls. From across the tent, I heard the hollow *thop* of popped champagne.

I dashed to the bathroom and stole a quick glance at the other booths en route. The art was contemporary, mostly emerging, and Elizabeth and Rob's hunch was dead-on: They'd opted for a solo booth of abstract photos because they bet other galleries would hang group shows and figurative work—figuration being all anyone in New York was talking about these days. I passed a tapestry of a dog flashing its hot pink erection at a naked woman, a puppet show starring a talking burger, a drawing of a Dolly Parton–ish poodle, and a painting of a pink man in tighty-whities. My retinas sizzled on all the color, and I wanted to detour to a booth in back to see an Oriental rug that seemed to be melting off the wall, but there wasn't time.

Back at Denny Dimin's booth, Elizabeth was closing a sale to a museum trustee, Rob was bragging about getting to know the curator of Apple's corporate collection, and I was being asked, "So, who owns the original?" and having to explain that yes, these were digital photographs of painted wooden blocks—"sculptural arrangements," I suddenly remembered O'Keefe calling them—and yes, I guess you could in theory print an infinite number of each photograph, but no, the gallery would *not* do that because we and the artist had committed to making only three editions of the image he saw for sale—three physical copies of that photograph, *ever*, plus two artist's proofs—and that the first edition would cost $4,500, unframed, while the second edition would cost slightly more and the third even more. Scarcity pricing, Elizabeth called it. You were incentivized to buy early. My explanation was unconvincing, apparently. "I don't believe in prints," sniffed the VIP.

Prints are real. It's the prices that require faith. Elizabeth and Rob did not arrive at $4,500 by sitting down with O'Keefe, tallying her costs (her time, printing fees, and so forth), then calculating how much to sell the photos for so she could at least break even. During a brief breather, Elizabeth told me she and Rob priced art "through comparables first and then through market forces." In other words, they checked what everyone else was charging for photos by artists who were at a similar point in their careers as O'Keefe. Great. Let's go with that. Next question: Was O'Keefe's work selling well? If yes, they could think about bumping up the price, probably in 10 to 15 percent increments, likely before some big event, like a show. (The prices had nudged up before Miami.) If no, hold steady. Prices could rise with a career coup—a solo show, a museum show—but not on any random Tuesday. (Getting into a museum is synonymous with breaking into the annals of art history—"If a museum has shown it, just 10x the price," whispered a museum director.) Lowering prices was to be avoided at all costs. Bigger work tended to be more expensive than smaller work, and Elizabeth showed me a spreadsheet she used to calculate paintings' prices according to their surface area.

Another common strategy for deciding the price of an artwork: Pull it out of thin air. "The prices are fabricated. None of this is real," Jack had said once. I'd thought this was another one of his deflections until, over dinner one night with Rob and some of his gallerist friends, the dealers described the complex reasoning behind pricing art as, "Like, three of us get together and are like, I think someone would pay that." They send out offers to a few people. "If they write back and say it's too high, we take five hundred dollars off the price." More expensive art was touted as easier to sell, since lots of zeroes on a price tag could signal *lots of Very Important People approv*e. "*Real* art shouldn't cost less than $3,000," one of the gallerists at dinner had quipped over his sashimi. I heard about a collector couple who wouldn't consider a piece unless its price made them wince.

Asking nicely could get you a 10 percent discount, though keep in mind that discounts eat away at what the gallery *and* the artist get paid. *Maybe* you could push for 15 percent if you were buying multiple pieces. Art advisors could get 15 percent off. (They might pass on a 7.5 percent discount to clients, and get 7.5 percent in commission from the gallery.) Museums could get 20 percent off. The more money people had, the less they generally expected to pay for a work: Wealthy VIPs figured that the good context an artist got from being in their collection could make up for the money lost on that sale. (One artist told me that a gallery acquiesced to a collector's demand to get several pieces for free, simply because the collector was a V, V, *V*IP.) Nothing peeved Elizabeth like the New York collector couple who touted themselves as committed champions of emerging artists and then demanded a 30 percent discount on a single painting. "Makes me want to vomit," she fumed. "I mean, HOW IS THE GALLERY GOING TO PAY THE ARTIST IF YOU'VE BOUGHT THE THING FOR NOTHING AND THE GALLERY CAN'T PAY THEIR BILLS?" To say nothing of the artist's expenses. A $4,000 painting is nothing to sneeze at, but if Jack had sold all nine paintings in Haley Josephs's show, given no discounts, and paid himself the standard 50 percent cut, Josephs would have taken home about $18,000, before taxes. It likely wouldn't cover a year's rent.

Another piece sold. Two pieces? By 3:00 p.m., I'd upgraded from "O'Keefe photographs her sculptural arrangements and then destroys them" to "she *dismantles* them." I gave "demolishes" a whirl. I tossed in some art-historical flair I'd picked up working with Jack. "I think there's elements of de Chirico, but she also talks about Fra Angelico with these very matte, powerful colors."

Still no sales.

I was starting to get worried. I wanted to make myself useful, so I volunteered to run out to get everyone lunch. At the VIP desk, I passed VIPs turning scarlet as they endured the public humiliation of waiting in line while no doubt contemplating alerting the United Nations to human-rights violations in South Beach. Someone whispered to me that she'd seen a man start throwing things—hell hath no fury like a VIP scorned.

When I got back to the booth, I tried channeling Jack's gravitas. "They look very painterly, but they're photographs of physical materials." I figured physical materials beats "cardboard"—right? I referenced Piet Mondrian, with a silent thanks to Julie, then threw in "Mondrianesque," just because. I was beginning to annoy myself. "That work has been placed," I told a woman. "Does 'placed' mean sold?" she asked. I wanted to fire myself on the spot.

"I'm so tired because we've done nothing except sell art," Elizabeth groaned, glowing. Seven minutes later, Rob sold two editions. At 5:00 p.m., the fair hit its VIP attendance record: Six thousand people had walked in the door.

In a momentary lull, Elizabeth emailed VIPs who'd liked, but not yet bought, O'Keefe's work. "You just have to write the same canned thing... *It was a pleasure to meet you at Untitled today. Thank you for your interest in the work of Erin O'Keefe.*" She tried to avoid using gendered pronouns—"Making someone aware of an artist's gender, especially for a female artist, is not helpful to them"—and tried not to call attention to the fact that O'Keefe made photos—"Sometimes emphasizing that something is photography undermines it as art." (Photography is an infant compared to painting and has had to fight to be considered fine art—see, for instance, the "I don't believe in prints" man.) Elizabeth allowed herself one exclamation point per email. "I think that as a woman, if I do fewer than one exclamation point, they think I'm being unfriendly, but if I do too many, I'm not serious." Alerts popped up on her screen as she typed, showing collectors perusing her emails in real time: *Someone just viewed Erin O'Keefe with Denny Dimin Gallery at Untitled . . . Someone just viewed Erin O'Keefe at . . . Someone just viewed . . .* She and Rob used software that let them see when, where, and how often a client read their emails.

At 6:39 p.m., Elizabeth tried to flag down the fair's PR person to plug how much Denny Dimin had sold and to whom. "It's very important, as you're doing these fairs, to brag publicly about how you're doing, because then press might want to talk to you about how the fair is going market-wise, and you start this whole rolling ball of visibility." She'd feed good sales numbers to the fair's PR people, who'd feed good sales numbers to journalists, who reliably fed those good sales numbers to their readers. Here and there, Elizabeth heard from a reporter who wanted to fact-check. In general, all news was good news. Gallerists told me that no matter how much money they hemorrhaged at a fair, the press always reported "brisk sales." (Fact-check: False—technically, I've also seen "*strong* sales" and "*robust* sales.") Since fair organizers made their money off galleries like Denny Dimin's paying for booths, "They're only going to include the people who are doing well," Elizabeth acknowledged.

As the day went on, I kept noticing all the ways Elizabeth and Rob were different from other gallerists I'd encountered thus far. For instance, they smiled. "I loooooooove being friendly because people are *so* offput by it in New York," Rob crowed. "It's the funniest thing in the entire world. People think a smile means you're *dumb*." They were also—get this—openly enthusiastic. "You have this calming moment," Rob said to a VIP considering O'Keefe's photos, "And then you learn what you're looking at, and you get this WHAT THE *FUCK*! moment that's like *really* amazing." They also openly listed their prices and gave clients a checklist that showed what had and hadn't sold.

At 7:11 p.m., I counted nine pieces sold that day, none by me. I was determined to prove myself. I had forty-nine minutes to sell something before the fair closed for the night.

In the seconds in between let-me-know-if-you-have-any-questions, I pumped Elizabeth for sales advice. I'd heard gallerists try to sell work by mentioning that *this* artist was beloved by *The New York Times*'s art critic or was in the Dallas Museum of Art's collection or was currently dating a more famous artist.

None of that was Elizabeth's speed. She didn't like context-forward spiels that focused wholly on the artist's résumé. "Too aggressive." Focus on the art, she advised. "I think it's more important to stay in the art until they *need* you to go out of the art."

She conceded that she'd broken her own rule earlier in the day. "She's sort of premuseum," Elizabeth told a VIP, after mentioning O'Keefe's work was being collected by museum trustees—"which is what happens right before someone gets a museum show or is added to a museum collection." But she only shared that because that VIP kept pushing for that information, she insisted. Some people, "they just kind of like that dance, dance, dance." In that vein, hovering was good: Use body language to signal someone has your full attention. "They like to see you work for it. Don't *ever* think that they want it to be easy." Even busy clients made time to boss Elizabeth and Rob around. A real-estate mogul (and museum board member) pointedly replied to one of Rob's sales emails with orders to immediately stop signing his emails "Best" because it was "neither meaningful nor distinctive." ("Rich person flirting," cackled Rob, who was less irked by it than Elizabeth was.) And don't say *placed*, Elizabeth told me. "It sounds too pompous," she said. "A lot of the works have just been *bought*, and there's nothing wrong with that." Elizabeth reiterated her golden rule: "I don't leave the work until someone asks me a question that leaves the work. Until then, I stay in the work." It was a kind of Hippocratic oath: Stay. In. The. Work.

If you're talking to someone and they seem overwhelmed, try focusing them with narrow questions. "Which one are you really drawn to?" Elizabeth might say. "Where are you from?" Innocuous. Polite. Calculating. "That starts *so* much information. That starts a *cascade* of information," Elizabeth stressed. "You can get everything from, 'Oh, I have a second home in Miami, I'm from New York.'" She translated: "That means art collector."

"Or," Rob cut in, "'I'm here with a collectors' group from Washington, DC; we come down every year—'"

"That means collector," Elizabeth translated.

"It's important to know if they're art advisors, if they're individuals thinking about collecting, if they're artists," Rob said. "It's important for you to get as much information from the person that you're talking to." Rob studied shoes, coats, and jewelry for clues. "I can tell 60 to 70 percent of the time if someone who's going to walk into our booth is actually interested in buying."

"I just—I just—" Elizabeth was turning pink. "I just don't think it's the way to do it."

"I can tell if someone went to boarding school in Europe," Rob bragged.

Elizabeth was unconvinced. I hadn't seen her and Rob vet buyers with Jack's NSA-style intensity. If anything, they seemed thrilled to sell someone their first piece of art. "Once people are in the ballpark of discretionary income, it seems to me that they're all fair game. And it's all magic," said Elizabeth. Take the woman who'd just bought two O'Keefe photos. Elizabeth shrugged. "I didn't know she had a $14 million house on Fifth Avenue."

Rob frowned. "I don't want to say I *definitely* would have known," Rob said, in a tone that suggested he *definitely* would have known.

AT 8:43 P.M., I was standing at the sad end of a line snaking through the lobby of the Pérez Art Museum Miami feeling dejected I hadn't sold anything and waiting to get into a party sponsored by Christian Louboutin. "We went back to their apartment and did—I can't remember the name of the drugs," said a brunette in a crop top next to me. A foursome in leather jackets arrived and marched to the front of the line, and a woman with a guest list waved them through. I think? Without a pair of binoculars, the front of the line was hard to make out. Every few seconds, a woman with a walkie-talkie whisked people out of line and through the entrance.

Eventually, I was inside. *Where are you going later? Where are you going tomorrow?* rang out around me. Someone had just gone to an opening at the Bass Museum, which was confusing because I'd also RSVPed for an opening at the Bass Museum, only my invitation said the opening wasn't for another few days. We compared invites: Hers was to an "exclusive unveiling," while mine was to a plebian "opening reception." A gallerist I knew from New York asked whether I'd be going to the main fair, then took one look at my hard-won Art Basel VIP badge and laughed in my face. "That won't do anything!" he guffawed. "That's worthless!"

What an innocent I was. Art Basel Miami Beach hosted not one but *two* invitation-only VIP days: The more exclusive "Private Day," which was tomorrow, would be followed by the less exclusive "Vernissage," which would be followed by Who Cares Day, when the public could come. Private Day—try to keep up—was further subdivided into three tiers of exclusivity: Ho-hum VIPs were allowed at 4:00 p.m., exceptional VIPs could come at 2:00 p.m., and extraordinary VIPs were welcomed at 11:00 a.m.—theoretically to be the first to lay eyes on the art, though, in reality, galleries had been selling their wares for weeks already. Art Basel, evidently running out of synonyms for *special*, called the 11:00 a.m. passes "First Choice VIP." Mine, which got me in more than twenty-four hours later, should have been called "It's Cute You Tried."

There was a hierarchy of entrance times and a hierarchy of days of the week. No self-respecting First Choice VIP would be caught dead in Miami after Thursday. "You go Wednesday, or you don't go at all," sniffed a collector. Even deigning to set foot in Miami this year—*sharp inhale*. A museum employee, whose boss forced him to come, regarded my excitement with pity. Hadn't I heard Miami was over? First the fashion people crashed the party, then the party people crashed the party, then "this year the art people pulled back, and the fashion people pulled back. So like, who's it for?"

Mind you, no one had to physically show up in Miami to buy the art. Those First Choice VIPs weren't lining up at starting blocks at 10:59 a.m. so they could race to the booths and claim the paintings they wanted. Weeks ago they'd been sent PDFs with thumbnail-sized photos of the artwork that galleries were "offering" for sale, and many did their shopping from that. Yet another hierarchy determined when (and whether) you got those preview emails—an even finer-grained classification of Pre–First Choice and Second–First Choice VIPs, and so on down the list, with your status determined not by your love of the work, or by how early you asked to get on the waitlist, but by a nebulous ranking based on... criteria. Your fealty to the gallery, for example. (Buy a lot of work, advance one space.) Your future plans for the art. (Donate to a museum or start your own, advance three spaces.) Your current art collection. (Own a work by KAWS and you'll have to move back several spaces, at least according to a rumor about one megagallery's criteria.) Your track record with past purchases could factor in. (Resell at auction, go directly to jail—and know that some galleries put clauses in their sales contracts to try to stop you from flipping.) Your hometown might play a role too. (Sprinkling an artist's work around the country is good, since it makes it more convenient for regional museums to put the work in shows.) For in-demand artists, the gallery—not the buyer—picks who buys what, based in no small part on that human's context.

Miami was heaving with art. It dangled off buildings and sunned itself on the beach, yet the whole affair seemed designed to make you think the world was running out of art. *That's on reserve for an institution, the next tier of VIPs are coming in an hour, the fair will be over in three days, so hurry! Because this offer won't last long.* Collectors had obediently learned to want what they couldn't have—"I know when they tell me I *can* buy something that I shouldn't buy it if I can have it," one VIP confided—and gallerists went out of their way to intimate that buyers were about to lose out on a once-in-a-lifetime chance to own the modern version of the *Mona Lisa*. "If you sit at a desk on the computer and you just look busy, people are like, 'Ooohhh shit! Something's going on there!'" was Jack's advice on behaving at an art fair, and he parsed his words carefully to avoid letting on how much he hadn't sold. I was with Jack when an art advisor, who'd come to see some of Haley Josephs's work, paused in front of a painting and asked what pieces were still available. Awkward silence. "That one is still available," said Jack. They were, to my knowledge, *all* still available.

No matter where you were in line, someone was ahead of you. Jack had told me I was the outsider. But did anyone feel like an insider? I was starting to have my doubts. Bridget Donahue, the most heady Head, insidery insider I knew, told me she felt self-conscious about her lack of art-history education. Elizabeth's art-historian friend— credentialed with a PhD in art history and lots of academic bylines— insisted it was too bold to call himself an art historian. ("I can almost say that—I'm *getting* to the place where I could say that—no, I still wouldn't, actually.") Collectors fretted about being in the outer circle of the inner circle—"I finally have someone to kiss! She's been saying hello to people all morning," pouted a First Choice VIP at one of the fairs, leaning in to air-kiss someone just as her companion was doing the same. Even artists, without whom none of us would be in Miami, felt insecure in the art scene. From the exclusive unveilings to the scorecard of VIP rankings, it all seemed part of a deliberate strategy to curry insecurity. Comfort is complacency, and complacency doesn't sell art. Give people something to prove, a new tranche of VIP to shoot for, and you get a private museum with someone's last name over the door.

It was liberating to realize this. Seeing the Miami machine in action made the pretention less intimidating, like watching a film crew apply an actor's zombie makeup. Now that I understood how the system worked, going along with it no longer felt like the only option. You could play the game, or you could make up your own rules.

Just after 11:00 p.m., as I was leaving the party at the art museum, my roommate texted to say she was heading to the White Cube beach party—a bash hosted by a London gallery that was *the* place to be and impossible to get into. Don't wait up, she told me. I wouldn't. I had art to see bright and early the next morning: I was hoping to scope out some other fairs before reporting for duty, and I found myself looking forward to that more than any party.

ROB CAREENED INTO the booth in the morning. "I did lots of drugs last night," he declared, all smiles. He did not seem as hungover as I would have been and was already hyping a party on some island that was "the *real* party to go to. *That's* the party. There's a bunch of other things, but *that's* the one. Oh hell-LOOOOOOO!" He bopped over to a woman who said she'd seen his quote on tax law in *The Art Newspaper*, then bopped back to announce, "I have to send a bunch of invoices out."

"I don't even *know* how much we've sold," Elizabeth burbled, sounding delighted.

I knew exactly how much I'd sold: zero.

I resolved to study our customers more closely. Not only did my sales pitch clearly need finessing, but I hoped that tapping into what made a human want to own a photo of colored blocks would reveal more about art's place in our lives, beyond its value as a status symbol.

I met one of Rob's clients—thirties, ex-physician—who called art a "full body high" and bought art because it was the right thing to do. "If you think contemporary art is important, I believe you have to support contemporary artists."

I overheard two collectors discuss art as if they were trading stock tips. "*Loooottt* of cool artists coming out of Detroit," one offered, while the other insisted Mexico was the place to look. His highest compliment for an artwork: "It's bankable."

A few people picked out paintings like they were choosing wallpaper—one couple said they needed to fill a spot in their apartment with art that had "low intensity of content" and "more squiggles and less blobs." Others bought whatever the art advisors hovering at their elbows told them to. "How do you know what to buy if you don't have an advisor? You need intel in *some* way," tsk-tsked one advisor, implying the intel you got from your eyes was wholly inferior to context.

People bought what their friends bought—Elizabeth grumbled about a couple who trailed their friends around asking for one of whatever *they* got—but that was amateur hour. The pros relied on museum curators to tell them what to buy. Beth Rudin DeWoody's advice to art newbies was to join a museum's acquisitions committee so you could "look and see what museums are collecting, what curators are looking at." (Beth belonged to the Whitney's board, and if that sounds appealing, be forewarned it's apparently considered polite to donate $5 million within a few years of joining.) At Untitled, I watched as the chief curator of a museum steered his trustees (that means *collectors*) through certain booths and then over to ours. Elizabeth told his group about O'Keefe's work, and the curator quietly put a photograph on hold. A little while later, one of the trustees returned. She announced she'd buy two editions of that same photo: one to be shipped to the museum, one directly to her home. A little philanthropy, a little polite corruption—in that an institution's stamp of approval is precisely the sort of context that can make prices (and demand) jump. "We're all white-collar criminals," said the gallerist at a nearby booth breezily, not long after admitting he'd never paid a dime in sales tax. Except in the art world, as people frequently reminded me, insider trading is perfectly legal.

I listened to buyers speak possessively about their collections, as if they owned the artists, not their work. "This is Daniel Arsham," they said, holding up their iPhones. "*My* Tom Sachs." For the price of a painting, you could buy a lot more than just the work. Cognizant of the fact that I was representing Denny Dimin and wary of alienating any credit-card-carrying VIP, I forced my face into a polite smile while a prodigal collector's prodigal son, whom I'd met while touring his family's art collection earlier in the week, mimed his technique for going down on a girl. "You look like my sister—*delicious*," he told me, and invited me to dinner. He treated me to a rundown of his professional endeavors. "I don't work the five to—" He hesitated. "The six to..." He looked perplexed. "What is it?" His face brightened. "Oh yeah! Nine to five."

The gallerists didn't go out of their way to bring it up, but anyone half paying attention had to realize that all over town, art that criticized the massive accumulation of wealth was being sold to individuals who embodied it—the same individuals who "can so easily use the art produced against them as a means of demonstrating their distinction," wrote Bourdieu. As far as I know, strangers don't gather in your living room asking you to give speeches because you bought yourself a nice yacht, but splurge on enough paintings and you may get a round of applause. Clement Greenberg called it the "umbilical cord of gold": In this part of the machine, the art cost a lot because making and showing the art also cost a lot. Even though Elizabeth didn't calculate her prices by adding up O'Keefe's expenses, galleries still had to make rent, and Elizabeth's $8,000 framing bill wouldn't pay for itself. Who could afford what was being sold in these tents? Probably not public-school teachers. Possibly doctors. With art, VIPs could have their cake, eat it, make a tax-deductible donation of it, and have their friends marvel at how elegantly they chew.

In the late afternoon, after scarfing down a sandwich while hovering next to the emergency exit, I took up my usual spot in the booth, waiting to talk to anyone who so much as paused at the photos. The crowds had thinned, and during a brief moment of calm, I let O'Keefe's work wash over me.

And then it hit me: Despite Elizabeth's advice to *stay in the work*, despite everything I'd learned in Julie's studio, I'd taken the easy way out and outsourced my opinions to context. No wonder I hadn't sold anything. I'd never really looked at O'Keefe's art.

While trying to appear available to passersby, I stared at a small photo, twenty by sixteen inches, just to the left of my shoulder. *Stay in the work*, I ordered myself. *Five things.*

O'Keefe had photographed three objects positioned on a watermelon-pink surface that butted up against a brushy, hollandaise-yellow expanse. On the left-hand side of the image rested a half-moon of canary-yellow cardboard, behind it was a long skinny brown pole thing, and to the right of that was an hourglass-shaped chunk of wood painted red with a curvy swoop of green. Or at least I think the things were cardboard and wood. As I've said before, O'Keefe's photos could pass for paintings and consistently made me second-guess what I was seeing.

Now *that* was interesting. From some cobwebby corner of my brain, there surfaced the memory of an old college professor lecturing that photographs were duplicitous by nature. In theory, photos faithfully capture a snapshot of reality. And yet photographers, like journalists, inevitably frame each scene in a way that cuts out some details and calls attention to others. O'Keefe's photos seemed to be toying with photography's untrustworthiness. I kept staring at her photo, transfixed. There, hovering on the yellow backdrop was a shape I'd never noticed before: a mysterious pale circle, some kind of tiny glowing orb. I had no idea how it got there. Was it painted on the backdrop? A reflection of light? I couldn't trust what I was seeing. And for the first time, I felt the thrill of being lost.

Doubts immediately rushed in. Look at the pretty colors! The preciousness of the paper!

O'Keefe's photos were beautiful, I realized with a sinking feeling.

I'd grown suspicious of beauty over the last few months. It had become increasingly clear to me that polite society (including but not limited to the art scene) considered beauty to be toxic and that seeking it out—by wearing mascara, splurging on flowers, or hanging a pretty picture of waves over your couch—was a sign of moral weakness. Philosophers, art critics, scientists, and your garden-variety intellectuals have, over the past hundred years, teamed up with artists to declare beauty both corrupted and corrupting. It's "superficial and consoling," "tainted by bourgeois values," and "manipulated by those in power," writes professor Rhett Diessner in his book on beauty—where, on page one, he feels compelled to reassure readers that beauty really is important to think about. "Today," he writes, "it is simply treated by the art world as a joke, a con, an idiotic, old-fashioned idea." I worried that enjoying a beautiful artwork meant I wasn't *really* moved, the way Jack was by Michael Blake's bathroom sculpture.

The art world hasn't always treated beauty as its sworn enemy. For hundreds of years in the West, beauty was virtually synonymous with art, to the point that art practically wasn't *art* unless it was beautiful. Then, in the twentieth century, a spectacularly messy breakup ensued: Many artists, lots of them reeling from the carnage of World War I, wanted nothing to do with beauty. Keep painting sunsets? Our brutal world didn't deserve more beauty, and with everything going to hell in a handbasket, pursuing pretty things was a frivolous waste of time. A whole generation of modern artists like Barnett Newman (whose paintings include a red canvas intersected by a single orange line) and Ad Reinhart (whose works include a painting of black squares on a black square) picked up the antibeauty baton. They made pieces that defied traditional ideas of what art should look like and they waved away beauty as a shallow bourgeois hang-up. *Real* art concerned itself with politics and ideas. "The impulse of modern art," said Newman in 1948, "was to destroy beauty." By the time I showed up to the art world, beauty didn't need destroying. Artists knew it was off limits. In art school, the artist Clinton King told me, it was "almost shameful to produce something beautiful or well-done."

But what *is* "beauty" anyway? Honestly—who knows: We've careened between definitions across cultures, minds, times. Beauty is linked to goodness, asserted Plato, Confucius, and communities throughout Africa. (In southeastern Nigeria, the Igbo term *mma* translates into both "beauty" and "good," and similarly, the beginning of Genesis features a Hebrew word that could be translated as either "beautiful" or "good." Imagine: The whole tenor of the Bible's opening shifts if, after making light, land, and man, "God saw that it was *beautiful*.") Beauty can be measured, argued Pythagoras, Plotinus, and various other Greco-Roman philosophers, who thought it was an intrinsic property based on certain beautiful proportions. No, beauty lies in blemishes, simplicity, and the subtle patina of age, contended Japanese tea master Sen no Rikyū. Or rather it's subjective and in the eye of the beholder, said Descartes, or an innate quality that brings us pleasure disconnected from any practical purpose, said Kant, or whatever activates the Al region of the medial orbitofrontal cortex (a brain region linked to pleasure), say neuroscientists. Freud said we recognize beauty because we want to have sex with it; Elaine Scarry said we know it because we want to draw, photograph, or replicate it; and Rilke called it "nothing but the beginning of terror." In short, beauty is a mess. I struggled to come up with my own definition, though when it came to art, I had the vague sense that beautiful pieces were pleasant and agreeable—the visual equivalent of a vanilla cupcake.

All these conflicting definitions can obscure the fact that our concept of beauty appears to be hardwired in our brains. "Beauty is one of the ways life perpetuates itself, and love of beauty is deeply rooted in our biology," writes psychologist Nancy Etcoff in her book *Survival of the Prettiest*. Like the innate preference for sweetness that makes newborns smile when they drink sugar water, scientists like Etcoff hypothesize that humans have evolved to find certain forms more attractive than others (a theory that undermines the idea, espoused by some, that what we find beautiful has been imposed on us by a corrupt cabal of Don Draper types). Exactly which visual features constitute the "aesthetic primitives" that humans innately consider beautiful is still being researched, but there are a few promising candidates. People across diverse cultures and age groups prefer curved shapes to angular ones—a preference that holds constant across things, rooms, patterns, and abstract shapes, as well as one we share with rats, chimps, and gorillas. Humans—like squirrels, crows, and capuchin monkeys—also prefer symmetrical designs to asymmetrical ones, and, perhaps unsurprisingly, we prefer colors (like blue) that we strongly associate with pleasant things (like clean water), while we dislike colors (like brown) that we strongly associate with things we avoid (like feces). In the 1990s, a pair of artists, Vitaly Komar and Alex Melamid, surveyed citizens across fourteen countries, from Denmark to Kenya, and found that each nation rated blue as their favorite color. Green came in second among everyone except the Danes (who preferred red—perhaps not coincidentally the color of their flag). The artists famously used their survey results to create each country's "Most Wanted" painting. All of these were practically identical in that they featured vistas of blue skies and blue water peppered with lush green trees—the sort of landscapes that make good habitats for humans. Rob and Elizabeth, in their ongoing study of New York art buyers, had noticed that blue and pink pieces sold better than works in green or yellow—"shades of nasty body experiences," Rob speculated.

I considered O'Keefe's photo, which had a few aesthetic primitives going for it. There were the gentle curves of the cardboard, along with the swoop of fertile-valley green near the horizon line. Was *that* why I liked it? Because I did: I liked it. The more time I spent with it, the more time I wanted to spend with it. Being around O'Keefe's photos just *felt* good, like lying on a beach towel in the sun.

Only that wasn't necessarily something erudite art connoisseurs were supposed to say. The reviews of O'Keefe's work that I'd memorized and repeated had praised her references to cubism and "carefully structured architectonics." None of them alluded to the way O'Keefe's photos could make you feel warm, tingly, and relaxed, and we can blame the modernists for that too: Along with turning us off of beauty, they implanted the idea that looking at art should be a philosophical, not a physical, experience—intellectual and a little bloodless. Even if an artwork affects you so deeply it makes you decide to quit your job and, say, run off to Tuscany to become a puppeteer, the proper response is to arch your eyebrow and say *Hmmm*. Mind you, the ancient Greeks had no such qualms: As one philosopher recounts, "Pliny tells us that Praxiteles' statue of the Cnidian Aphrodite"—a naked portrait of the goddess of sex and beauty—"caused such lust in one man that the stains that marked the consummation of his passion were still visible in the marble hundreds of years later."

Screw those killjoy modernists and their cold-blooded philosophizing, I decided. We may think we're done with beauty, but beauty definitely isn't done with us. Most of us don't wake up each morning in a concrete box with the bare minimum of functional furniture, skip all grooming, and throw on whatever shred of fabric will keep us warm and cover our naughty bits. "Wherever you look, and however far back we look, there seems to be evidence that people care to decorate things beyond their simple utilitarian value. And that feels like something really core. Something I think has been perhaps deemphasized in our culture," says Anjan Chatterjee, a neurologist who specializes in the burgeoning field of neuroaesthetics. Beauty may be far more essential than we realize: In France and Canada, doctors have been prescribing their patients visits to art museums and letting them pick art to hang in their hospital rooms. "Encountering beauty," says the neuroscientist who runs one program, "can have a therapeutic effect."

I started to think swearing off beauty in art was like a health nut cutting out salt. Sure, you could get used to eating flavorless soy sludge three times a day, but why would you want to? Beauty, like a pinch of salt, can bring out other flavors in a work. Come for the curves. Stay for the sense you'll never look at a photo the same way again. O'Keefe's photos were a pleasure. And what was so bad about that?

———

MY SALES PITCH CHANGED. The next day, I stayed in the work, and people stayed there with me.

Eyes bugged, mouths gasped, heads swiveled. But I can't take all the credit. By Thursday, the VIPs had been joined by a more diverse crowd that included visitors who'd hitchhiked here from New York, said things like, "I don't get hungover from Molly," and, among certain gallerists, might be referred to as Schmos. These viewers didn't immediately jump to context. In spite of the overstimulating chaos of the fair, lots of them circled the booth over and over, jaws slack as if they'd been hypnotized, then came back later tugging friends behind them. "These are *photos*?" I got asked a lot. "Wait—*that's* not a painting?" Yep. "What about *that* one?" Still a photo. "Do you have a layaway plan?" asked an artist who couldn't pry herself away from our booth. We did. "I'm going to kill off a relative. No—I'm going to take out a life-insurance policy and *then* kill off a relative." It wasn't O'Keefe's work that did it, but I'll never forget watching a lanky woman in a long skirt stop abruptly in front of an abstract collage of golden triangles and black squares outside a booth. Her eyes widened until they were as big and bright as full moons, and it took me a few moments to realize she was crying. "It's so beautiful," she told her friend. She left to get a paper napkin to blot away her tears, then came back and just stared. An artist I'd met before coming to Miami had fretted that people "aren't actually looking at things." I wanted to reassure him that some were.

Partway through the day, a middle-aged couple, dressed like matching sailboats in crisp white button-downs and navy loafers, wandered into Denny Dimin's booth. I hovered beside them as they paused in front of each photo, eyes rarely traveling from the work.

The woman stopped at one of O'Keefe's biggest pieces—a photograph of squiggly cardboard shapes that made me think of cubist houseplants. She didn't move. She didn't even blink.

"The gallery—so this *is* a New York gallery?" she asked at last.

Lower East Side, I confirmed.

"Her studio's in New York?" Yes. "Do you do a lot of fairs?" Yes. "How long have you been representing her?" Four years. Silence. I sensed she needed a tiny nudge. Context, I understood, was also a way to try to securitize your investment, a way to be sure you weren't the only one who thought this work was special. I murmured a sweet nothing about O'Keefe's "institutional support."

The woman turned to the man she was with. "Is it going to Boston?"

"Or Palm Beach?" he said.

And that's how I sold my first piece: $9,800, thank you very much. I felt giddy, like I'd just been called onstage to accept a prize, but I was cool as a cucumber, tight smile and firm handshake, while I swiped their credit card.

Elizabeth and Rob cornered me as soon as the buyers left, huge grins on their faces. "Good job!" said Elizabeth.

"Thanks," I said curtly, trying not to sound overly enthusiastic, even though on the inside I was tossing confetti and leading a marching band in my honor. "Exciting," I added in a Jack-ish monotone.

"*More* than exciting, Bianca!" Rob crowed. "Fuck, dude. Nicely done."

That first sale chummed the water and I got a little bloodthirsty after that. Something clicked. I'd gone from regurgitating lines to doing the dance, dance, dance. As the hours ticked by, I sensed a part of myself emerging from a deep freeze and thawing in the warm Miami sun. I was . . . helping? I'd almost forgotten what it was like to feel capable.

Elizabeth told me to go eat my lunch, which had been stewing in its juices for the better part of an hour. I waved her off. "I just want to wait to see if this woman comes back," I said, scanning the crowd for the lady I'd pegged as a promising buyer. Elizabeth and Rob exchanged a look and burst out laughing.

"You *drank* the Kool-Aid," said Elizabeth in between giggles.

"That was like, real fucking art-dealer stuff," said Rob.

I sold two more pieces and put one on reserve for a woman I'll call Isabel. I gobbled down dinner—"the unnecessary speed bump," Rob called it—and was on my way to another Pérez Art Museum Miami cocktail party when a sexagenarian named Poodle—smokey eyes, crocodile purse—tried to steal my Uber, but Poodle was going to the party, too, so I invited her to tag along. Poodle couldn't stomach American rosé, traveled with a few hats in case of a horse race, and had a recently deceased partner whose art collection was two thumbs jerked several times in the air expensive. I flashed her pictures of O'Keefe's photos and declined a phone call from my husband. ("Literally she's not coming home. You should prepare the divorce papers now," a friend texted him in our group chat.) Rob found me at the museum and took me to the *real* party he'd raved about, where I pitched O'Keefe to the guy next to us in line for tequila sodas whose reply was "A lot of my art is in storage," which also translates to *collector* and immediately got him our full and undivided attention. "The Tate reached out to ask if they could have this for their upcoming retrospective," he said, showing me a sculpture on his phone, and Rob couldn't pull out his business cards fast enough. Drinks by the pool with gallerists from Germany ("Have you seen O'Keefe's work?" I asked, rummaging for my phone) turned into the back seat of someone's Escalade destined for Soho Beach House, which was surrounded by a wriggling mass of thrashing limbs as though Miami were sinking and Soho House the last lifeboat. "I fucking hate the weekend in Miami," groaned a gallerist beside me. My phone buzzed with a text from Isabel saying she wanted to buy the photo she'd put on reserve, just as someone beside me in the Escalade noisily *hrooonfed* a line of cocaine. Dive bar from 12:30 to 1:30 a.m. Gay bar dancing with half the population of Brooklyn from 1:30 to 4:13 a.m. Drive-by threesome from 4:13 to 4:15 a.m. (aggressively necking couple; uncomfortably small hotel elevator). Home just as my roommate was leaving for the airport. Friday morning—time to get the hell out of dodge.

"Coffeecoffeecoffeecoffee," Rob was chanting when he got to the fair a few hours later. "We ended up going down to the beach at five thirty in the morning."

Isabel came by to pay for her piece. There was the debate over which residence would get the art (Philadelphia? Miami?), and Rob, gold medalist in small talk, got her chatting about her move to Philly, and next thing we knew, she was telling us how she'd joined the photo committee at a *major* museum and couldn't wait to show O'Keefe's work to the curator. "I just drooled all over this sales sheet, I'm sorry," Elizabeth said, as soon as Isabel left. According to the rules I was learning, galleries and their clients could only do so much to nudge their favorite artists into the canon. Ultimately, museums held the keys to the kingdom.

I made another sale. Scarsdale or Florida? "You have too many houses!" chirped the clients' art advisor.

I sold a piece to a couple in their forties who came back three times before taking the plunge. "This is the first time we're *actually* buying a serious piece of art, so it's like, very stressful for us. I want to pick the right one," said the buyer, who kept staring at O'Keefe's photos and repeating the word *love*. I sold a piece to a young couple who decided to splurge on a small O'Keefe print. Scratch that—make it two, they decided.

We ran out of the red dot stickers we used to mark pieces as sold, and I bounced between booths asking if anyone had some to spare, which was obnoxious, but I did it anyway, dizzy and manic off the high of selling.

IT'S EASY TO SNEER at the absurd spectacle that is Miami Art Week. The whole scene has a ludicrous cartoon-villain vibe, what with the sprawling lairs, the copious stroking of tiny inbred lapdogs, the cackling about world domination while demanding to be paid $2 million— no, *$3 million!*—for the Kusama or else innocent civilians get zapped with the laser beam.

What's harder to admit, especially if you're with folks who worship the holy trinity of Marx, Foucault, and Deleuze, is that Miami is fun. Are the parties a distraction from the art? Well, people *are* going to museums, aren't they? So they've had a few drinks, and they're taking selfies. That doesn't make the paintings invisible. I could see how doing Miami every year for a decade would make you want to lock yourself in a closet and scream into a pillow. But like a prim chaperone hissing at giggly teens to be quiet, there was a prissiness in categorically denouncing the extravaganza. I wasn't sure where else you'd find thousands of people shouting about art over dinners, over dance floors, overnight, and at all hours of the day.

As the week had worn on, instead of feeling exhausted, I was exhilarated. Miami was boot camp for the Eye—Art Basel Miami Beach had 268 booths alone—and whenever Elizabeth and Rob could spare me from the booth, I'd careened through the city on a Supermarket Sweep of art. I was a person possessed. I woke up early to tour the Rubell Museum before it officially opened and skipped breakfast to beeline for the main fair, where I saw a $50 million Mark Rothko painting that warmed me from the inside like I'd swallowed a chunk of the sun. I spotted one of Julie Curtiss's paintings, a conga line of Paola Pivi's feathered bears, and a whole lot else that I could tell you about, but truth be told, I left the main fair sooner than I'd expected. I dashed back to Untitled, excited to venture beyond Denny Dimin's booth for the first time in days, and as I made the rounds, I lingered over a papier-mâché sculpture of a man licking a woman's nostril. Weird, but I wanted weirder.

I don't know whether it was Elizabeth's advice or the sheer quantity of art I'd seen or the contact high from all the drugs in the air, but as the week neared its end, I found myself craving art I didn't know, by artists I'd never heard of. Most of the art at the fairs, like the art in collectors' homes, looked like art. I'd spent a week gorging myself on a very specific diet of art that could sit politely in a living room: a lot of colorful painting mixed in with the occasional fuck-you piece that was now famous enough to not scare house guests. Which was great. The work was tasty and rewarding and easy to sell, and I was thrilled to have seen it. But at the NADA art fair, I noticed my attention sliding off wooden bonsai trees in *Sesame Street* colors and coming to rest on a black sleeping bag, slumped against the wall, that inhaled and exhaled of its own volition. Bizarre. Sick? Also entrancing. On Saturday, I was late getting back to Untitled because I'd hurried over to a pop-up fair housed in a shopping mall and got wrapped up talking to the artist Norberto Rodriguez, whose artwork consisted of him living out of an empty storefront above a Cole Haan—part of an ongoing project, he said, in which he was attempting to turn his entire life, "from my birth to my death," into a work of art. He tried to sell me his suitcase as a sculpture.

Like a lot of contemporary art, these pieces made me feel as if someone had kicked out my legs from under me. But that helpless, grasping feeling had stopped being painful. It was a rush. Unknown artworks were a challenge, a dare, and for the first time that I could remember, I didn't want to back down. Maybe it helped that, after a week in Miami, I finally felt as if I'd peeked behind the curtain and discovered that the high priests and priestesses of contemporary art were as flawed as the rest of us. They took a few hits of weed vape before talking to a VIP, whooped when "Like a Virgin" came on at the club, and showed up late to work reeking of cigarettes. They weren't special or scary. They were tired, stressed about bills, and often making it up as they went along. I was beginning to see that the Heads were not infallible, and that emboldened me to trust myself more.

My tastes, I realized as I scanned Untitled from my spot in the booth, were changing. I couldn't wait to get back to New York and see whether my relationship with the city's art had changed too.

SUNDAY, the last day of the fair. A steady stream of artists filed through the booth, chatting warmly and pressing business cards into our hands while stressing their deep interest in the gallery's program. Sean Fader, an artist represented by Denny Dimin, whom I'd had dinner with earlier in the week, dropped by the booth. He was curious to know how I was feeling now that the fair was nearly over.

A little shell-shocked, I confessed. I wasn't familiar with this Bianca who woke up excited to see a show of video art and could confidently tell a collector that edition two of *Book of Days #21* was on reserve for an institution, but if they wanted to buy the piece now, we'd sell them edition three at edition-two pricing.

"You never thought you'd be wheeling and dealing art in Miami," Sean said.

"*Definitely* not."

Sean got very serious, which was unusual for him, and he leaned in close so our foreheads were practically touching. "Every red dot means an angel gets its wings. And some fucking artist can pay their rent, okay?" he said. "It means that somebody who's a maker gets to keep making."

In the final hours of the fair, I learned that the gallery across from us, which hadn't sold anything, would be shutting down for good at the end of the year. Denny Dimin was not closing. We'd had a blowout fabulous fair. I'd sold seven pieces. The gallery had sold more than two dozen pieces for a total of—Elizabeth was still totaling all the invoices—more than $200,000. They'd live another day to share artists' work, and that, in the absence of a more perfect system, was something.

Also, they wanted to promote me.

CHAPTER NINE

So when we reflected on Miami, it felt like you were doing the equivalent job of an assistant director, so I think we should just give you that title," said Elizabeth when we got back to New York. My new role came with an email address, the keys to the gallery, and the fancy new "Assistant Director" title, which was a slick way of saying helping Rob, Elizabeth, and Dylan with whatever they needed on the two or three days a week I'd come in. I scanned press mentions, drafted art-fair applications, and met with clients, where the gravitas of my new title really came in handy. I sold another two O'Keefe photos while Rob and Elizabeth were at a fair in San Francisco and delivered art to Fifth Avenue addresses.

Most importantly for my purposes, I got to keep learning from Elizabeth and Rob. Not only were they open to the point of letting me rifle through their bills, but I sensed they cared more about helping someone develop her own Eye than imposing the Denny Dimin view. I couldn't claim to be an expert, but after a few weeks with them, I no longer felt like I was hanging on for dear life.

As for what they saw in me: I wasn't so naïve as to ignore the possibility that Rob and Elizabeth might be going out of their way to be nice to a writer. (At galleries, mutual back-scratching took lots of different forms; Jack had told me that if he wasn't as ethical as he was, "my go-to intern hire would be hiring the daughter of like a wealthy art collector. Can't tell you how often that happens.") But at the risk of flattering myself, I think I was lending a hand. Jack's tough love had whipped me into shape, and far from royally screwing up Miami, I'd sold nearly $50,000 of art. "You're really good at this. Like, *really* good at this. I have no doubt you could sell a $5 million painting," Rob told me. An exaggeration, but I appreciated his enthusiasm.

What Rob didn't say, but which I could see as plain as day, was that Denny Dimin needed all the extra assistance they could get. Between renovating the new space in Tribeca, launching their outpost in Hong Kong, and prepping for another art fair in Dallas in the spring, Elizabeth, Rob, and Dylan were practically sleeping at the gallery, if they slept at all. "I feel busy at a level that isn't fun anymore. It's just really scary," Elizabeth said during a late afternoon slump more than a month after getting back from Miami. Her voice was crackly with exhaustion.

That evening, Elizabeth put on her coat to go home and was about to step out the front door when she doubled back to the office. She stood next to the skinny desk we all shared, crossed her arms over her chest, and glared down at Dylan, Rob, and me.

"I'm having a memory of a meltdown," Elizabeth said slowly, "where I told you all that there was absolutely *no way* that we could do a new gallery, Hong Kong, *and* the Dallas Art Fair."

We nodded. We remembered.

"And *FUCK* all of you!" said Elizabeth, her face bursting into a giant grin. Somehow, we were doing it all.

I CAME BACK from Miami craving weird, boundary-pushing art—stuff that was a little ugly, a tad rude—but the artist Mandy AllFIRE made work that sounded like too much, even for the open-minded new me. I first learned about her art in the course of what had become my new routine of seeking out shows at New York's most off-the-beaten-path galleries—places, usually run by artists to support their talented artist-friends, that tackled the problem of high rents and a shortage of chances to show by staging exhibits in dumpsters, trees, bathtubs, shipping containers, broken payphones, and a microwave. I spent one Saturday at Catbox Contemporary, a gallery based out of a cat tree in a guy's apartment in Queens, where I contemplated a video of scrotal hairless cats padding through a bathtub full of frosted donuts. I hit it off with the artist who'd made the video, Deirdre Sargent, and she texted me a few weeks later to say this artist called Mandy AllFIRE was having a solo show, and would I like to come along to the opening?

I skimmed the press release Deirdre sent me. AllFIRE, whom I'd never heard of, had on her résumé a master's in visual art from Columbia (one of the top art schools in the country, if you're counting), a stint at the prestigious Skowhegan residency, and a track record of performing at some of the city's most precocious arts venues, places that on other nights would host luminaries like Patti Smith or Philip Glass. More recently she'd been performing on Instagram as an ass influencer, and her camera unshy booty had charmed nearly three hundred thousand followers, who were coming tonight to be squished as part of a "live face-sitting." "She aims to sit on as many people as possible, for as long as possible," declared the impressively straight-faced press release. "Each participant will be sat on until they can't take it anymore." The gallery was offering the artist's previously worn underwear for sale because—get your mind out of the gutter—it formed part of All-FIRE's ass-forward exploration of societal ills, such as the "obsession and desperation to achieve the often misappropriated, oppression-based aspirations and exaggerated objectification of the female body."

The answer was no, I did not want to go to AllFIRE's opening. I fancied myself a budding art connoisseur and liked to think that I was well on my way to appreciating whatever avant-garde tomfoolery the kids these days were up to, but really, this was too far. Used underwear? Face-sitting? Be reasonable.

Still, it wasn't every Saturday night a real-life artist asked me to hang out. I felt like a gauntlet had been thrown, and God forbid I should seem like an antisocial square just in case next time, Deirdre might invite me to something worthwhile.

"I'd love to join," I texted Deirdre. We made plans to meet around 7:00 p.m. at Haul, the gallery that was showing AllFIRE's work. I kept my strong aversion to AllFIRE's show to myself.

HAUL GALLERY WAS down the street from the toxic sludge that is the Gowanus Canal, kitty-corner from a check-cashing spot, and nowhere to be found. My only tip-off that I'd come to the right place was the gaggle of people milling outside a janitorial supply store smoking cigarettes and dressed in the typical Brooklyn-opening uniform— hoodies, beanies, patchy dye-jobs that made them look like their moms had caught them bleaching their hair in the bathroom and grounded them before they could finish. Someone in a leather jacket materialized out of the sidewalk holding a Budweiser, and I understood the gallery was down there—between two metal doors in the sidewalk, down a steep flight of steps, in a squat room with low ceilings and lumpy white walls. Once upon a time, Haul Gallery had been an underground storage unit.

People were lined up three deep around AllFIRE, and I bobbed and weaved for a view. Orange wires dangled from the ceiling next to pairs of AllFIRE's lacy underwear. "Work that ass, work it, work it!" called a man's voice over the autotuned rap that thumped from a speaker somewhere. I spotted a gallerist friend of Jack's cradling his chin thoughtfully, an artist I knew from Jack's gallery tilting her head in concentration, and Deirdre, who whispered a hushed introduction to some of her friends. At one end of the gallery, behind a red velvet rope and on a cot fitted with a wrinkled white sheet, was AllFIRE herself.

The art was already happening. AllFIRE's ass faced the audience. She wore gold hoop earrings, black eyeliner, and lacey black lingerie. A middle-aged man, slick as a manatee in nothing but leopard underwear, was stretched out on the mattress with AllFIRE straddling his face. Her bare feet dangled over the front of the mattress, her knees pressed the cot, and her ass crack smushed the guy's receding hairline. Like a discerning mattress shopper testing the merchandise, AllFIRE bounced gently on his nose.

"Rich, you're next, right? You're next, right? You only live once, Rich," babbled a guy a few inches from AllFIRE's left foot, while Rich stayed mute. The crowd was equally split between men and women, with approximately a million raised iPhones, as well as some *National Geographic*–quality digital cameras.

"Have you ever been sat on before?" asked AllFIRE. She held a microphone up to her butt.

"Mhever," said a muffled voice from under her. "Mshurh biggest fan."

"Can I push harder down on you?"

"Wuhwoo! Hordor, hordor!"

For fifteen minutes, AllFIRE roosted on the man's head while she read fan mail from her followers. ("Wow, your ass makes me crazy I would love it if you put it in my face.") There were occasionally whistles, a few *woo*s! ("Rich, do it Rich, do it Rich, do it, c'mon Rich, c'mon, you only live once, man," said Rich's friend, while Rich, I assume, wanted to die.) AllFIRE swiveled on the man's forehead and tossed her booty-length black hair over her shoulder. She put her hands on her hips and looked over her shoulder at the crowd.

"Is anybody else going to participate?"

I have this moment on video. I've watched it at least fifty times, trying to make sense of what happened next. The blurry twenty-two-second clip pans jerkily over someone's dirty white Converse and over a woman filming with a steadicam, then back to AllFIRE's cot. All-FIRE adjusts herself on the guy's face, flips around, says, "Is anybody else going to participate?" and stares directly at my iPhone. Then the recording cuts off.

That's when I raised my hand.

When I try to think back to that moment, all I see is a solid black expanse where my brain should be. Did I think it through? I wouldn't have done it if I'd thought it through. Everyone and their mother was videotaping, I remembered belatedly as my feet carried me to the front of the room. Any hope of a political career was over, I thought—the least of my worries, but that's where my addled mind went. I thought of my poor oblivious husband, knitting quietly by the fireside at home.

I couldn't have said what I expected to discover by having my airways squished by a pantsless woman I'd never met, but I guess I figured art would never change my life unless I took a few chances, and anyway, before I could figure out how to politely tell AllFIRE I'd made a terrible mistake, thank you but no thank you, I was stretched out on a wrinkled white sheet, covered in a full-body sweat, staring up at AllFIRE's bare thighs.

Darkness descended.

Wet warmth spread over my forehead, nose, cheeks, mouth, and chin. After a few moments, a tightness cinched my chest. I couldn't breathe. Panic gripped my lungs. I snuffled weakly at the blackness and got nothing, then parted my lips slightly—panicking even more as I debated whether this was crossing the line—and sucked in thick, melted air.

The room was silent.

"Alright, all the men are getting real quiet," I heard AllFIRE say.

There were a few scattered laughs.

"You might have a girlfriend after!" someone called.

"Make this sexy, please!" said another voice.

That creeped me out. I reached for my *notice-five-things* safety blanket. It was extremely dark. A minute went by. Come to think of it, I'd never been anywhere so dark. AllFIRE was back to reading fans' messages ("I want to smell your farts"), and it dawned on me that I could feel AllFIRE laughing before she laughed, could sense my forehead trembling before my ears heard the *ha ha*. It was primal. It was like being in the deepest pit of a hug. Or a cave. A few more minutes passed, and my mind drifted. Was this like being in the womb? A reverse womb? Something about being born again? Seven minutes went by. My breathing had slowed. My heart had stopped thudding. AllFIRE's body pressed mine securely. It was surprisingly peaceful. Truth be told, I wouldn't have minded taking a nap.

THE MORNING AFTER Mandy AllFIRE sat on my face, I showed up to work at Denny Dimin and discovered I was locked out. I'd been distracted while leaving the house that day trying to process the significance of spending seven minutes with a lingerie-clad performance artist on my nose, and I'd forgotten my keys.

Elizabeth was running late that Sunday—the subway refuses to work weekends—and while I waited for her outside the gallery, I pulled out my phone to try to learn more about this AllFIRE character.

AllFIRE was, to be clear, a character. The artist, whose real name I still didn't know, had spent the last two years performing on Instagram as the booty influencer @ThugLifeThickBaby, whose 270,000 fans sent her gifts from her Amazon wish list, including pink ruffled underwear that hollered, "YES DADDY!"

I scrolled through AllFIRE's Instagram posts. She had a fringe of dark bangs, a small nose ring, and a very gregarious butt. Here it was hanging out of a window. There it was balancing two donuts. Now it was riding a tractor or in bed or trying to escape from a shower. The ass donned an elegant lace thong one day, a racy neon bodysuit the next. Regardless of outfit or setting, AllFIRE's butt was front and center, usually bare.

Some say romance is dead, but AllFIRE's fans were devoted. "I'm sure there's still some tribe somewhere that would drag their nuts across a mile of broken glass and rusty nails for the opportunity to hear your fart," one wrote her. Truly, her fans were poets. "Gave a whole new meaning to the big apple," one commented. They were curious. "On a scale of 1–10 how horny r u rn?" They creeped me out. "Can I fuck your eyes?" one inquired. They didn't ask before volunteering portraits of their dicks.

Nothing alluded to AllFIRE's identity as a performance artist, except for a few posts earlier in the week inviting fans to come to the gallery so she could sit on their faces. She'd tagged various art outlets: *Artforum*, *The Brooklyn Rail*, *Artsy*, *Artnet*. Her fans loved the idea. "I kill to be smothered by your beautiful 🍑." If I'd stumbled on AllFIRE's account without the context of last night's opening, I'd never have guessed it was a conceptual artwork.

When Elizabeth finally arrived, I didn't even wait for her to take her coat off before bringing up AllFIRE.

"So I went to a very interesting performance-art piece last night," I began. I set the scene. Haul Gallery was a labor of love run by two artists who kept it afloat with the money they earned teaching and working at another gallery. They were trying to come up with a business model that didn't rely on selling only to the ultrarich ("wealth criminals"), was transparent about money (they listed all their costs on their website), and sold affordable art to anyone. (You could buy AllFIRE's worn underwear, packaged with a self-portrait of her in that pair, for around thirty dollars.) Haul had hired a security guard to handle the flash mob of wannabe smotherees they'd expected at AllFIRE's opening, and since I'd gotten there fashionably late, I figured I'd been smothered only after a long line of fans who'd dragged their nuts across a mile of broken glass and rusty nails to be sat on. I'd discovered only afterward that nuts had not been dragged in quite the anticipated numbers. Despite her fans' catcalling and swagger online, they'd refused to show their faces. I was the third of three people AllFIRE squished at the opening.

"I actually think it says something about how threatening the gallery context is," Elizabeth mused. "I think if it had been in a club and not in an art context, she would have had a different turnout."

So did that mean the art had failed? "Was it good art?" I asked. I wasn't sure whether that was even the right question. "Was it effective?" What yardstick was I supposed to use in measuring the quality of the art, or was measuring quality even the right way to think about it?

Elizabeth scooted over to my computer screen to read over Haul's press release, nodding as she went along. "I really like this." She read a section out loud—*AllFIRE has recruited a small selection of her online fans to participate in a live-face-sitting event*—then glanced up from the screen. "To fulfill what they want. Their desires." Elizabeth saw parallels between booty influencers and emerging artists. "I'm speaking very off the cuff here, but I think trying to manage desire is a *huge* part of the art business and the art world. And this is an interesting reflection on it." She read another passage: *This event is about smothering*. "I find that *super* interesting," Elizabeth grinned. "Because smothering is also, you know, putting your art in someone's face." She got to the part about AllFIRE's worn underwear being for sale and laughed out loud. "And it's really fucking funny too!" Elizabeth said. "Humor is very underrated in art."

Elizabeth thought it would be helpful for me to consider AllFIRE in the context of some seminal performance-art pieces, so she cracked open the art encyclopedias she kept in her head. A quick disclaimer here: The definition of performance art is slippery, but generally the genre includes work that is ephemeral (even if there are videos or photos, it's often more of a "you had to be there" thing), work that is dynamic (a performance could be different every time), and work that can consist of pretty pedestrian actions. (Staging Alison Knowles's performance piece *Identical Lunch* means eating a tuna sandwich on wheat bread with lettuce, butter, and either soup or buttermilk on the side. In 2011, MoMA hosted a performance in its second-floor café.)

AllFIRE's face-sitting made Elizabeth think of Vito Acconci's *Seedbed*, which involved Acconci wedging himself under a gallery floor and masturbating while audibly describing his fantasies about the people walking above him. Oh! And Marina Abramović's *The Artist Is Present*: Eight hours a day for nearly three months, Abramović sat at a table and locked eyes with anyone who sat across from her. Elizabeth kept rattling off names and titles. Chris Burden spent five days squished inside a locker for *Five Day Locker Piece*. For *Untitled*, Andrea Fraser arranged for an art collector to pay her a sum of money, then had sex with him in a hotel room, which she videotaped in an hour-long film she later exhibited at a gallery—a commentary, perhaps, on what artists feel they have to give of themselves to the market.

Many artworks vanished from my memory as quickly as new names at a cocktail party, but there were occasionally pieces that took up residence in my brain and declared squatters' rights. They threw parties and played loud music and stomped on the floor and couldn't be evicted or ignored. AllFIRE's performance was like that. I couldn't stop thinking about it, I told Elizabeth. "Does that mean it's good?"

"No." Elizabeth got very serious. "You literally had your face sat on. You're going to be thinking about it for a while."

I mulled that over while I got to work assembling a price list of work for an upcoming show. That wasn't it, I decided. AllFIRE's practice intrigued me in part because it reminded me of my own process: I sensed we were both hoping for insight by immersing ourselves in a community we hadn't figured out. And I was fascinated that her art didn't obviously look like art. Or did it?

I realized there was an extremely fundamental, superannoying question I still didn't know how to answer: What made something art?

I turned the question over to Elizabeth.

"Did it feel like art?" Elizabeth said.

Did it *feel* like art? "How do you know if it feels like art?" I asked, panicky that I couldn't answer that for myself.

Elizabeth shrugged. She sighed. Shrugged again. We had artists' CVs to update and invoices to send, and my conundrum seemed unlikely to resolve itself anytime soon.

I needled her again. "What's the moment something feels like art?"

Elizabeth just shook her head. She grinned at me mischievously. "I guess once you're reading a long press release, and at the bottom it says that she went to Columbia and Skowhegan," she said, poking fun at the art world's tendency to trust fall onto context. "I guess that's it."

I DECIDED I needed to go directly to the source. With Deirdre's permission, I crashed a studio visit she'd scheduled with AllFIRE, whose offline name was Amanda Alfieri. Maybe Amanda could tell me why face-sitting was art.

The studio visit took place at a Lower East Side bar, and, after settling into a couch near a pool table, Amanda, Deirdre, and I dissected the smothering. I was shocked to hear that some of the artists I'd met at Amanda's opening—emerging, at the vanguard of hip, with unorthodox art practices involving materials like mummified rats—had been confused and even unsettled by Amanda's performance. The signifiers, so to speak, were "all off," they'd said. They didn't think Amanda had clarified whether participation was problematic or encouraged, and the ambiguity made the whole performance uncomfortable. That instantly got my attention. Artists were constantly telling me they *loved* ambiguity and art that made them uncomfortable. What gives? I got Amanda's phone number and resolved to learn more about what she was up to.

I met her for coffee one Thursday morning before she headed to her job at the New School's photo lab. We had coffee again a few weeks later, after she finished work. Then again. We started meeting regularly.

Amanda often seemed drained when she showed up. She alluded to inappropriate comments she got at work and tumultuous meetings with HR. She was hunting for a new job while also working full time, performing as AllFIRE, and having a life, though what she really wanted was to focus on her art. "Trying to work full time and work on my art is just getting too much," she told me after dragging herself to coffee one afternoon. Her voice sounded hollow. "It's hard for me to be fully invested in this project simply for monetary reasons. Like, I have to work." She made about $52,000 a year working at the New School and had so much debt from school—"like over $120,000"—she didn't even want to think about it. "I know that I'm going to probably die with this debt. Ha ha." As a performance artist, Amanda didn't necessarily make the sorts of sellable objects people could buy to hang on their walls, and the path to turning a profit from her art (albeit not every artist's goal) was a bumpy one. Performance artists might try to support their practices via grants, residencies, and day jobs, while courting opportunities to show at institutions and museums. Eventually they might parlay that into a show at a gallery, which would probably try to make money by translating their performance practice into physical items that could be sold—like photographs or used underwear.

Amanda grew up in Los Angeles. Her mom worked with disabled kids, her dad was a commercial fisherman, and Amanda, in her words, was different. "I kind of had a hard time growing up in the sense that I'm Mexican and Italian, and I grew up in a predominantly Hispanic community, and I had a lot of issues with other girls," she said. "They didn't like me. I looked different… I just *was* different. So I had a lot of issues. And I wanted to do acting when I was little." Amanda asked her mom to get her out of public high school and into a magnet program so she could study drama. When Amanda showed up at her new high school, she learned acting wasn't an option: Apparently her mom had ticked "visual arts" instead of "performing arts" on the application—"she didn't know what the hell the difference was"—but Amanda stuck it out. "I started getting into art as a way to sort of deal with what was happening at home," she said. "My father is a drug addict, so there was a lot of turmoil going on at home. My way of escaping was taking photos and being an artist and being in the dark room at school during my lunch and all that." In college, she discovered performance art and "just kind of fell in love." She left the San Francisco Art Institute after a year—she'd lost her financial aid, right after an audit turned up accounting irregularities at the school—and transferred to the University of Southern California to study photography. She briefly debated pursuing an art career while also working as a forensic investigator; one of her early performance pieces involved interning at the coroner's office so she could track down her dead grandmother's crypt. But Amanda decided juggling the two career paths wasn't realistic. "That's when I realized I just needed to get back into the arts… It's going to be hard, and I'm probably not going to make money, but that's my passion." She built up her CV staging shows in an empty karaoke bar with a friend, then applied to grad school to get her MFA. "I felt like it was necessary if I wanted to be taken seriously as an artist."

In grad school, Amanda started embodying different personas in pieces that stretched over weeks or even years. While many of her classmates at Columbia were prepping canvases and mixing paint, Amanda watched twenty-three seasons of the reality TV show *Survivor*, submitted an audition tape based on the types of contestants she saw cast, and got flown to California as one of about fifty semifinalists to try out for the show. (She made a video about the audition process, in character—"My character believed that as a performance artist she had the training in endurance, pain, and humiliation to be the ultimate survivor," Amanda wrote in an artist's statement on the piece.) For another performance, she gave a TED Talk–style lecture that argued that to become the "next great artist," your work had to be deep, painful, nude, edible, and a sex tape, and Amanda incorporated each element into her talk. (For pain, she used a broken wineglass to carve YOLO on her stomach while someone in the audience shouted, "Don't forget the hashtag!") A few years after graduating, Amanda decided to compete in an amateur bikini competition. She fasted, counted calories, fake-tanned, and fanatically exercised—two hours a day, six days a week, for twelve weeks—to the point that, on the day of the contest itself, you could count the tendons in her forearms. "I was thinking a lot about Marina Abramović's work and her whole philosophy in the way that she preps for a performance. Sometimes she fasts, sometimes she doesn't eat," Amanda told me. "Of course, I see it as art, right? Your body is the sculpture. You're molding your body to what you want it to be." Amanda's pieces didn't always involve a performance at a gallery. Over and over, they raised questions about the distinction between art

and life, which for Amanda, is exactly the idea. "Everything that I embarked on is a performance that blurs the borders between art and life,
and fiction and reality," she wrote in an artist statement. "Performance
art has become an intrinsic part of my life. It is no longer something
that I do, it is who I am."

Scrolling through Instagram after competing in the bikini contest,
Amanda noticed beauty standards changing. Six-packs and thigh gaps
were out; curves, D-cups, and pneumatic asses were in. "Everyone was
like, who can be slim thicc? You've still got to be skinny, but you've got to
be thicc too in all the right places." She studied the #thot canon (Insta
for "that ho over there") and women who were getting famous—like,
millions and millions of followers famous—posting fetishy photos of
their feet or 32K-cup breasts. Belfies (butt selfies) were a classic of the
genre. Amanda decided she—or rather, the persona she developed and
named AllFIRE—would try to become a butt influencer. She wanted to
explore the "dangerous" influence of social media on self-esteem and
mental health, and "the way that women choose to display themselves,
objectify themselves, empower themselves." Also, "for me, the ass was
something that I've always been interested in for some reason."

Asses and Instagram intrigued Amanda more than, say, querying
the boundaries of painting for the umpteenth time. "I'm not interested
in 'an object in relation to space,'" she told me. "I feel like in the art world
it's so easy for artists, or for people who are involved in the art world, to
dismiss these things that they don't see as important or valuable, but I
think it's so [much more] important than some fucking abstract painting or sculpture." She wanted her art seen by as many people and as
many different people as possible and, by the time we met, already had
more Instagram followers than Untitled Miami had had attendees.

Three years before she sat on me, Amanda had landed a coveted

$5,000 art grant that she used to pay a glute expert and she'd started doing thrice-weekly workouts tailored to get her a thicc physique. She spent hours photographing herself, doing squats, studying #thot trends, and flattering fans by answering their questions in flirty videos, all while documenting her life as AllFIRE for what she hoped would be a feature-length film. Her photo series *Feed da Booty*, which shows her stuffing ice cream and French fries into her ass, got shown at the Bronx Museum. She hit one hundred thousand followers. Two hundred thousand. Her goal was one million, but her fans demanded constant titillation and were easily bored by anything that happened above All-FIRE's neckline. "I noticed that if I talk too much in my stories, or I post too many videos of me speaking, my count will drop. Or people will say, 'Show me your butt, I don't care how you're feeling.'"

If you don't see how becoming an ass influencer is art, you're not alone. Allow me to briefly advertise my hard-won art-history knowledge by saying that, after reading up on performance art, Amanda's work made me think of famous artists like Orlan (who live streamed herself getting plastic surgery), Lynn Hershman Leeson (who spent five years pretending to be the fictional character Roberta Breitmore), and Lee Lozano (who, for *Decide to Boycott Women*, decided to boycott speaking to women—initially for a month, though it turned into a twenty-nine-year project that ended only with her death). Abramović hasn't yet done a face-sitting, though she did do a piece where members of the public had to squish themselves between her and another artist standing naked at the uncomfortably narrow entrance to a museum. Yet even performance art devotees who fawned over the genius of a guy masturbating under the floor thought Amanda's latest piece was ass-backward, so to speak. "Like, why is this art?" Rob asked when I showed him AllFIRE's Instagram. "If an artist is calling something

art, it's art," he told me. "But this is borderline slightly *too* far. I'm having a hard time with it. I understand that there's a certain level of sub-
version of the male gaze and all these different things. But I don't see
this as anything other than, like, attempting to be sensational."

So was it art or just an attempt to be sensational? I was still facing
down the question *how do I know if it's art.*

I couldn't put it off any longer. I went shoveling through art theory
for answers, hoping to find a straightforward definition along the lines
of Rob's "if an artist calls something art, it's art."

Cut to me trudging back and forth from the library, pasty and
rickets-prone from lack of sun exposure, muttering about institutionalism while facing all-but-certain death under the tottering skyscraper
of books on my desk.

And yet the more research I did, the more my quest looked futile:
After centuries of arguing, the experts have pretty much thrown up
their hands on defining art. Small wonder in an age when the term
"art" gets stretched to include everything from Michelangelo's *David*
to Duchamp's urinal to AllFIRE's belfies. "There is no way to unques-
tionably tell whether an object is an artwork or not," declared a rather
unhelpful paper titled "The Ambiguity of Artworks."

Don't get me wrong, lots of definitions of art have been proposed. I
won't attempt to explain them all here—it's for your own good, trust
me—but picture a swarming nest of -isms: essentialism (there are formal, physical properties that make art *art*), intentionalism (it's physical properties *and* a viewer's mental impression that make art *art*),
functionalism (satisfying a specific purpose, like an aesthetic experience, makes art *art*), historicism (relating to a past piece of art makes
art *art*), institutionalism (connoisseurs dub art *art*), and the "cluster
approach" (some hodgepodge of all of the above makes art *art*). That

barely scratches the surface, but believe me when I say: No definition has satisfied. Lots have been considered and rejected for being circular, inconsistent, sexist, racist, classist, or obsolete, among other flaws. On top of that, so much contemporary art is dedicated to questioning what's contemporary art that the debate has largely devolved into a self-licking ice cream cone. And then there's the problem that art keeps shape-shifting across different cultures and times.

Case in point: Today we hail Picasso's *Les Demoiselles d'Avignon* as art and dismiss a needlepoint pillow that says "NAP QUEEN" as lowly "craft"—certainly not the sort of thing we should stare at in museums, waiting to feel transformed. Yet the notion that fine art exists in a special category unto itself and moves us more deeply than mere stuff is actually a recent invention, one that's newer and more European than the cuckoo clock.

Rewind to ancient Greece and Rome. "Art" meant any activity requiring human ingenuity and skill. Training horses, painting vases, passing laws, writing poems, singing songs, sewing clothes, blowing glass: art, art, and more art. While in ancient Egypt the "chief sculptors" who worked on royal tombs enjoyed a privileged status, among the ancient Greeks and Romans, painters and sculptors got lumped in with farmers, cobblers, and other manual workers who did physical labor for a fee—"suppliers of a commodity on par with shoemakers," writes one archaeologist, describing Greek artists circa the fifth century BCE. And for thousands of years in Europe, that's the way it was, as historian Larry Shiner chronicles in *The Invention of Art*, a book I couldn't put down. Artworks had a practical function—they inspired devotion to God or obedience to authority—and you could hire Leonardo da Vinci the way you'd hire a decorator these days. When, in 1483, Maestro da Vinci was picked to paint a new altarpiece for a chapel in

Milan, he had to sign a contract that specified the painting's due date (December 8), its composition ("Our Lady in the middle" with "mountains and rocks" in the background), and its color scheme (the Virgin Mary's "upper garments" should be "ultramarine blue, brocaded with Gold"). Also, he'd be collaborating with two other painters on the job.

But over the next few decades, writes Shiner, European tastemakers decided that "art" and "craft" were different things, made by different people, to be appreciated in different ways. People love to go on about the cultural upheaval of the 1960s—hippies, free love, you know the story—but after reading Shiner's book, I'm convinced it doesn't get wilder than the 1760s. Novels were the hot new reading technology of the day, art museums were being born, a new class of traveler called the "tourist" was crisscrossing Europe to look at old paintings, and art critics were in hot demand as class-conscious audiences struggled to figure out what was worth their while. The Industrial Revolution churned out a growing middle class that tried to ape the nobility's taste in art—it's around this time that "popular culture" becomes synonymous with *Schmo*—and as the number of art collectors grew, standalone art galleries started to emerge. (According to Shiner, they cultivated "an aura of exclusivity" from the get-go.) In the middle of this arts feeding frenzy, Europe's elite came up with a cultural hierarchy that elevated "fine art" to a throne from which it's waved smugly at that peon "craft" ever since. (What we now call "art" is short for "fine art," which comes from the French *beaux-arts,* meaning "beautiful arts," which for a time was translated as "polite arts.") *Art* was narrowly defined as painting, sculpture, architecture, poetry, or music that audiences appreciated for its pleasure (not its practicality) and that was made exclusively by honest-to-God artists—which is to say, creative white male geniuses free to pursue their inspired personal visions. All the leftover stuff, like needlepoint and cobblery, got lumped together and demoted under the heading of "craft," which was considered the useful (but not soul-shaking) output of rule-following tradespeople with skill (but no imagination). In 1740, the Académie Française—then and now the official referee of the French language—very expansively defined an *artiste* as "one who works in an art . . . in particular, those who perform chemical operations." By 1762, the Académie Française had revised its definition to read: "he"—cough, *he*, cough—"who works in an art where genius and hand must concur."

Redefining *art* also redefined how we relate to it. Craft could keep us warm and dry, but art could elevate our existence. Uprooting artworks from chapels and sticking them inside art museums solidified art's status as an object meant for pure contemplation, divorced from daily life. For hundreds of years, viewers kneeled before da Vinci's altarpiece in the church in Milan, praying to receive salvation from God. Then his painting of the Virgin Mary moved to London's National Gallery, where museum audiences stood before it waiting to feel moved by the grace of the artist. A century or two later, that's basically where I'd found art. (At least in the West, though these ideas got exported over the years through the additional -isms of colonialism and imperialism. And to be fair, connoisseurs in China had already beaten Europeans to the punch somewhat on developing a hierarchy of "arts": As early as the ninth century, painted murals and portraits were already starting to be associated with craftsmen making utilitarian works at the direction of state and religious leaders, while landscape painting, calligraphy, and poetry—especially in the hands of the educated elite—were celebrated as far more noble pursuits. One seventh-century figurative painter, wary of his sons following in his footsteps, allegedly cautioned them not to "practice this lowly skill.") Even as numerous East

Williamsburgers wrung their hands problematizing the distinction between "high" and "low" culture, there was still the unmistakable sense that silently appreciating abstract paintings was a different experience—and far more refined—than hollering for Mickey Knuckles at WWE's Gorefest of Death.

So much for finding a tidy definition of art that put neat boundaries on the concept. I was jazzed by the idea that art could be lurking in places where I least expected it. But the idea was disorienting too. Learning this history made everything I'd set out to do so far, the whole premise of developing an Eye so I could appreciate art, seem absurd. I wasn't on a journey to discover the spiritually transcendent in a pair of Nike sneakers. And yet my expectation that I should feel something profound when I looked at art was apparently based on a rather arbitrary idea of "art" I'd inherited from class-conscious European snobs. Art has meant many things to many people—to Mao Zedong, art was a tool for class struggle; to prehistoric humans, art meant something we can only guess at—and it is dangerous to assume what we now call art was seen as such by humans before us. Hence, in part, our struggle to define it. "The modern system of art is not an essence or a fate but something we have made," writes Shiner, noting that the Japanese language lacked a word for "art," in the European sense, until the nineteenth century. "Art as we have generally understood it is a European invention barely two hundred years old." So how *should* I understand it instead?

A MONTH PASSED since the face-sitting. Two. I kept meeting Amanda for coffee and following AllFIRE on Instagram and wondering where one stopped and the other began. Amanda had dropped hints that she was considering plastic surgery, which was the only way to keep up with the ass race, and even though she'd avoided full nudity until now, her latest outfits were only a strong sneeze away. I'd started helping Amanda with her performance piece in the hopes of understanding it better. One week I revised her artist statement. Another I brainstormed foods (twinkies, cakes, pies, pizza) that Amanda could film herself smothering for a photo shoot we were planning in Times Square. Hot dogs, she decided, with mayo but no ketchup—"because people right away associate that with something else."

During our chats, Amanda and I circled the "what is art" question over and over like lion tamers trying to subdue a snarling beast. She'd been wrestling with it, too, ever since creating AllFIRE. "Is it art because I say it is, and I happen to have an MFA from Columbia? Or has it been art all along, and nobody's realized it?" she wondered aloud one afternoon. "I don't know what art is any more, especially in these current times, when everyone's an artist. Everyone is an artist with their iPhone."

One Wednesday, Amanda came to meet me for coffee and slumped into a chair at a rickety wood table surrounded by bearded guys on laptops. She seemed on edge. She'd just been to her sister's wedding in California, where from the sound of it, she'd fielded a lot of questions about why posing nearly naked on Instagram was art. Amanda admitted AllFIRE had been interfering with her romantic relationship too. "My boyfriend right now, he's supportive, but also disturbed too," she said. "Where he's at—and where I think a lot of people in my life are— is, 'Are you doing this and enjoying it and just calling it art so you don't feel bad about it?'"

"And what do you say to that?" I asked.

"That happens to me a lot when I do these projects. I do get lost in it," Amanda said. "Sometimes I feel like people close to me get so frustrated because they're like, 'Wait a minute. This is not art anymore. This is you just fulfilling a fantasy or something.' Which..." Amanda sighed. "A part of it is true, but a part of it isn't. Like I *do* see what these women are doing as performance art."

That caught me off guard. Ass influencers didn't exactly fit into the "polite arts" category bequeathed to us by eighteenth-century Europeans.

"Performance art in what way?"

Amanda whipped out her phone and opened Instagram. She showed me a looping video of two women prancing innocently through the aisle of a supermarket, then pantsing each other so their bouncy butts mooned the camera. That reminded her of performance artists from the 1960s and 1970s, like Bas Jan Ader—"He would do these things where he would like, ride his bicycle into a canal, I mean *how* many videos do you see like that go viral?"—or Allen Kaprow, who staged loosely planned "happenings" in public spaces, where people performed everyday actions like breaking plates or sweeping a courtyard. ("The line between art and life should be kept as fluid, and perhaps as indistinct as possible" was Kaprow's motto.) Amanda lingered on a video of a woman in a supermarket getting her skirt flipped up by someone in a Cookie Monster costume—"Like, the performance artists who disrupt public space, that's what these people are doing with their videos"—then clicked over to an influencer who resembled a doe-eyed Pixar character allergic to clothes. Amanda showed me how each influencer developed a signature style: This woman did splits in shopping malls, this one squatted over her phone. "I feel like it's also very similar to the way an artist works. Like, they get fit into this type.

You're the abstract painter... You're the Latino performance artist..."
Inwardly, I gave Elizabeth points for picking up on that same thread.
"I don't see what these women do—or anybody who's trying to gain
some kind of notoriety, Instafame, make money, or use Instagram as
a tool for branding themselves—as any different from what an artist
does, when they go to grad school and try to sell themselves to the art
world." Amanda tapped on a photo of a brunette whose ass struggled
to free itself from a bathing suit: "This girl, she says she's 'creating art
for your pleasure.'" We fell silent as Amanda scrolled past breasts
straining against silk and butt-cheeks splashing through a bathtub of
rubber ducks. "I do see it as art," Amanda said finally. In Amanda's
world, the Kardashians weren't reality-TV stars. "I see them as performance artists."

Did *I* see it as art? I was intrigued, which surprised me. Less than
a year earlier, if you'd sat me down with someone who claimed Kim
Kardashian was a performance artist, I'd have injured myself rolling
my eyes. But I'd had my face sat on since then, and, more to the point,
I'd been searching for a more expansive definition of art.

Down the rabbit hole of my research, I'd stumbled into an odd conundrum: Even though art experts can't agree on what art is, a large
number of them are convinced that making and experiencing art is an
innate human impulse. It's not a learned pastime we dreamt up once
we got bored of staring at blank walls or figured out how to live past
age twenty, but a biological predisposition that has helped our species
survive. (One we may share with songbirds, parrots, whales, and other
animals that have their own "aesthetic culture," writes evolutionary
biologist Richard O. Prum.) One survival-of-the-most-artistic hypothesis contends that art is our version of peacock feathers: An extravagant, frivolous display by which paleolithic humans showed potential

mates that they were fit enough to hunt and gather *and* have time left-over to paint warty pigs. Another theory is that our art-inclined ancestors survived, thrived, and reproduced because making art offered a dress rehearsal for grappling with hostile conditions. (Nine-thousand-year-old Libyan rock paintings of spear-wielding figures sprinting after horned beasts come to mind.) The scholar Ellen Dissanayake, who's dabbled in anthropology, archaeology, psychology, and art history, argues that art is a social glue that bonds communities together and thus increases its members' odds of survival. Also, she thinks the concept of "fine art" is a travesty that's made us forget that "engaging with the arts is as universal, normal, and obvious in human behavior as sex or parenting."

I kept coming back to Dissanayake. She's for banning the word *art* altogether on the grounds it's uselessly vague, and argues we shouldn't treat art as a thing but as a behavior. Art, she claims, occurs anytime we take ordinary things and transform them into extraordinary experiences through a process she calls "making special." Making special happens when words turn into poetry, flesh gets painted for a shaman's ceremony, a B-flat meets a middle G to form the tune in a Peking opera. I liked her definition, which seemed less arbitrary than others I'd read and didn't turn up its nose at blockbuster movies or Super Bowl halftime shows—which Dissanayake calls "the arts of our time." As she sees it, art results from several key "operations" that can apply equally to painting caves and photographing your ass: Artists repeat (Amanda posted hundreds of photos), formalize (a pet's-eye view of her butt was a hallmark composition), exaggerate (she tailored her workouts to enlarge her rear), elaborate (she riffed on the theme of underwear by wearing spandex one day, lace the next), and manipulate expectation (her bare butt popped up in surprising places, like in a car or in an art gallery). Break dancing, leading a tea ceremony, designing *Grand Theft Auto*—to Dissanayake, it's art, art, and more art.

I thought about Dissanayake at night, in bed, while I browsed Instagram and watched AllFIRE spray water over her ass, then smush it against her shower door. Questions bubbled up in my brain: Why did I feel so squeamish seeing AllFIRE's bare ass? Would I feel differently if those photos were at a gallery? Or if she didn't have an MFA? When did a performance-art piece become a lifestyle, and what was the difference? Was AllFIRE empowered or exploited? Upholding unrealistic beauty standards or subverting them? And, for the millionth time, was this art?

I still didn't have a pithy, one-size-fits-all definition for *art*, though I'd started to agree with those who thought that art wasn't solely the result of an artist's behavior. It depended on the viewer's behavior too. You needed to be willing to follow where the artist was taking you. To make a leap of faith. Certainly to have an open mind. Art seemed like the result of a handshake between a creator and her audience. The artist put forth something as art, and you, as the viewer, had to choose whether you'd relate to it as a deformed rock or as a sculpture. Maybe that's why the definition of art could feel so personal.

As unorthodox as it was, Amanda's work made me wrestle with meaty questions about art, beauty, sex, society, and myself, which is more than I could say for 90 percent of the polite art I'd passed in galleries. Her work confused me. It made me uncomfortable. It took me on an extraordinary journey. And that, to me, was enough to make it art.

But was it good?

That, unfortunately, was a question I still couldn't answer.

CHAPTER TEN

I nstall, deinstall. Install, deinstall. Openings, open studios, sales pitches, PDFs. Monday–Tuesday was the art world's weekend, first thing in the morning was 10:00 a.m., and I could anticipate what Elizabeth needed even before she asked. I was getting the hang of the cycle. The fifth law of thermodynamics: There is always an art fair.

January's fair in San Francisco had crushed Elizabeth's hopes and dreams. Silicon Valley apparently had the money but not the inclination to buy art, which Rob thought was very rude. "They all need to go to billionaire school. They need to learn what's expected of them now that they're rich," he fumed when he got back, the gallery many thousands of dollars poorer.

February had brought Frieze, ALAC, and Felix in Los Angeles, kicking off the cyclical speculation about whether the art world's beating heart was moving West, which Rob thought was, as the cultural commentators say, LOL. "It's California in general. I don't think they appreciate culture the same way we do in New York," Rob told a complete stranger on the subway. And Los Angeles itself—LMFAO. "They drive from strip mall to strip mall in traffic and call it a city!"

We all complained about the fairs—too many, too expensive, awful way to see art—and we all begged for VIP passes. There were six fairs in New York the first week of March, including the Armory Show, which Denny Dimin didn't get into, despite Rob's backchannel lobbying via long calls with collectors. I bumped into Jack at an Armory Week mixer and thanked him for inspiring me to audit that art-history survey class at Barnard. He assured me I wouldn't learn anything. A survey class was *waayyyy* too broad. By April we were prepping for the Dallas Art Fair, and I watched New York gallerists wipe drool off their chins thinking about all the wall space in big Texas homes.

During all this, a hazy daydream of an idea solidified into a yappy, un-shut-uppable chihuahua of want. I wanted to curate a show.

I hear you. It felt bold to me, too, like hitting on a glamorous stranger at a bar, only the stranger was the New York art world, and I was toilet paper stuck to a shoe. But the question of how to judge the quality of artwork had lodged itself in my brain. There were pieces I liked more than others—pieces I wanted to take home with me and pieces I couldn't stand being around—but I wasn't sure what made some artwork better than others, outside of my personal whims.

I didn't think I could lay claim to having an Eye without some hypothesis about what "good" art consisted of, and at the same time, I craved imposing some sort of order on my taste. Lately, it'd run amok: I'd begun second-guessing things that I'd always loved implicitly—the watercolors my mom painted on vacation, the song "Strange Days" by The Doors—and I felt caught in an ambiguous muddle between my own opinion and what I thought I was supposed to like according to the Eyes around me. I should note that by now I'd turned my entire life over to art. Besides working at Denny Dimin, I was meeting artists for studio visits, helping Amanda with her practice, and carving up my days off to tour Chelsea or watch a performance artist dance around with chains in a U-Haul parked outside a cemetery. To everyone in my former life, I was a deadbeat—one editor of mine emailed me to inquire after my health—and I felt like I was having an identity crisis, especially when it came to matters of taste.

I tried to get answers by joining Crit Club, a community-minded group that brought a dozen artists together every Wednesday night to spend four hours critiquing each other's work. Seeing how artists revised their pieces and what they sought to improve seemed like a promising way to wrap my mind around the idea of quality. Each artist kicked off the discussion of their pieces by posing a question, which, I discovered, was never, *Is this good?* Instead, they asked, "Is this ambiguous enough?" or "How could I make these"—veiny, fetus-like bundles of fabric—"really nice for children but not nice for adults?" And the answers they got back were never *um, that's not working.* "What's the meaning of these drips?" the group might ask an abstract painter. One woman presented us with her sculptures of houseplants balanced on skinny white towers. "Why do they need to be white?" Crit Club's members asked. "What if it's about the plants' personality?" "What would your plants do if they had an office job?"

Artists danced around the question of quality in the studio, and yet outside it, that issue was fair game. "There's so much *bad* art," I kept hearing from art connoisseurs who apparently knew enough to say so, and that phrase was driving me demented with curiosity. *How did they know?* I envied their certainty, their ability to look at an artwork, compare it to some mental scorecard, and confidently pronounce it "bad."

To Elizabeth, this skill was irrelevant.

"Calling something bad art just doesn't make sense to me," she told me. "You can say you don't enjoy it or you don't like it. But it's just art. It *can't* be bad."

Fair. But she and Rob were implicitly judging quality every time they put on a show, such as when they'd decided to show Paula Wilson's work over another artist's back in December or when they'd selected *those* photos of Erin O'Keefe's out of countless others to bring to Miami. "Curating" was International Art English for *picking*, and picking, to me, meant having some criteria for what made one thing superior to another. I thought if I could just help curate a show, one measly little show, I'd absorb what I needed to know to tell good art from bad. By the spring, I hadn't yet worked up the nerve to mention the idea. But maybe soon.

IN THE MEANTIME, I focused on Denny Dimin's business, which was impossible not to do. Constantly, hourly, Elizabeth and Rob were scrambling to sell art. Before starting at Denny Dimin, I'd assumed galleries hit payroll each month by flogging what they had on the walls at that month's show. "*Huge* public misconception," Rob told me. The shows were bait: Elizabeth and Rob made payroll by selling paintings they'd had sitting in the basement for years, prints they'd never exhibited, and old photos yanked from dark drawers. They flirted with secondary-market sales, and Rob was quietly helping a client resell a

KAWS print, for a commission. Some artists' work sold much more frequently, and I learned it wasn't uncommon for galleries to survive off sales from just a handful of the artists on their roster. I tallied that in the first few months of the year, two artists had sold more pieces than Denny Dimin's sixteen other artists combined, though that wasn't unrelated to who'd just had a show or whose inventory was running low.

Jack had clamped his hands over my eyes for anything money-related, but given the frequency with which Dylan was flagging down the FedEx guy to ship art, I surmised that Denny Dimin was selling a whole lot more art than Jack had during my tenure. Jack appeared to have fewer expenses—there'd been only one of him and no Dylan—but I couldn't figure out how Jack made the numbers add up. I kept replaying an artist's observation: "There's this thing that I call 'magic money,' which is money that you have no idea where it comes from and how people live their lives." The art world, she said, was full of magic money.

A curator had told me that there was no better training for one's Eye than seeing art with artists, and, starting that spring, I'd established a standing date with the painter Liz Ainslie to go see shows. (At one point we stopped by the newly christened Jack Barrett Gallery, but Jack's chilly reception convinced me to keep my distance.) As Liz and I toured galleries, I was struck by how many of them had a take-it-or-leave-it stance on money. Instead, as far as I could tell, they relied on *magic* money. Liz and I chatted with an artist showing with a gallery on Bowery that, she whispered, was run by big-hearted billionaires who wanted to support emerging artists making "market unfriendly" work, only they couldn't be bothered with pesky details like sales. Another artist griped about the time she'd shown with a moneyed descendant of Dutch royalty, who didn't lift a finger to sell the work. *I needed the money*, the sculptor stressed. Pure was often a privilege in its own right. Independently wealthy gallery owners could turn up their noses at money, which was a luxury the artists they showed couldn't always afford.

The New York art world was populated by people so loaded that little things like money slipped their minds. Elizabeth was not among them.

"Tomorrow is going to be one of those days that I do the magic trick, which is paying the bills with no money," Elizabeth announced at the end of the month. A month when, thanks to a sold-out show, she should have been backstroking Scrooge McDuck–style in pools of gold. "It's my least favorite magic trick," she grumbled while staring dead-eyed at an Excel doc. "I've been doing it for six years."

She read off the names of clients who owed money. "We should have, like, a bazillion dollars. But because we sold to a lot of 'serious collectors,' in air quotes, we have *no* money." Serious collectors were a dream because they sat on museum boards and inspired their friends to buy whatever they got, but also a gigantic pain because they could buy art on their word and would forget about bills. "You have to, like, chase them down and three months later, *maybe* you get paid. And they make you feel bad for it."

Not everyone wanted to work with serious collectors. The two artists who ran Haul Gallery—and funded it off their day jobs—prided themselves on not having to sell art to stay in business and considered the "wealth focused, blue-chip, megagallery art industry to be inextricably tied to global capitalist systems that are oppressive and violent."

At the other end of the spectrum was a place like Gagosian gallery, where an ex-assistant said she had to memorize flash cards of VIPs so she could instantly recognize individuals inextricably tied to global capitalist systems and summon a salesperson to say hello.

On a quiet Sunday, I asked Rob to walk me through the gallery's math. Elizabeth had told me she calculated her salary based on her projections for the year's sales. "And on months I can't pay myself, I just don't pay myself." That was less tenable now that she had two kids. "It *totally* fucks me over." Rob's base salary was $45,000 a year, plus a 10 percent commission on work he sold. Last year, his pay had just brushed six figures, which was a record high. In prior years, he'd relied on "supplemental family money"—disbursements from a trust fund that were "not a lot of money" but money that worked magic all the same. "To get to this point without the family support—hell fucking no." On top of cold hard cash, there was the fairy dust of growing up "upper-upper-middle class," he pointed out, which had given him comfort schmoozing Fifth Avenue collectors, a network of wealthy friends to sell art to, and people to fall back on if disaster struck. (In short, the ol' cultural-social-economic capital trifecta.) Lots of people in the art world elided their privilege, and I found Rob's candor refreshing.

I recognized I was no exception: My ability to be at Denny Dimin hinged on my getting money elsewhere. Yes, I was making money off writing projects past and present, but my lifestyle would have looked vastly different if the philosophy major I met in college and then married hadn't spent years at a lucrative corporate job, or if I hadn't had parents with stable white-collar careers, or if I hadn't had an Ivy League education, or . . . The list goes on. To say nothing of my own comfort and ability to blend in as a gallerist, to get Elizabeth and Rob to put their trust in me, to stand up to pushy collectors who demanded

20 percent discounts. To be a chameleon stepping into a role at an art gallery knowing as little as I did was only possible because of all I did know.

Jobs in the art industry, where people with advanced degrees get paid starting salaries that make them eligible for food stamps, tended to favor individuals who started off wealthy. (One accountant referred to art galleries as a "princess business"—since profits are so iffy, it's best you came from inherited wealth.) "We *chew* people *up*," Rob told me. "Because nobody gets paid. So the only people who can afford to not get paid are people who have access to money."

That could limit who pursued a career as a gallerist, which Rob believed contributed to the overwhelming whiteness of his profession, which includes me. Black artists were underrepresented at galleries. Black gallerists were even rarer. Out of 176 members who belonged to the Art Dealers Association of America, only 1 was African American, according to a *New York Times* report, and Rob estimated there'd been only a couple Black gallery owners among the 133 galleries at Untitled in Miami. "There are very few African American art dealers, and it's because of the systemic racism and wealth inequity and disparity that's existed for multiple generations," Rob said. "To get here is *such* a fucking point of privilege." Jack once told me, "Most observations about the world apply to the art world. They might even be magnified." He was right: Look at the extremes of wealth, the often unacknowledged advantages of skin color, the boost of privilege, the inequality of access. "So if we're one of the more progressive sides of the world," Rob said, "and we are *so* segregated?" He shook his head.

Our conversation was cut short by a Serious Collector barging into the office with his wife and daughter. I knew the guy—I'd met him and his entourage in Miami.

The man had taken time out of his day to travel to the Lower East Side so he could scream at Rob for liking—not posting, *liking*—a meme on Instagram that, the Serious Collector blustered, kinda sorta vaguely poked fun at an organization he supported. Rob paled and stammered out an apology. The collector's wife and kid piled on with more outrage. *Delete that*, the collector commanded. He peered over Rob's shoulder as Rob unliked the post, supervising Rob's iPhone to verify his will was done.

MY SHOT AT curatorial fame and glory came unexpectedly. One minute Rob was talking up the rave he was going to tomorrow. The next Elizabeth asked whether I might like to help her curate the upcoming show at Denny Dimin's new Hong Kong space, and I didn't let her finish her sentence before I said yes, definitely, absolutely, *yes.*

In retrospect, I think there had been little dry runs to test my Eye, like Elizabeth asking me to recommend artists for a client who was buying art for a new home or having me draft the shows' press releases, which until now had been her job. "I love when you talk about art," Elizabeth said to me one afternoon after she shooed me out to tell some visitors about our current show. I couldn't help but beam.

Elizabeth laid out the parameters for the exhibit we'd curate together. It'd be a group show, we had six months to work on it, and it'd be at DDHK, a.k.a. Denny Dimin Hong Kong. DDHK was a gallery, though it would be equally accurate to call it the living room of the apartment that Elizabeth and Rob's business partner lived in with her family. I clicked through photos of the space and tallied five walls that could hold at least ten pieces, plus a flat-screen TV wedged between bookshelves filled with art books and a *Lonely Planet* guide to Thailand.

Elizabeth opened a new Google Doc and shared it with me so we could start adding artists' names. For the show's theme, she put, "artists referring to mapping or global movement in different ways." For criteria she wrote, "artists we're either interested in in a larger sense or have a real market."

Those were my marching orders. They seemed . . . broad. I wasn't entirely sure where to begin.

EVERY DAY, Elizabeth and I promised we'd discuss the show, and every day we ran out of time. She was wrangling Denny Dimin's move to Tribeca and all the threatening calls to exterminators that entailed, and she gave me vague orders to just research artists on my own. "Great!" I chirped. I wanted so badly for it to be great. The show felt like it could be a milestone for how far I'd come. Also, I was coming up on five months with the gallery, and out of loyalty or gratitude or both, I hoped to see Denny Dimin succeed. Elizabeth confessed that sales in Hong Kong had been sluggish since the gallery opened in late March under the guidance of an old friend of hers. "She finally sold her first thing to not her parents," Elizabeth said in a tense voice, worry glinting in her eye.

Coming up with artists' names wasn't the problem. It'd been months since I'd seen the bottom of my purse, which was covered in sedimentary layers of press releases from shows that blew my mind, and the photos in my iPhone should have concerned the local authorities: disembodied heads, hovering ceramic bombs, bleeding canvases—offbeat, mostly market-unfriendly artwork that I'd photographed in the hope of returning to the sparks of surprise it offered. Elizabeth wanted names? Oh, I had names. Dozens of them. Except I still wasn't confident what metrics I should use to deem an artwork "good"—or at least "better" than some other thing.

I decided to seek professional help. Museums, I felt certain, were run by responsible, objective stewards who could give me pointers for how to separate crap from grade-A culture.

I scheduled a meeting with Rujeko Hockley (who goes by Ru), a curator at the Whitney Museum of American Art. She'd just finished assembling the group-show-to-end-all-group-shows: the Whitney Biennial. Every two years, the Biennial assigns itself the punishing task of narrowing down the nation's population of artists to several dozen individuals whose work is supposed to provide a "snapshot" of contemporary art in the United States. Ru and her cocurator, Jane Panetta, had spent the better part of the year crisscrossing the country doing studio visits, and if Ru could pull off the Biennial, surely she could offer some wisdom on the comparatively straightforward task of curating a few artists into a group show in Hong Kong.

Ru, who met me inside the Whitney, was Wizard of Oz chic in red shoes, a blue-and-white gingham dress, and long braids with purple highlights. After circling a few rooms of the Biennial, we took a seat on a low bench overlooking a huge lavender wall hung with nearly a hundred squirming metal pictographs. I recognized them immediately as the work of Maia Ruth Lee: Jack and I had seen this work during our tour of openings back in September, and I'd helped Lee hang these "Glyphs" during a stint at Jack Hanley Gallery so brief I haven't bothered mentioning it. Now, museum visitors paused to ask me if I could photograph them in front of Lee's artwork. I mentally congratulated

Lee—being picked for the Biennial came with a $1,500 honorarium and could do for artists' careers what the Fairy Godmother does for Cinderella. I couldn't help congratulating myself too. I'd seen more of the machine than I realized.

I quizzed Ru about putting together the Biennial. The early part of her process sounded a lot like Elizabeth's and mine: She and her cocurator separately brainstormed a wish list of artists, then highlighted overlapping names and began doing studio visits—ultimately more than three hundred over the course of a year. They solicited suggestions from artists and other curators, and they received unsolicited suggestions from collectors, Instagram followers, and whoever got hold of their emails. Did they consider the unsolicited tips? "Everyone we looked at, but some of them we were more interested in than others," Ru said diplomatically. Do people who donate money to the Whitney get to weigh in? "We made all the decisions and all the invitations without really any external input." I built to my key question: What were they looking for in the art?

Ru said that she and Jane kept hearing about the challenges faced by emerging artists as small- and mid-sized galleries had closed, and they'd decided to use the Biennial to promote emerging artists who could benefit from being associated with the Whitney's "institutional machine." But other than that—Ru shrugged. They didn't set out with any strict criteria, which Ru realized was "unsatisfactory for people, especially because people want to be in the Biennial." Ultimately, she said, "The people that we invited are people whose work we felt really strongly about."

My spirit deflated. I didn't doubt that was true, only it was such a slippery standard. I pushed: But—but—how do you cross people off your list? Not *everyone* gets in.

"It's a *totally* subjective experience," said Ru matter-of-factly. "Like, I think two different people who were doing the same studio visits, doing the same kind of travels, making the same exhibition, could have come up with a totally different list of seventy-five from the three-hundred-plus people we visited. Or they could have come up with the same list of people and different artworks. I think it's really an exercise in subjectivity. Deeply." She didn't sound apologetic or embarrassed. "I mean, honestly? I feel like if anybody tells you differently, they're kind of lying to themselves."

Her answer caught me off guard. I'd imagined Ru would say these were, without question, the seventy-five most exciting artists working today. Instead, she'd leveled with me.

It's subjective. The process is flawed. The Whitney—no museum, really—ever advertised that fact. The wall text mounted on white placards next to each piece spoke with an almighty Voice of God that declareth, "Thou Shalt Not Doubt Our Taste." But Ru was telling me to question, to doubt. Going to a museum, "it's very important to be cognizant that this is a filtration mechanism and that you're seeing a subjective view of art and of the art world. You're seeing the product of many, many decisions made by humans, which means there are inherently flaws to those decisions," Ru said. "Like, there is no 'best.' I don't think that's a real thing. And I don't think it's responsible that that's kind of the way we talk about these sorts of exhibitions."

I left the Whitney grateful for Ru's honesty, but also bristling with frustration. Ru, like Elizabeth, was urging me to give up on the whole idea of "best," which should have felt blissfully liberating. But it didn't. I didn't want freedom. I didn't want to muddle around trying to invent my personal idea of quality. I just wanted the right answer.

I was supposed to relish art's ambiguity! Seek out discomfort! Uncertainty was *good*, remember? And yet no matter how dreamy I thought it'd be to toss off convention and splash around in the fountain of who-knows-who-cares, I just couldn't. Deep down I still believed that if I hauled each artwork into my brain's interrogation room and badgered it under hot lights, it would eventually confess to being great or terrible—and, with a bit more prodding, give up its correct interpretation. I'd come so far in some ways—I'd befriended a few fuck-you artworks and learned to savor the beauty of colored rectangles. But in other ways—namely, my attachment to my brain's narrow comfort zone—I felt like I'd progressed barely at all.

I STILL DIDN'T KNOW precisely how to judge art "good" and wanted to keep hunting around for answers, but we had a show to curate, and we were way behind.

I got to work. I began with the highly biased, thoroughly unscientific ritual of writing down all the artists whose work I knew and liked. Names poured out of me: artists I knew from studio visits, open studios, crit sessions, friends of friends, fairs, shows, and residencies. Ru was right: This was totally subjective. No one on my list didn't go to college. No one worked out of the Midwest. No one was over fifty or getting their first-ever shot at showing. I tried again, hoping to cast a wider net. Hong Kong artists, I decided. We needed artists with some connection to Hong Kong because this was, after all, a show in Hong Kong.

A few days later, Elizabeth and I huddled around her laptop to compare our lists. She went first, pulling up paintings by the artist Nicolas Grenier. Disembodied bar charts with labels like "eat drink" and "shit piss" floated over hazy, screen-saver expanses of color.

"I LOVE him," Elizabeth said. "So the works all have these weird logic they're exploring with graphs and maps. This is *totally* my brain."

Grenier was in. The artist who'd just stopped into Denny Dimin to drop off a collage of do-rags was not. "They're all made on *very* heavy panel," whispered Elizabeth, glancing at the piece. "The works only *cost* like $4,000, and it's going to be *so* much just to ship them to Hong Kong."

Elizabeth had come up with some additional criteria for who to include. "We should figure out A: who's the best, B: who we can ship the most cheaply, and C: who it's in our best interest to have something by in Hong Kong for a while." She skipped right over an explanation of how we should determine "who's the best," which would have been helpful, and continued on with a list of other criteria—including D: Since shipping is so expensive, the works we pick should be lightweight and easy for Elizabeth to pack in her carry-on or a checked bag. "Probably not sculpture." E: Pieces should be thirty inches by forty inches big, *max*, since the gallery space wasn't huge. Obviously the works needed to be on theme, and F: They'd ideally earn Denny Dimin good money or good context. Changing lives and the entire course of history would be nice and all, but Denny Dimin had bills. A budget to follow. Logistical headaches to consider. Elizabeth liked the idea of including a bunch of artists that Denny Dimin already represented, because that would give her business partner in Hong Kong an inventory of art she could hang on to for a while and, fingers crossed, sell.

My turn. In spite of Elizabeth's suggestion to focus on people with a "real market," I'd been drawn to artists who were, for lack of a better word, risks. They weren't well-known, weren't necessarily represented by galleries, and didn't specialize in colorful painting. (They'd shown before, but even an artist with a dozen solo shows on her résumé can, according to the art world's nebulous standards, be considered "emerging.") One by one, I pulled up each artist's website. Here was an artist who made room-sized installations that mapped restricted airspace. ("She seems like a great fit," said Elizabeth, eyeing some of the smaller pieces.) Here was a painter who mapped time through layered renderings of toppling birthday cakes. ("I'm totally into this.") Here was someone who'd made a trippy video featuring hands massaging bread dough ("I really do like the artist"), someone else who'd dressed up in a gold leotard and filmed himself pouring beer over lily pads (Elizabeth nodded), and someone who did needlepoint portraits on mosquito screens. ("This work is *amazing*.")

Elizabeth was quiet as she considered each artist's website. She did not check for MFAs, confirm who had a real market, or ask if I'd want to hang out with this artist before saying yes. She stayed in the art. I noticed that in each case, she made a decision even before clicking over to their résumé.

I started emailing artists after our meeting, and the yeses, nos, and maybes rolled in. One painter was getting ready for a solo show in Milan and had only works on paper to offer us. No can do, said Elizabeth—a work on paper would need a frame, and frames cost money. (Framing follows trends, and the convention since the 1960s has been that paintings on stretched canvas or wood panels don't need to be displayed with frames.) The painter Jon Key, whom I'd met via his solo show at the Spring/Break art fair, had a couple works to offer. We'd take both. One artist gave us two paintings to pick from, and Elizabeth picked the one in universally beloved blue.

Bit by bit, I noticed Elizabeth ignoring her own rules. The painter Ho Sin Tung had only a large 44-by-48-by-8-inch piece that was treacherously heavy and would need various rental trucks and storage spaces to work. Make it happen, Elizabeth told me. Super-emerging? Fine. Sculpture? Pack it up. Elizabeth was all in to show a piece that wasn't even for sale.

She flew over to Hong Kong with art in her luggage and, moments before the opening, emailed me photos of the show. It was six in the morning in New York, and I clicked open her email before I got out of bed, anxious to see where the works I'd picked had ended up. We'd finalized the list of artists ten days before—way too close for comfort—and exactly half were my suggestions.

I can't say you would have guessed the show's theme. "On the Map" was all over the map. Just inside the front door hung Key's painting of a Black man staring dead ahead with piercing white eyes. Dannielle Tegeder's painting—a mesh of delicate lines that looked like a blueprint gone wild—was near the kitchen. Here were Jessie Edelman's Easter-egg-colored paintings of women in pools (good inventory to get to Hong Kong); there, Brent Birnbaum's collage made from shredded board games (small enough to fly with Elizabeth).

Was this the best work? It was the best we could do given our constraints. We'd had to make compromises, but then so did places like the Whitney. "We're two people who have likes and dislikes, who go and do our job, and that's what we base it off of," Ru had said of the Biennial. Her comment was a reminder that whatever "good" art was, you couldn't just assume it was whatever happened to be nicely hung inside a white cube. In the end, the only Eye you could trust was your own.

What held our show together, besides some hand-wavey explanation about mapping, was that this was work we wanted to share. These weren't artworks I'd necessarily want to live with. These weren't artworks I totally understood. These were just artworks that had turned me into a shaken-up bottle of warm Coke that would explode, *now*, if I didn't get to discuss these pieces with as many people as possible. Was that a reliable metric by which to judge the art "good"? Honestly, the question no longer felt pressing. It felt small, a little crumb of a query, that dwarfed in comparison to this strange new urge I felt to thrust art in front of people and say, *Get a load of this.*

I'd left Jack's gallery not only distrusting my opinions on art but convinced that sharing them was an existential threat. Now, after quality time with Elizabeth and Rob and Amanda, I was having trouble shutting up.

And yet as spring thawed into the armpit of summer, I started getting antsy.

BY THIS POINT, I'd spent nearly a year working at galleries. I was fluent in International Art English, skilled in handling exotic tape species, and able to hold my own with a piece of art. Yet after months with people like Jack and Elizabeth who interpreted the results of the creative process, the creative process itself still mystified me. My day in Julie's studio had given me a peek at how little I really knew about making art despite my passion for painting in a previous life, and the reverence with which Elizabeth and Rob spoke about artists made me itchy to get closer to the black box of what went on in their studios. I'd been taught to analyze art as a viewer. I wanted to understand it as a creator.

I scheduled my last day at Denny Dimin, which was bittersweet for all of us. And then, in the early part of the summer, I flew to Asheville, North Carolina, with the idea of throwing myself into making art.

My destination was the School of the Alternative, an anti-hierarchical, we're-all-teachers-here art-school–meets-utopian-commune run by artists, for artists, that I hoped would teach me to think more like an artist. "It's like the underground Hogwarts for adults," said one of the faculty members, as he drove with us from the airport to a YMCA campus at the base of the Blue Ridge Mountains. Thus began my week scrubbing pots, primal screaming, lucid dreaming, and recording an album that consisted largely of us slamming chairs. During class, we drew portraits of each other using our nondominant hands, linked arms and shuffled around the buildings to embody slime, and group-hugged a vending machine while harmonizing with its hum—all of which made me squirm with unease. But to my surprise, I was able to relax a little into the discomfort, the way you might into a no-recline airplane seat on a flight bound for an exciting adventure. Sure, there was the voice of petty, always-be-optimizing Bianca whispering, *What's the point?* But she was quieter than she'd been in a long time. "There's no immediate need for results," said the artist Carolyn A'Hearn, inter-rupting my knee-jerk *why* questions after she had my classmates and me tie ourselves together with plastic bags. "That's something we've been conditioned into needing: a takeaway or result."

In spite of my inner wet blanket, I came back to New York feeling as if I'd been nudged off my axis. Artists, I'd concluded, approached reality in a way I still couldn't make sense of. And I was convinced that all the studio visits in the world—I'd done dozens by now—wouldn't provide the answer. What I needed to do was to work for an artist.

Part III

The Studio

CHAPTER ELEVEN

The job of studio assistant had long intrigued me. On its face, the role meant helping more established artists with whatever weasels they needed taken care of: washing brushes, painting hands, answering gallerists' annoying emails. But artists who'd been studio assistants described the job as an indispensable rite of passage that had transformed their relationship with art. One studio assistant who'd spent eight hours a day for years mixing paint for a famous painter made it sound as if her boss had done *her* a favor. "Like, the thing it does to your brain and to your eye?" she marveled. "It just trained me really well."

I'd been toying with the idea of trying to work as a studio assistant for going on a year, and even though I'd been doing lots of studio visits, my time with Jack had rattled my confidence to approach artists about taking me on. But the show in Hong Kong—a wild success, Elizabeth had confirmed when she got back—gave me a jolt of encouragement to try again. Lately, I'd also noticed that more and more artists were flipping the script during studio visits and asking *me* advice—on negotiating with galleries, revising press releases, promoting their upcoming shows.

Still, there were a number of obstacles to my getting hired. For starters, help-wanted ads made it clear that hard skills were a nonnegotiable. Hoping to brush off the cobwebs, I enrolled in a class and oil-painted for the first time in many presidential administrations. The results were hard to look at. Truly—I'm not being modest. "It's hard to look at," said our mild-mannered teacher when she saw my painting. The next time she passed, she told me it was "painful"—high praise if I'd been going for something like Picasso's *Guernica*, but my subject was a pink Dunkin' Donuts coffee cup. Bit by bit, though, I felt as if I was getting back into the swing of things.

But then there were logistical difficulties. I'd hit it off with an artist, then she'd disappear to a residency. Get too busy to return my emails. Move to Berlin, return date TBD. And there was the sad reality that more than a few of the artists I'd gotten to know were burning out—not emerging but submerging under the weight of shuttling between adjunct teaching jobs or restaurant jobs or studio assistant jobs, or all three, while wondering when, if ever, they could exhale. They didn't want to stop making art. But the question of how much longer they could live like this would get stubbornly more persistent. I managed to get a daylong studio-assisting gig helping the artist Alexis Dahan hang a ceramic ear on a defunct payphone outside the Guggenheim Museum, but just as I was about to contact him to see whether I could help out again, he emailed me to announce he was taking an indefinite break from making art. His email doubled as a screed on all the ways the system was stacked against emerging artists. He wrote that his "fire had been put out" by the art world.

Yet through the summer and into the fall, I managed to convince some artists to let me in as their helper. Besides Amanda, who asked me to brainstorm ways to make AllFIRE go viral, I spent a few weeks with an artist who had me sand sculptures, mix epoxy, and wrap hunks of clay in moist towels as if they were customers at a spa. That is, until my presence as a journalist had her so on edge she threw me out. I helped artists write grant applications, make paper infused with birth-control pills, and source hundreds of plastic onions for an installation at the New Museum. Only, I left each time thinking about the day I'd spent with Julie Curtiss.

Julie's work had been following me around for more than a year now. When I went to Central Park, the high-heeled legs from her painting hovered near the bushes. Her work wasn't pleasant like Erin O'Keefe's or shocking like Haley Josephs's or confrontational like Michael Blake's. But her pieces wouldn't leave me be, and I couldn't figure out why.

I decided to pay her another visit.

I'd seen Julie quite a few times since I'd last been to her studio. We'd bumped into each other at a museum fundraiser Rob took me to, at a gallery closing party, and at various openings, including her own. (I'd been lied to: The art world isn't "small," it's microscopic.) Lots of artists were coyly evasive about their work and treated my questions like I was a cactus running after their balloon, but Julie was so excited about the paintings she'd made that she'd tell you all about her work, even if you didn't ask. At Julie's show, I watched her respond to a throwaway platitude—*Oh, I like that piece*—by leaping up onto a countertop to get closer to her painting, then gesturing wildly as she relived every plot twist in its creation. She bobbed and weaved as her outstretched finger flew around the canvas to show where she'd changed the color of the hair right *there*, redid that whole patch after messing up the border *here*, and used acrylic instead of oil over *here*—building to the high drama of some last-minute disaster with varnish that she recounted while grinning from ear to ear.

For some of us, igniting our creativity involves assembling some kindling, rubbing sticks together, then hunting around for lighter fluid. Julie seemed to have a pilot light burning bright blue at all times. An artist once asked Julie why she painted, and Julie's answer was "too little time." Making art was such a nonnegotiable that *why* concerned her less than finding more hours in the day. Besides painting, she dreamed of making installations, animations, prints, more ambitious sculptures.

One Thursday morning, I met Julie at her studio, then trailed her to a coffee shop, then followed her back to her apartment while, like a magician pulling scarves out of his sleeve, she kept tossing out new projects she couldn't wait to work on. She whipped out her phone to show me a box she was making in the shape of a woman's head, then padded around her apartment draped in a bile-green blanket chattering about how excited she was to enroll in a ceramics class, start work on a new show, and visit Buddhist temples during an upcoming residency in Japan.

Go on, *ask her*, I nudged myself. My stomach wobbled with worry that she'd say no.

I've been wanting to work with artists, I began.

Julie's face broke into a wide smile. "Do you feel like you should start making art?" she asked eagerly, with a leading *obviously the answer is yes* tone.

I've been wanting to work as a studio assistant, I said. Then, as I usually do when I'm nervous, I projectile-vomited information and talked for way too long about all the reasons why. I wanted to see where her ideas came from. I wanted see how an artwork started and where it ended. I wanted to work with my hands. I wanted to see what it meant to be an artist now, in the flesh, in the twenty-first century of our Lord.

Julie listened patiently. "I saw you work," she said, when I quit yapping. "I'd hire you tomorrow."

We set a date. She told me to show up at 10:00 a.m.

CHAPTER TWELVE

Julie is approximately five foot three, would lose a wrestling match with al dente spaghetti, and struck fear into my heart. Not deliberately. ("Would you like some coffee or tea?" she asked me with grandmotherly concern the moment I stepped into her studio for my first day.) It's just that I knew that artists jealously guarded the energy and ambience of their studios, and even though we'd spent a great day together more than a year before, I wasn't sure how long her warm welcome would last. I desperately wanted to make a good impression so she wouldn't kick me out.

I'd come to learn that artists were extremely picky about who they let into their studios as assistants, or let in period. They didn't abide by any equal-opportunity employment blah-di-blah. The artist who'd let me care for her sculptures before asking me to leave had summarily ruled out hiring a male assistant. "Unless it's a gay man," she said. Artists could hire by feel and fire on whims, and they leaned hard into the idea of "culture fit." "Whenever I get an assistant, I put them through hell the first day," said the painter Jamian Juliano-Villani in an article I'd read. "I make them watch people die online, do poppers, and see if they can wake up the next day at 9:00 a.m. If they do, they are hired."

Julie didn't offer me poppers, but it was clear she liked her studio just so. She greeted me with a stack of Ikea boxes—cabinets she wanted me to assemble so she could hide the clutter of her tools—and announced she didn't think she could get going on a new body of work until we'd repainted her floor. "The ground is just so *dirty*," she groaned. "It's preventing me from focusing on the work." She glared at the ground resentfully, and I immediately followed her gaze. The floorboards, probably gray at one point, had faded to a dead-tooth yellow, mottled with mysterious black smears. "It's bugging me. It's the stains." She was gearing up to make work for a solo show the following fall and said she wanted to "create the right atmosphere."

Julie's residency, where I'd stretched canvases, had ended, so she was back in her old studio in a part of East Williamsburg that felt like the buzzing backstage supporting Manhattan's all-hours cabaret show. Nearby businesses sold feather down, metal railings, Carrara marble, bags of rice big enough to swim laps in, and supposedly "NATURE'S FINEST FABRICATED VEAL & LAMB CUT'S"—though the warehouse's bricked-up windows and streamers of barbed wire made me suspicious. Julie's studio looked out over a gas station and, beyond that, Pumps Exotic Dancing. In a former life, Julie's squat brick building had housed a printing press, but now it was heaving with artists. I'd done seven studio visits here already, way more if you count the building next door. Montmartre, eat your heart out: If there was an epicenter of the emerging-art world, this had to be it.

The inside of Julie's building had a lived-in disheveledness I'd come to recognize as artists' way of marking their territory. The entryway

smelled of freshly cut wood and weed, a mixture that made me nervous for someone's fingers, and the hallway by Julie's studio was lit-
tered with plywood slabs, empty wine bottles, and boxes of olive-green
Styrofoam balls someone had left for the other tenants to forage. Studios were separated by white walls as sturdy as bed sheets, which allowed Julie to get to know her neighbors. The guy upstairs, for instance,
liked soda, which Julie learned the hard way when he spilled his drink
and sticky brown liquid rained down on her head while she was painting. That was better than the time a fire broke out and the fire department showed up with hoses. "People were like, ARGHHHH, WATER!"
Julie recalled. They all helped salvage each other's work.

By step three of the Ikea instruction manual, I'd lost feeling in my
toes. Julie's studio, like lots of New York studios, had no heat. Julie mer-
cifully plugged in a space heater, which, alas, turned out to be powered
by a lone asthmatic hamster. I didn't say anything, determined to make
myself as little trouble as possible, and tried to discreetly slide back on
my winter coat. Julie noticed. Obviously she noticed: The studio was
one room, shaped like a shoebox, and approximately the size of one of
those elfish "Tiny Homes" from Pinterest fever dreams. Julie looked
puzzled and hitched up a jean pantleg to reveal purple long underwear.
"You don't have—?" she asked in a tone of voice that suggested not having worn two pairs of pants for a day spent indoors made me a few
brain cells short of a quorum. "I *always* wear that under," she chided.
She hospitably plugged in a second heater. The studio plunged into
darkness—blown fuse. Lights back on, back to one heater. After a little
while, she plugged in a fan to try to circulate the heat. Darkness, again.

I got to know Julie's studio inch by inch on my hands and knees
while we repainted the floor a sidewalk gray. Even with my back to
Julie and my face so close to the floor I could make out fossilized

crumbs, I tried to radiate cheery can-do helpfulness, since I knew creating the "right atmosphere" wasn't only about sprucing up the floors.

Life updates floated between us as we painted. After nearly a decade in New York showing little and selling less, Julie had recently started being represented by Anton Kern, a gallery based out of a slick townhouse in Midtown that was a regular at Miami's main fair, several rungs up the ladder from Denny Dimin, and not unfamiliar with loaning its artists' work to famous museums. "I just never in my wildest *dreams* thought this would happen," Julie said. She grew up "very middle class"—her mother was a librarian at a social workers' school and her father, an orphan from Vietnam who emigrated to France after being adopted, was a technical photographer at an architecture firm. Julie was an anxious, comics-loving teen who struggled with depression and got bullied in junior high. She took refuge in drawing—"a therapy," she called it. Yet even after graduating from Paris's École des Beaux-Arts—a school so exclusive Rodin was rejected three times—Julie balked at calling herself an artist. "I felt almost like an imposter. I didn't have examples in my family of people making money as artists, so I never could imagine I could just *live* off my *art*. The thought—it was impossible."

She had to live off something though, so, after graduating, she made art at night and on weekends while she also tutored; worked as a receptionist; taught art; and, after moving to New York, sold pastries, then shoes, and then clothes before getting hired as a studio assistant for Jeff Koons and then KAWS. She was ambitious—she rented a studio the moment she got settled in Brooklyn—but her work didn't get out much. "I was a nobody." One of her earliest studio visits with a gallerist—"when I didn't have *anything*"—was with a friend-of-a-friend named Jack Barrett who was "really respectful and very sweet and really got the work," Julie told me as we worked. But nothing came of it. Julie applied to grad school in the hope of jump-starting her career with a second, all-American MFA. But she got rejected. She kept plugging away at her art, which evolved from sinewy landscapes evoking postapocalyptic Disney films to melty figures with knobby knuckles and pointy breasts, and kept trying to get eyes on her work however she could. She sent her art to open calls; applied to residencies; joined crit groups; participated in open-studios events; and, as Jack advised, went to lots of openings around the city. "People are really open here and very dynamic, and they really respect hard work. So if you are going to shows, if you are part of the community, if you go do studio visits, if you're interested in other people, you can create a community," said Julie. "You can't be a lazy artist in New York." I didn't yet know how she'd ended up showing with Anton Kern. But I did know that, this past spring, she'd had her first solo show with the gallery, and it'd sold out.

Julie wasn't doing any victory laps. If anything, she seemed on edge. "Yeah, so—I don't know if you saw the article on *Artnet*?" she asked me, her eyes flicking up from the floor to gauge my reaction. "What did you think?"

I'd avoided bringing it up.

The *Artnet* article, which I'd read earlier, recounted how more and more collectors were selling Julie's paintings at auction for larger and larger sums of money—which, to much of *Artnet*'s readership, was considered the first sign that a terminal disease had infected Julie's career. (More on that later.) A painting that Julie had sold two years before for $1,350—and pocketed $600 for—had just been resold at auction for more than $100,000, of which Julie got zero. As opposed to, say, probing what drew people to Julie's paintings, the *Artnet* article had gone on to catalog all the shitty things anonymous "high-end dealers and critics" had been saying about Julie's work: It's derivative, it's tacky, it's "a bubble that could burst." There was a bloodlust to the article, which read more like cutthroat opposition research than sober art analysis. It mentioned naysayers who'd boycotted even seeing Julie's most recent show at Anton Kern—thus making the totally reasonable, highly mature decision to dismiss art they hadn't laid eyes on—and it highlighted the trolls who'd been anonymously attacking Julie on Instagram. "Am I the only person that thinks Julie Curtiss makes sad knockoffs of Christina ramberg and dominco gnoli???" wrote one account after Julie's art went to auction. Another repeatedly posted Julie's paintings beside other artists' work with the snide caption "#whoswho." (Like Julie, Ramberg, who died in 1995, often painted women's heads of hair while Domenico Gnoli, who died in 1970, did detailed close-ups of hair, shirts, ties, and other everyday household things.) I'd seen paintings of Julie's that bore more than a passing resemblance to both artists' work, but when you stepped back two inches and considered her body of work as a whole, the criticism seemed histrionic. And yet Instagram bubbled with such vitriol that it seemed people were rooting for Julie to fail. "I'm having a little bit of Instagram phobia," said Julie, with a forced laugh.

I began to suspect Julie was taking her stress out on the floor. "I feel like psychologically, I need to clean this floor," she said, as we ran foam brushes along the wood. Julie hadn't been sleeping well; her insomnia, which she'd struggled with for decades, had sunk in its teeth again. She seemed to be steeling herself for her streak of good luck— the shows, the sales, the time to work on her art without juggling other jobs—to come to a sudden, abrupt end. "I'm getting used to it, so that worries me," she said quietly. "I don't want to get too used to it. Because I really don't know if it's going to last."

CHAPTER THIRTEEN

U pon the successful completion of my painting masterpiece, *Untitled ("Julie's Studio Floor")*, Julie, astutely
recognizing the budding artistic virtuoso in her midst,
entrusted me with priming four huge new canvases. That is: Take each
one, and paint the whole thing white.

Primer is a painting's underwear. It goes on first, beneath all the
layers that'll be seen by the public, and though you can go without it,
you might be uncomfortable. Priming with a few layers of acrylic
gesso, as I'd be doing, smooths the canvas's stubbly surface and pre-
vents it from soaking up paint like a sponge. Julie wanted exactly three
layers of gesso—enough to make her paintbrush glide. Any more and
it'd be too shiny; any fewer and it'd guzzle paint like a frat kid under a
beer bong and be just as annoying to deal with.

Paint a white thing white? I'd done that before. I'd learned a thing
or two since my "dog-shit" wall fiasco at Jack's gallery, and besides,

Julie didn't seem like the hazing kind. For a Michelangelo of floors such as myself, this promised to be a simple task.

It was no such thing.

The less said about this ordeal the better.

Okay, wait. I'll say this, but only to help conservators who, years from now, may be puzzling over the strange condition of four Julie Curtiss paintings dating to the early decades of the twenty-first century: I couldn't do anything right. That isn't a passive-aggressive snipe at Julie for being overly demanding. I'm just saying, objectively: all wrong. I won't go into detail about what happened when I poured the gesso into the plastic palette Julie gave me, because I'd prefer to keep Julie in the dark on precisely how much gesso I rinsed down the drain in an attempt to make it look as if I hadn't blanketed myself, the palette, and the entire sink in white paint. (I returned to her studio sopping wet and shivering, my fingers numb.) Julie asked me to tape the sides of the canvas with blue painter's tape so they'd stay pristine, which someone else could probably do without interrupting her eleven times to ask if the tape is too crooked, but I am not that someone. She told me to paint the entire canvas white. I proceeded to paint the entire canvas white. I called Julie over to admire how I'd painted the entire canvas white and, after an awkwardly long silence, heard: "Don't worry. It's going to be covered by the next layer." In fact, I had not painted the entire canvas white. (Raw canvas *really* absorbs paint.)

Julie walked me through all the things I needed to do differently the next time around, and even though I'd done a lousy job, I was electric with the thrill of getting to handle her paintings. I wasn't painting a white thing white, I realized. I was putting down the first layer of a painting, which meant I was getting to witness the moment of creation, the act of bringing art into the world. I felt as if I was finally getting to see an artwork face-to-face—with less artifice and more mystery than I ever had before.

The primer on Julie's big new canvases barely had time to dry before Julie hung them on the wall and started sketching out paintings. She'd need about nine paintings for her next show—a solo booth Anton Kern was planning for the Parisian art fair FIAC, or the Foire Internationale d'Art Contemporain, if you've nailed your uvular trill. She'd need another painting for a group show that same fall and at least two paintings for various art fairs, and she also wanted to get going on some sculptures and works on paper. She'd set herself some deadlines to ensure she got it all done. Was it... three paintings a month? "Actually, I did the calculation, and I already forgot about it." A solo show was a chance to make a "complex statement" with multiple pieces that all spoke to each other, and for Paris she already knew she wanted to show pieces that felt "darker... edgier... a little more sexy... more Paris," she said. "There are a lot of artists at FIAC and you kind of need to stand out a bit." She didn't know ahead of time exactly which artworks would end up in the show, but, like a lot of artists prepping a new body of work, she had a theme in mind she wanted to explore. Another way to assemble a solo show, which I'd witnessed while assisting a different painter, was to cast an eye over all the work you'd accumulated the past few months and pick whichever pieces work well together—or *dialogued nicely*, as a gallerist might say.

Watching Julie settle into the studio each morning was like tuning in to a boho Mister Rogers. She'd swing open the studio door all smiles, then hang up her coat, slip on a red button-down over her layers of wool and long underwear, and swap her black leather shoes for scuffed sneakers. She'd offer me tea, crank up the music, and start singing—

never "Won't You Be My Neighbor," but she did harmonize with Nina Simone and *doo-doo-dee-doo*-ed to psychedelic French jazz. Then—no Instagram, no reading the news, no fucking around on the internet whatsoever—she got right to work. Except she didn't see painting as work. "When you're doing your thing—it feels like a luxury."

New pieces kept appearing, and old pieces kept evolving, and I usually got to Julie's studio early, tugged there by my curiosity to introduce myself to whatever new painting might be waiting. Within a few weeks, Julie had six paintings in progress, and her studio was starting to feel like a boisterous party full of scintillating guests—at least to me. To Julie, all the unfinished work made the place feel more like an ICU. "All of them are like, 'HELP ME! I'm in a bad place! I need HELLLLLP!'" she moaned, taking stock of all her patients. Some pieces were dead on arrival, or so I assumed after I glimpsed the painting of the hairy croissant that Julie had sketched the first time I helped out in her studio. It hadn't progressed beyond a black outline. I never saw the painting again.

One especially unwell painting was a portrait of a woman sitting at a table with her legs parted to reveal an illicit patch of crotch, her thighs and undercarriage made entirely out of hair. Julie had sketched the piece onto a primed canvas using watery black acrylic paint, but the composition didn't look right, and now Julie was, quite literally, back to the drawing board. She sat hunched over her table surrounded by sketchbooks and fluttery squares of tracing paper, storm clouds gathering over her head as she kept drawing and redrawing different versions of the same scene. One sketch had the woman's torso *and* legs made out of hair. In another, only the crotch and legs were hairy. Julie kept flipping back and forth between pages of her sketchbook to compare ideas. Crop out the knees or include them? Now you saw the

woman's chair, now you didn't. I did some filing while Julie fumed silently behind me. She grew suspiciously quiet. She was very focused on
something. Julie was googling porn.

"I was just looking at kinky images while you were working so
hard," said Julie, who sounded quite pleased with herself, when I finally interrupted to ask what was going on back there. She'd googled
"woman spread legs under table," which delivered exactly the sort of
smut you'd expect, and was carefully scrutinizing each picture for inspiration. "I just want it to feel more like a moment, an instant, where
you saw something and you weren't supposed to see it," Julie said, her
eyes glued to the pictures on her phone. "Kind of disturbing, basically.
Like it's another world. But I couldn't figure out her body, you know?"

I knew it was risky to offer. It could creep Julie out and get me
fired, but there was also a chance it could save the day. I went for it.

"Want me to sit for you?" I volunteered.

Julie's head snapped up from her sketchbook, her eyes gleaming
with the wild-eyed look of an overexcited terrier who's cornered a squirrel. "*Yeah!*" She hustled me over to her plastic folding card table and sat
me down in a rolling office chair, then she backed away a few feet and
considered me and my open (but clothed) knees from the waist down.

She crouched, then stood up straight, and then crouched again.
"*Arrgh*, it's so frustrating. Now I'm thinking maybe it just doesn't make
sense." Her face scrunched with focus. "Lower your chair a little bit?" I
did. "Shift your knees in different angles just so I can see different
options… Bring your arms more forward…" In a flash of inspiration,
I thrust my pelvis forward in a move straight out of Pumps Exotic
Dancing, and Julie's face lit up. "AH! Yeah! That's better! *Cool!*"

She hurried back to her drawing table, glowing triumphantly.
"*That's* what I wanted," she said happily.

Watching Julie's pieces evolve in the studio made me think I'd missed a crucial step in my art education thus far. I knew to pay attention to artists' decisions. Only I still didn't fully grasp what those decisions added up to. I'd developed a sense for *what* artists do to an artwork, but not *why* they make those moves.

When I got to the studio a few days later, I immediately noticed that the bare-bones outline of the woman spreading her legs had disappeared under a new, full-color version of the piece. The gist was the same, only the woman, who'd previously been sitting with her body directly pointed at the viewer, had swiveled slightly in her chair so she was now sitting at an angle. That shift changed everything, and I could see now what Julie was after. In the old version, it appeared as though the woman was deliberately spreading her legs in a come-hither, *Basic Instinct* pose. Now I wasn't sure if I was being flashed or being a voyeur. Was I a victim or a predator? The painting was more ambiguous, and I could see how that made it far more interesting.

Julie wanted us to get going on the painting next to it, a piece she'd just recently sketched out of two people, seen from the ankles down, sitting on toilets in adjoining bathroom stalls. One pair of feet wore high heels, the other men's loafers, and both rested on a checkered tile floor, half of which Julie had already painted a mottled asphalt gray. She produced three rolls of yellow tape she'd picked up in Japan ("the *best* tape") in three different sizes, then delivered a half-hour lecture on how to place teensy-tiny pieces of tape over the gray painted squares so she could neatly paint the remaining squares black. "So you'll help me with that today—placing the tapes—now that you're becoming more expert at this."

While we placed minuscule shards of tape with surgical precision, I asked Julie what inspired the piece. I must have had a lot more pompous gallery rhetoric coursing through my system than I'd realized because I instinctively expected Julie to trot out at least one dead German philosopher and a line about institutional critique.

"It feels so alchemical where ideas come from, how the vision appears," I mused to Julie, stick lodged solidly up my ass. "How did this piece come about?"

"Oh, this one?" said Julie, her face inches from the painted floor tiles. "Just from, you know, taking a shit in the bathroom."

Excuse me? Julie, too laser focused on the tape to notice my surprise, was plowing ahead on a lengthy tirade about public bathrooms. "You have the stalls and you can see all the peoples' feet and you can hear them, and I found that *completely* inhibiting." Like, why do we get all gussied up in our pretty shoes and nice clothes, she demanded, then go to some shared room where we crap in unison while pretending like it's private, only "it's *not* private anymore, it's sharing something really intimate … it's so *absurd!*" Julie's French accent leapt out with the force of the word to make it sound even stranger—ahb-*zoord*! "That's such a domesticated way of doing it. Like, we've forced ourselves into it."

I'd never pondered the absurdity of group pooping in public bathrooms and the way they make defecating a team sport—when you've got to go, you've got to go. But I was beginning to grasp that Julie's brain latched on to moments where our primal needs hit the conventions of culture and our animal impulses got tweezed, teased, or tied into submission. It was my first glimpse of the fact that Julie did not process the everyday in a way I found remotely familiar, but before I could probe further, Julie stuck a paintbrush in my hand. She wanted my help painting the bathroom tiles black. As in I, Bianca Bosker, would get to place colored pigment on a Julie Curtiss painting.

Julie rattled off a list of warnings. I should be sure not to leave streaky brushstrokes, or zone out and accidentally paint the wrong squares, or load the brush with so much paint that drippy snots of black roll down the canvas. ("Painting with a loaded brush," it's called, an expression that always made me think of guns and mortal danger.) I tried to pay attention to what Julie was saying so I could do a better job than I had with the primer, but my brain was too busy sprinting in circles like an over-caffeinated toddler screaming, PAINTPAINT-PAINTPAINTPAAAIIIIIIIINT!

I'd been praying this moment would come and had dropped a lot of unsubtle hints (*Did you know I painted in high school? Would you like to see more pictures?*) that I could be trusted with a paintbrush. I was happy to help Julie with whatever she needed and had been doing a lot of impromptu vacuuming with a methy Mary Poppins vigor I don't typically bring to chores, but *painting* an *artwork*—it felt like bonding with Julie's art at the most intimate level.

Julie mixed black paint and a splurt of white into a palm-sized plastic cup, and she got me a skinny foam brush from a sackful she'd salvaged while working at KAWS's studio. ("I felt so bad because we used them once and then we threw them out, so I rescued them.") I dipped the brush into the black paint, stopped breathing, then brought the brush to the canvas and pulled it sideways.

Black bled out in a line, darker than it had looked in the cup, which made Julie frown. She stirred in more white paint. I dipped the brush back into the cup, then stretched another black line across the glowing white of the canvas. A stroke. My stroke. My mind flickered to something Liz Ainslie had said once while staring at her own works in progress. "This is a record of the human hand," she'd told me. "This particular hand, in this moment, and there's no other hand that touched this in this way." Each stroke felt strangely permanent, even monumental. I wouldn't have been prouder riding a steel beam into place on the Empire State Building.

You might be thinking that Julie was somehow cheating by asking me to paint her black squares, and if so, you wouldn't be alone. *Two* people working on the same canvas? It just doesn't fit with the popular vision of the lone genius, solitary and suffering over his art. I noticed a lot of gaspy pearl clutching whenever an article reported that, say, Jeff Koons employed a team of 150 assistants to make his work ("I'm basically the idea person," he said once. "I don't have the necessary abilities, so I go to the top people"), or that Yoko Ono didn't personally create the one hundred sculptures of body parts that made up one of her exhibitions. ("How did you enjoy making the piece?" she asked, according to her fabricator, when she showed up at her opening and took in her finished work.) And yet for thousands of years, at least as far back as Ancient Egypt, making art (or what we now consider art) has been a team effort. Raphael, Rubens, Rembrandt, and lots of other celebrated Old Masters had plenty of younger masters painting robes and touching up hands, often for the same reasons that artists rely on assistants today: They needed to keep up with demand or required additional technical expertise to help execute their visions. In Europe, signing an artwork didn't become a thing until the seventeenth century, and even then many artists were no more likely to autograph their work than a cobbler would a shoe. It was those swooning, hike-taking Romantics circa the late eighteenth century who really pioneered the image of "lonely, forlorn, brooding artists struggling to make ends meet but producing powerful art at great personal sacrifice," writes the art historian Noah Charney. The impressionists doubled down on the idea that artworks were supposed to channel the artist's innermost spirit—an extra pair of hands was both unnecessary and inappropriate. The solitary artist is obviously a stereotype with staying power, even if it's often wrong. Practically every artist I spoke with either had a studio assistant, was a studio assistant, or used to be a studio assistant. And now I was one. That black line felt like my admission ticket into art history.

TWO WEEKS LATER, Julie threw out the painting.

I showed up at the studio and found the canvas with the bathroom stall tipped on its side against the wall. Starting over, she announced. "Too many problems with the composition."

She'd already hauled out another one of my primed canvases and outlined a new version of the same scene—this time with three feet in the bathroom instead of two. She'd also enlarged the floor tiles ("to be more dramatic") and angled the floor (to make it "more as if you're looking from lower," she said, miming peeking under a bathroom stall). "I have something in my head, and I don't know what I'm looking for, but I know when I've found it," Julie said. My job for the morning—I tried not to take it as a referendum on my painting skills— was to email her accountant.

CHAPTER FOURTEEN

My first few weeks in Julie's studio, I ate lunch standing up in between my various tasks, but as we settled into a rhythm, she started inviting me over to her apartment for a sit-down meal. Julie lived in a three-story walk-up a few blocks from the studio—past NATURE'S FINEST FABRICATED VEAL & LAMB CUT'S, past an impound lot, past stringy guys in peacoats hand-rolling cigarettes. "It's a pretty ugly neighborhood, in fairness," Julie said on our walk over one afternoon. I disagreed. Look at that cute Hansel and Gretel house! And she was next to a charming little community garden and a very pretty brick church. I'd just completed my rousing defense of the loveliness when we both spotted a man drop his jeans to his ankles and crouch. "Oh! Oh!" Julie yelped. "And someone taking a shit!"

Her apartment was a one-bedroom that she and her husband, the artist Clinton King, had lived in since moving to the city seven years before. It had a dresser in the kitchen, a shoe rack under the fruit bowl, and art everywhere. I repeat: *everywhere.* Balanced over the fridge, peeking out from behind doors, watching Julie from above the stove as she threw together her lunch of spinach, ground beef, and soy sauce. I excused myself to use the bathroom and peed with my shoulder in an oil painting while staring at a sculpture of ceramic breasts and flashing a gnome sculpture on the toilet tank behind me—all under the supervision of the abstract painting mounted over the medicine cabinet. "We have more art," Julie quickly assured me, as if I might have found this insufficient. "We actually like not having too much art on the walls." I had to wonder what too much could possibly look like.

I loved it. It felt like she and Clinton had a few dozen rambunctious roommates running around, and as I ate my leftover chili with a side of Julie's homemade kimchi, I immediately pitied anyone—myself included—whose idea of living with art was color-coordinating pieces with the couch and stopping once all the big walls had things on them.

Lots of the artwork was by friends of Julie and Clinton's, which they'd traded their own work to get. "That's a Liz Ainslie . . . That's mine, that's Loie, that's Hein Koh . . ." Julie said, pointing to a small canvas over her desk, then to a constellation of pieces that hung over the kitchen table. Interspersed between artworks by brand-name artists were pieces that a smaller mind would have called craft: a black abacus, antique French guignol puppets. And then there were pieces that a truly tiny mind might have called trash, given that they once were in fact trash. "Oh, that we found in the street," Julie said when I complimented a tiny concrete house on the floor beside her bedroom door. "There's a *lot* of stuff we find in the street." Clinton brought home a taxidermy ram's head he found on the sidewalk, and Julie shampooed and blow-dried it before mounting it on the wall of art beside the kitchen table. Back in Julie's studio, I marveled at a haunting sculpture of a wooden cathedral with wire mesh over its steeple and doors. Who's it by? I asked. Julie eyed me suspiciously as if to see whether I was joking. Uh, it's a mouse trap, she said. She'd found it God knows where and, in the tradition of Marcel Duchamp, repurposed it as a sculpture.

There is nowhere to hide in a one-room studio, and I quickly confirmed that Julie had the most omnivorous, most voracious cultural diet of anyone I'd ever met. One night she had tickets to *Swan Lake*, another to the Westminster Dog Show. She was off to a club to hear dub techno; she was counting down the minutes to a "Baroque Spectacular" featuring early choral music's greatest hits. "IT'S FUCKING TRANSCENDENT!" Julie yelled, grinning giddily, as she blasted *O Magnum Mysterium* as a teaser. I heard about how much Julie liked the 1972 space drama *Solaris* at least seven times, even though it took her three tries to get through the film without falling asleep—"I'm so inspired by it visually right now," she raved. Multiple times a day she'd step away from a canvas to gesture wildly at the air with her paintbrush while explaining why I absolutely *had* to watch this "fucked up version of *Little Red Riding Hood*" done by Soviet Claymation animators or check out architect Freddy Mamani Silvestre's flamboyant Neo-Andean LEGO-like homes. Her passion swept you off your feet and dragged you along like an undertow, and I left our conversations reeling, unable to focus on anything until I'd followed Julie's instructions to watch *This Is Spinal Tap* ("one of my favorite movies") or read Carl Jung's *Man and His Symbols* ("a *huge* discovery for me").

A self-described introvert, Julie could seem reserved, and she was constantly trying to weasel out of nights out—"Thank you. Already have a dinner or some excuse," she instructed me to email a gallerist who'd invited her to an opening's after-party. But mention you thought

Eyes Wide Shut was overrated, as I did, and she'd talk your ear off for half the width of Manhattan, waving her hands in the air while lecturing about the hidden logic of the Double Rainbow costume store at a volume that made other pedestrians turn and stare. (Clinton, she wanted me to know, deserved credit for turning her on to the film's genius.) I gathered we were growing closer, because Julie started lobbing questions back at me while she painted. What'd you think of *The Tree of Life*? Julie had walked out of the theater and drew a line between people who liked it and didn't. What'd you think of *The Irishman*? Julie liked it, I loathed it, and she loved that I'd argue the point with her. Julie had this openness to being moved by things she saw, read, and watched that made me feel as if I'd been experiencing culture through earmuffs and an eye mask. Just walking around the city was, for Julie, a chance to have your mind blown. She whisked protective plastic off some new sculptures that had been inspired by *sampuru*— the plastic food samples that Japanese restaurants stick in their windows to make your stomach growl. "It's almost an art form," Julie said. "It's so niche and so specialized, but also so artistic in a way. But also funny! And it's completely surreal." I peered over Julie's sculpture of two pieces of sushi wrapped in seaweed. Two unblinking brown eyes stared up at me.

The chaos of Julie's tastes caught me off guard. I'd gotten the sense from Jack that pop culture, next to the golden child of fine art, was at worst corrupting and at best a dumbed-down version of what galleries like his were showing. But Julie seemed to have moved past distinctions between polite arts and rude arts, art and craft, in a way that intrigued me. And yet she was still discerning. I wondered about her own standards of taste and, as things were winding down at the studio one evening, decided to get her take on the question of good art versus bad art that I'd failed to reconcile a few months before.

It was nearing 8:00 p.m., I was futzing around with a broom, and Julie was mocking up backgrounds for a painting that wasn't quite coming together. She'd snapped a photo of the piece—a faceless woman wearing pearls and a puffy red boxing helmet against a sky-blue expanse—and opened it in Photoshop. "I was thinking a padded room," she announced, pulling up a still from *Solaris* that had stuck with her: a view of a space station with puffy, marshmallow walls. She photoshopped it into the painting and frowned. Back to Google. She searched for padded rooms, padded blankets, quilted blankets, movers' blankets, and "upholstered wall pad 70s" looking for inspiration while she weighed my question: Is there good art and bad art, or is taste just totally subjective?

"*Is taste all subjective?*" Julie repeated. "Good question. *Is taste only subjective?*"

I reached for an extreme example, a painter I thought she'd despise, no question: Thomas Kinkade. If you, too, misspent your youth at your local mall, then you know who I'm talking about. Kinkade, who was alternately adored as America's most-collected living artist and pooh-poohed as a purveyor of pure unadulterated kitsch, specialized in mail-order landscapes so sweet they'll rot your teeth, where clouds are always close to orgasm and horse-drawn carriages never went out of style. His painting *Central Park in the Fall* (on sale for $550 to $5,350, depending on what I'm not sure) is the hallucinatory vision of a Midwestern granny who's come to New York to take edibles.

I didn't say any of this to Julie. I just nudged her away from her laptop, googled Thomas Kinkade, and let her click around.

Julie gave his work a few seconds and googled Bob Ross instead. Bob Ross—the guy with the poof of hair who hosted TV's *The Joy of Painting* and taught America to paint sunsets, fresh snow, and happy little trees standing guard over alpine lakes.

I toggled between Kinkade's paintings and Ross's. I shrugged. "Not so dissimilar," I said.

Completely dissimilar, Julie corrected me. "I fucking *love* Bob Ross," she said vehemently. She clicked on a Bob Ross painting of a snowy lake—"But look how well-painted this is!" she cried, thrusting both hands at the screen. "How it's making sense. The composition." Her voice rose with excitement. "It's tasteful in its own distaste! I mean, it's GREAT! And then you have *that*." She clicked back over to a Kinkade painting of a glowing cottage nestled between pink clouds and a burbling brook. "Compared to that guy, Bob Ross is like, so *restrained*. And so *conservative*. And so, like, *poetic* . . . There's an elegance to them . . . It's more open . . . You sense a real sense of wonder. It's not reducing things. It's opening them up. He's not too precious." She googled a video of Bob Ross working on another snowy mountain scene and breathlessly narrated him painting each tree as though she were a sportscaster building to the winning goal. "He makes them— *Bam!* He does another one. *Bam! Bam! Bam!*" Bob Ross smiled back at Julie from the screen. "I mean, I'm sorry—the *way* he found to do that with the fan brush? Those *trees*?" Her voice radiated awe. "It's very minimal. If you look at this"—she pointed to the scrawny branches of a Bob Ross evergreen and imitated what she imagined they'd sound like: *eesp eesp eesp.* "It's *abstract*!" She clicked back to Kinkade. "What he's talking about is smaller." She imitated the sound of his brush-strokes with a contemptuous nasal *myeh myeh myeh.* "His world is becoming so small. And so intricate. Intricated? *Étriqué*." But Bob Ross—"The way he sees things is *so* good."

I'd say the same about Julie. Until that second, I'd have dumped Bob Ross and Thomas Kinkade into the trash can of not good art and never looked back. Evidently I'd missed something. On second thought—had I ever really examined the work? Or I had outsourced my looking to someone else and simply fallen back on my vague sense that Bob Ross was on the motel-lobby side of good taste, whatever good taste was.

Poor Bob. He was just a victim of my tendency—and, who knows, maybe yours too—of letting my tastes default to the suggested, endorsed, and familiar.

I pressed Julie on taste again.

Yes, Julie allowed, taste could be subjective. "Because obviously, who are you to tell me what I should like or not like? I'm free to like whatever the fuck I want."

But she got agitated thinking about someone who wouldn't want to challenge her tastes by exposing herself to new things. "It's opening new dimensions into your brain," Julie stressed. "Otherwise, if you listen to the same thing over and over, all your life—um—maybe—" The concept seemed so foreign to Julie that she struggled to imagine a life with stagnant tastes. Her brain went immediately to mental illness. "I don't know if there's been a study—could you become depressed?" she ventured, not lightly, as someone who'd struggled with depression in the past.

Fresh experiences can lead to new tastes and a life that feels longer, Julie contended. Remember when you were little and an hour-long car ride felt like a lifetime? "I think it's because, truly, everything's new. When you experience new things, time slows down a little bit," she told me. "When you go on trips—which is my favorite thing to do—everything is new, and you feel so *young* again. And reinvigorated with new ideas, new perspectives, a new understanding of yourself."

Take Julie's first-ever trip to the United States, to study abroad in Chicago during art school. In America she discovered a new culture, and those new tastes gave rise to a new Julie. "You recreate yourself when you discover new things and you develop new tastes." Going back to France was miserable—"I was so depressed, I was crying all the time." She missed Clinton, who'd introduced her to a mind-blowing range of artistic expression when they'd met and started dating in Chicago, and she knew she had to get back to America. "Because somehow, I had discovered a part of myself here. A new self." With new tastes. "A new taste, it can be life changing."

Many of us wear our tastes like nametags. They identify us, and we'd rather not be known by anything else, *thankyouverymuch*. We are the sort of person who likes Lil Nas X or pastel porcelain cherub figurines or fourth-wave feminism—end of story. Especially as we get older, we relax into the warm bath of our preferences and then stay there, even as the water cools and our fingers turn pruney. Tastes become our identity, and the idea of changing them feels like an existential threat.

But "*I like this*" is such a dead end compared to "*Would I like this?*" Julie's answer alluded to the secret truth of taste, which is that it's malleable, ever-changing, and probably more honest to keep asking questions of yourself than to lay claim to *the* right answer. If you want to lose faith in the concept of "good" art, just consider all the artists who were brushed aside as feckless losers in their own day—El Greco, Van Gogh, Monet, Gauguin, Cézanne, the list goes on—only to get their own museum wings and their paintings plastered on tote bags today. Watching Julie watch Bob Ross dab icy blue on a patch of pristine snow, I realized that I had been thinking about taste all wrong. Instead of being an identity to be adopted, or an answer to be reached, what if taste was simply an idea to be interrogated? I liked the idea that "good" taste could just mean having tastes that were unpredictable and flexible—if you could always predict what someone would appreciate, well that sounded like rotten taste to me. I started to think that taste shouldn't be a destination but rather the starting point for a journey.

I knew Julie was far from the only person on this planet who could find joy in both Picasso and Pixar movies, but nights like that one left me feeling as if her eyes picked up on so much I still couldn't see. But was that true? Was I just drunk on the art world's Kool-Aid, or could being around art demonstrably change our outlook on the world?

A few months before, I'd sought out scientists to weigh in.

THE CLUNKILY NAMED Visual Science of Art Conference is an annual gathering of psychologists, physicists, neuroscientists, and ophthalmologists that, by all accounts, probably shouldn't exist.

For centuries, philosophy asserted itself as the key to demystifying our experience with art, so when a group of neuroscientists started poking around the subject two decades ago—proposing we stick some volunteers in an MRI machine, show them paintings, and see what happens—plenty of experts were none too pleased. Humanities scholars bristled at the interlopers trespassing on their turf. Scientists scoffed at the cockamamie notion that you could run experiments on a touchy-feely thing like art. Artists were plain outraged. One experimental psychologist I talked with sounded as if she was still scarred by the response to her study probing whether people can differentiate paintings by the artist Mark Rothko, a four-year-old, and a monkey. (They can, at a rate better than chance, even when the works were deliberately mislabeled.) "One artist took huge offense and said, 'You can't compare these things because you can't measure art!'" recalled the psychologist. "It was emotional. It was anger."

Yet a small subset of experimenters just plowed right ahead with their research. They strapped eye-tracking goggles on tourists at art museums, and watched peoples' brains while flashing Matisse paintings in fMRI machines—all in an effort to untangle our relationship with art and how it affects us. And a bunch of these scientists, I'd discovered several months before starting work with Julie, were gathering in the quaint Belgian town of Leuven to share what they'd found. I immediately booked my ticket.

It's not that I didn't believe what artists and art lovers had been telling me about the value of art to our lives, though admittedly I am the sort of person who'll fact-check a love letter. It's just that I was curious to get a second opinion, from a neutral party, on what—if anything—engaging with visual art does to our brains.

I landed in Leuven a few hours before the conference began, and after marveling at the fairy-tale dreaminess of the city's cobblestone streets, cooing doves, and frilly Gothic cathedrals, I went directly to a windowless auditorium where I would spend the next four days.

I learned about the aesthetics of graffiti. I learned about the Czech researcher who poked himself in the eye for science. (Jan Purkinje is his name, and you should really check out his drawings of the squiggles he saw while mashing his closed eyelids.) I learned that standing 5.49 meters from a big Jackson Pollock painting is considered optimal. That we can make reliable judgments about artworks in fifty milliseconds, faster than the blink of an eye, and that getting goose bumps while you look at art is called "aesthetic chills." I learned that lots of studies set out aiming to answer ambitious, age-old questions like *What do humans find beautiful?* and end with frustratingly narrow conclusions like *Subjects prefer paintings in the intermediate fractal dimension range.* I also learned that studying vision doesn't make you better at gauging whether the long black curtain walling off the side of a classroom is art.

"It's a modern artwork," declared a sober-faced scientist as he contemplated the expanse of black fabric.

"I thought it was a construction area," ventured a slender neurologist.

"No, it's a modern artwork."

"*No*, I think it's a construction area."

Art experts, I learned as I dove into the research, would not only be able to recognize that curtain as artwork but would likely prefer it to a painting of a fruit bowl.

After the presenters finished their talks, I'd corner them beside the podium and pester them for data on what, if anything, distinguishes art lovers' outlook. I learned that while the definition of "art expert" varies according to the study (it could mean art students, art historians, artists, art professionals . . .), years' worth of research has found that experts do appreciate art differently than "naïves"—the shorthand for novice laypeople who, in other circles, are known as Schmos.

Experts like abstract artworks more than naïves, who prefer representational pieces that depict the real world. Experts prefer "high art" from museum collections; naïves prefer wildlife photos and "sentimental portraits." Experts reject the belief that art should "provide warm feelings to a broad audience"; naïves think that's exactly what art should do. The two groups physically engage with artworks differently: Artists, for instance, pay close attention to an artwork's background and the relationships between the objects depicted, and their eyes scan the whole work to understand its structure and composition. Naïves' eyes tend to linger on a few salient details: a face, hands. (One study found that experts blinked less than naïve viewers while contemplating an abstract image, a lack of activity that apparently indicates the experts' "increased visual effort.") Experts focus on an artwork's style; naïves focus on its content. Experts pay attention to context, while naïves pay attention to their gut: Research has found that experts not only prefer an artwork when they think it belongs to MoMA but will override their biological impulse for beauty (by rating neutral faces more highly than attractive ones). Naïves like a beautiful face when they see it, whether it's in an artwork owned by MoMA or not. Also, unsurprisingly, studies show we like art more when we understand it.

This was all interesting to learn, but after hours of lectures and poster sessions, I still didn't have a solid sense of whether artists and art experts processed the world differently.

My breakthrough—though it didn't feel like one at the time—came midway through the conference.

After a brief break for dinner, a herd of us filed back into a lecture hall for the final talk of the day. The speaker, a renowned physicist whose blinking eyes I could just make out through an explosion of white facial hair, clicked through his slides while I slumped lower and lower in the warm, dark room, my stomach full of the bratwurst I'd just devoured, jet lag pulling at my eyelids, my notes devolving into a half-conscious jumble of cryptic phrases copied from the physicist's talk—"squid squirt ink . . . not just lambs and tigers . . . we really need our centaurs . . ." Then, through my haze, I heard the physicist say something that jerked me upright. "Most people think they don't miss anything, that they see what *is*," he said. "They don't realize: They see what they hallucinate."

Wait, what? I thought vision was our bedrock. Thanks to Plato, sight has long been celebrated as the most trustworthy of our senses. Taste and smell are animalistic; touch is downright obscene; and hearing, while slightly less offensive than those three, can't compete with sight— "the noblest and most theoretical of the senses," Plato declared. Cue generations of philosophers fawning over sight (the "spy of the intellect," cheered the Renaissance Jewish philosopher Leone Ebreo). Even now, we trust our eyes implicitly: "Seeing is believing," we say, while "I saw it with my own eyes" is supposed to put a stop to any argument. The idea that sight is synonymous with good data runs so deep that vision is our go-to metaphor for insight. (Ahem, in*sight*.) If we're "in the dark" about something, we'll ask someone to "shed light" on the matter and "make it clear." See what I mean? Vision is the sense that we rely on to insert pacemakers, to avoid plowing into oncoming traffic, to take our toddler home from day care and not someone else's. What could this renowned physicist possibly mean when he said vision was a hallucination?

I wanted to ask him to clarify, but a flock of grad students mobbed him after his talk, and I retreated to the snack table to wait my turn. A squat ophthalmologist, who'd challenged the physicist on a point during the Q&A and seemed pretty hyped up, inserted himself into my path. He wanted to ask me a question: What color was the lanyard around the physicist's neck? "You looked at him for more than ninety minutes," the ophthalmologist reminded me.

My mind raced. Maybe it was a trick question, because I couldn't remember him wearing a lanyard at all.

"You didn't realize the color of it!" the ophthalmologist crowed triumphantly. He jabbed a finger at the people standing around us. "We don't see it. Not you. Not *you*. Not even *you*. No one sees it." He sounded strangely happy about this. "That's the problem with visual perception," he crowed. "We think we see very well. We don't."

Before I go on, I need to show you this picture. What do you see? Got it in your head? Let's continue.

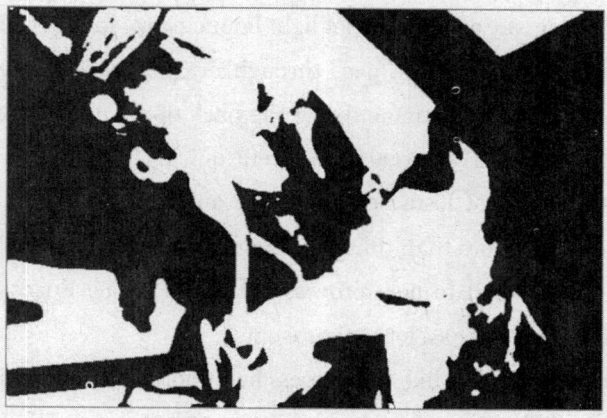

A COUPLE OF DAYS after the physicist's talk, I met Rebecca Chamberlain at Leuven's local art museum. Rebecca, an art student-turned-psychologist, researches the psychology and neuroscience of art perception at the University of London and has spent years examining how and why we engage with art. When I'd set up our meeting, I'd intended to pepper her with questions about her studies on artistic expertise. Now, however, the physicist's talk had made me realize I first needed a primer on how we see.

Let's look at this piece, Rebecca suggested, stopping in front of the first painting in the first gallery we entered. It was an oil painting by an unknown artist from around 1470 that depicted the stages of Jesus's crucifixion, albeit in a manner that presaged some of Berlin's more aggressive raves. Skinny guys in red tights moshed around a castle, various dudes with headbands waved their arms in the air, and, in the center, a bare-chested Jesus leaned against a post looking blasé.

I looked at the painting—which, as Rebecca explained to me, is just a simpler way of saying: I let light bouncing off the surface of the painting enter my cornea, pass through my pupil, hit my retina (a light-sensitive layer of tissue lining the back of my eyeball), and get translated into nerve signals that were quickly transmitted to my brain. As I stared at Jesus being poked at on the cross, my brain furiously recruited more than thirty different regions (around 40 percent of our gray matter) to help process the visual scene. Edges, colors, depth, motion: There's a lot to figure out.

If you want to feel like you possess heretofore undiscovered superpowers, I highly recommend looking at art with Rebecca. Did I realize how miraculous it was that I could tell Jesus's pale ankles from the peach-and-gold-tiled floor behind them? I did not. "Our brain's ability to know that that texture on the floor is all one thing is actually really, really sophisticated because it's broken up into all of these patches," Rebecca said excitedly. "How does the brain know that this tile area *here* is continuous with that tile area *there*? It's not a trivial problem at all for the visual system to work out." The process is so sophisticated that scientists still don't know how our brains manage to translate a painting's 580-nanometer wavelengths of light into a face, then recognize that face as *the* face of Jesus Christ. As best as scientists can tell, visual processing is not an orderly, step-by-step assembly line. It's a bustling feedback loop of crosstalk and collaboration between brain regions, more like a restaurant kitchen full of chefs shouting orders at each other during the dinner rush.

It was just after this point in Rebecca's explanation that I abruptly lost all sense of having superpowers. We might want to believe that we see like video cameras and go around dispassionately, accurately re-cording the scenes around us. We do not. Not even close. First off, the incoming data is "very impoverished," Rebecca informed me. Our view of the world is mostly blurry, with only a small area in focus and a black hole constantly hovering over our field of view. (We all have a blind spot where the optic nerve, which carries nerve signals to the brain, plugs into the retina.) And here's the thing: According to the lat-est theories, our brains are not faithful translators of those impover-ished light signals hitting our retinas. The incoming visual data passes through what Rebecca calls a "filter of expectation" in which our brains preemptively dismiss, ignore, sort, classify, and prioritize the raw data even before we get the full picture. "The expectations come before the information is even received," said Rebecca. "Traveling around this art gallery, I'm always going to have expectations about what things are going to look like and where things are going to be. That is already potentially having an impact on these lower areas"—parts of the brain that identify basic shapes, boundaries, or colors—"and constraining the way they're processing information." In other words, our brains' top-down predictions about what we *expect* to see ulti-mately shape what we think we see. I thought back to something the ophthalmologist had said to me: "We can see without the eyes. We can't see without the brain." I was looking at a piece that an artist had painted. But my brain was creating the artwork, too—tossing out in-formation before I'd even registered it, jumping to conclusions about what was where, overriding the data to give me a passable impression of the piece. Hence the physicist's claim that what we call "vision" is really hallucination.

Our visual systems take creative liberties with reality all the time. Take color, Rebecca said. The light in our environment changes constantly: It can be bluer at dawn, yellower at sunset, orangey by candlelight, and purplish when it's cloudy. And yet when you leave a supermarket's cool-white fluorescent lights and step into the dark blue of twilight, you don't marvel that your white shirt has suddenly turned purple (even though the light bouncing off your shirt may technically have a wavelength closer to what we call "purple"). You still perceive your shirt as "white," and you can thank a visual process called color constancy for that. Our perception of an object's color remains constant even as its hue changes because of shifting lighting conditions. If our visual system *didn't* adjust to changes in lighting conditions—"I guess you'd have almost like a hallucinogenic experience of these qualities of lights and colors changing all around you," Rebecca said. Research suggests color constancy may improve with age—it takes experience to figure out how light changes during the day, or that shirts don't spontaneously turn purple—and babies might constantly feel like they're tripping. They probably experience "radically big changes in perception of color and light," Rebecca speculated, only there's no easy way to ask them.

Context is, in a sense, hardwired into vision: The knowledge we amass from our lived experience is a crutch our brains rely on to decode our environment with split-second accuracy—even if that means dismissing some of the data. "The visual system is always trying to come up with the most efficient way of representing the world in the simplest way," Rebecca told me. Why? Because our vision evolved to save us from fast predators with sharp incisors and not, camcorder-style, to record the minutiae of slow dances at weddings. "The goal of vision is not to get things perfectly right all the time," writes the neuroscientist V. S. Ramachandran, "but to get it right often enough and quickly enough to survive as long as possible to leave behind as many babies as you can." Our visual system doesn't have to be good; it just has to be good enough. That means taking shortcuts and compressing incoming information by passing it through our filter of expectation. If you want to experience your filter of expectation at work, flip back to that black-and-white picture I just showed you. Did you recognize it as a picture of a woman in a cowboy hat (on the right) kissing a horse's muzzle (on the left)? If you did, you're cleverer than I am. If you didn't, good luck unseeing it now. Your filter of expectation will automatically descend to organize your perception into a hallucination of a horse.

But there are exceptions. Remember Anya Hurlbert's lecture earlier in the week?, Rebecca asked me. Hurlbert, a professor of visual neuroscience, had given a talk on color constancy that included two side-by-side paintings by Claude Monet of the Rouen Cathedral. Monet painted that same cathedral more than thirty times, at different times of day, to study how the color of its stone—what I'd call a whitish-beige—changed with the light. He painted it at dawn, dusk, noon; on cloudy and sunny days. In one of his paintings of the cathedral in the morning, its stone masonry is a deep blue. At sunset, it's a radiant poppy orange. That wasn't purely artistic license, Anya told us. Some people, she'd explained, seemed capable of overriding their brain's color constancy mechanisms. People such as artists. "Monet allowed himself to see all these different hues and brightnesses," said Rebecca. "Other people would just see the face of the cathedral."

It's no easy feat to stop the brain from settling into its default mode, which is to fiddle with the controls so that the stone facade remains a neutral beige. But Rebecca's own work had led her to a similar idea: that artists have the capability to access a "less top-down, constrained way of seeing," she said, one they could "switch on when they want." I tried to imagine it: What would the world look like if our filter of expectation could be yanked off?

IT WASN'T UNTIL I started working in Julie's studio that the information I'd learned in Belgium began to take shape in my brain. The turning point came the day I watched Julie embark on the dull task of mixing gray.

While I settled into my post at Julie's laptop to help her answer emails, Julie sidled up to her painting of the feet under the bathroom stalls. By this point, most of the painting's sheer acrylic base coat had disappeared under an unctuous layer of oil paint. The tiles were black and white, and the three sets of feet had slid into three pairs of shoes: green high heels, brown loafers, and flamingo-pink pumps. Today, Julie planned to tackle the bathroom stalls along the top of the canvas. According to her base coat, they'd be gray. Blah, boring gray.

Out of the corner of my eye, I saw Julie rummage around in her painting cart, fish out a couple tubes of paint, and squeeze out a curl of white next to a comma of black on her palette.

White and black. If memory serves, that should be plenty for making gray.

But instead of reaching for a brush, Julie went back to digging through paint tubes. She added dabs of chrome orange (the color of an orange peel), Naples yellow (a dollop of Dijon mustard), quinacridone magenta (evocative of 1980s' windbreakers), phthalo turquoise (picture the Caribbean Sea by the horizon line), and red ochre (the dusty brown of cave art).

Whoa, whoa, whoa. Seven colors for gray? I wasn't so naïve that I thought painters exclusively used paint straight from the tube, but please—all this for gray? A color that, I'm willing to assume, is the favorite of exactly no one. The word itself is a letdown, less adjective than whine—*greh.*

I briefly stopped typing the email I was drafting and watched as Julie used a palette knife to blend a bit of orange and turquoise into an army-tank green.

Julie made a face. "The chrome orange was the wrong decision," she whispered.

Yes, well, I could have told you that, I thought. She seemed to be seriously overcomplicating the matter.

Julie mixed in some white, then some black, then the whole gob of black. She fished more paint tubes out of her cart and squeezed out a dab of peach, periwinkle, and Payne's gray, which, actually being gray, seemed promising. I went back to typing and heard the squishy gloop of her palette knife swirling paint.

"*PFOOOOO!*" An irritated exhale shot out behind me. "I'm struggling."

Julie added a Wonder Bread yellow called jaune brilliant—the eleventh color on the palette.

"*CHOOOOO!*" she huffed, sounding even more annoyed.

She brushed a horizontal stripe of her new paint mixture on the canvas and stepped back to inspect it. No good. "*GHOOOOO!*" she breathed angrily.

Nearly half an hour passed. Julie kept struggling over the swirl of gray on her palette, and I gave up on the emails to hover a few feet away from her, openly gawking as I tried to figure out what she was after. Julie went back and forth between colors, picking up dabs of orange and turquoise with her brush. "So frustrating," she muttered. "So. Very. *Frustrating.*"

"I want to recreate the steel color here," Julie said, jutting her chin in the direction of her studio door. It was a dull, satiny steel streaked with dark and light grays. "It's kind of a weird, cool *and* warm gray." She squinted at the door. "See how that gray is so strange? I think it shifts according to what's reflecting on it, and according to the daylight... I kinda like it."

More time passed. This just seemed masochistic. Clearly, I was missing something, so I tried staring at her studio door. "We tend to be naïve realists," a grad student had told me in Belgium. As naïve realists, we implicitly trust our brain's filtered view of reality without ever questioning that we could be seeing more. *Was there more?* I stared at Julie's palette, then at the painting, and then back at the door. The gray door. The "gray" door.

It was happening, right in front of me, I realized. "You take away the filter of expectation," Rebecca had told me, "and you allow the world to be this chaotic stream of information." And here it was. The mess of colors, the long gazes at the door: Julie, I thought, was pulling away her filter of expectation so she could capture the full glory of the door's "gray."

I saw the gray door through my filter of expectation, and it was gray. Julie cast hers off, and the gray became a rainbow: a chaotic stream of turquoise, orange, magenta, and periwinkle. I was, I'll admit, jealous.

UNTIL NOW, I would have ranked color way down my list of interests, right near football and your decision to go gluten-free. Purple, blue, orange—who needs 'em? I liked dressing like a nun (I maintain there's a quiet dignity in always looking as if you're going to a funeral) and I'd successfully purged all color from my apartment such that you could live there, be color-blind, and never know it. A painter I met—a not-so-subtle hint, I realize now—sent me a copy of the book *Chromophobia* in which the artist David Batchelor argues that the West has "systematically marginalized, reviled, diminished, and degraded" color, and while I'm certainly not condoning that attitude—well, it sounded familiar.

But that was before Belgium and before I started spending most of my waking hours around artists. They perseverated over color. Left to talk among themselves, gallerists talked shit about other gallerists, but artists gossiped about colors. "I hate blue," the artist Kari Cholnoky declared. "I think it's gross, but it also has to do with its link to a really predictable, conventional relationship to beauty." Not since kindergarten had I heard the icebreaker "What's your favorite color?" trotted out with such regularity.

Julie had torrid affairs with certain colors, then cooled on them and moved on. Every so often she pulled out a mangled paint tube with a flourish, smiling to herself as she recounted fond memories of alizarin crimson or Persian rose with the toasty nostalgia of someone flipping through old vacation photos. "Some colors are just more special," she said, gazing at a squashed tube of Michael Harding–brand Pale Violet. Michael Harding paints were a splurge—the less-expensive Williamsburg was Julie's go-to—but Harding colors had "a sweetness to them that you don't find." She was embarking on a passionate fling with a resplendent, navy-inflected purple that made me think of kings in velvet robes. Looking around her studio, I saw traces of it in three different paintings.

Julie's enthusiasm had inspired me to read all I could about paint, and I eventually discovered that, in the grand scheme of history, Julie's was a low-grade fever relative to manias of the past. As a species, we've done crazy things for color.

Paint consists of two key elements. One is pigment, which gives paint its color and is made of teeny granules of things like ground rock or cancerous cadmium sulfide. The other is binder, a medium in which the pigment is suspended so it can be spread. The binder in Julie's oil paints was linseed oil, but other paints may use egg yolk (big among the ancient Egyptians), orchid juice (common among Aboriginal artists), ear wax (a favorite for Medieval monks), or milk from a lactating bovid (the go-to for painters forty-nine thousand years ago). Archaeological research shows that early humans were willing to risk it all for the right color. Even though Paleolithic painters living in Africa three hundred thousand years ago had easy access to pigments like yellow ochre and black manganese, they traversed more than a hundred miles—across valleys crawling with snakes, lions, leopards, hyenas, and other mortal threats—to retrieve glittering chunks of specularite, a mauve pigment archaeologists say artists used for no other reason than because it looked nice.

Our lust for color has turned us into poisoners, grave robbers, and killers. To make a flaming-red pigment the color of freshly butchered meat, ancient Romans forced convicts to mine cinnabar from mercury mines—a job so toxic it effectively doubled as a death sentence. To make a brilliant red the color of a bloody wound, the Aztecs and Mayas slaughtered countless cochineal insects en masse. (In an irony the cochineal wouldn't appreciate, the acid they secrete to defend themselves just so happens to dazzle artists.) Circa the 1800s, painters in India and elsewhere went wild for a radiant egg-yolk yellow whose mysterious source turned out to be the dried urine of cattle fed mango leaves— a diet that makes nice paint but is murder on the animals. But then corpses have come in handy for color too. Beginning in the 1500s, European artists like Eugène Delacroix delighted over a mahogany-brown pigment called "Mummy Brown," which was made from actual ground-up Egyptian mummies. Admittedly, Mummy Brown wasn't always mummy. On a trip to Alexandria in 1564, a French physician discovered that one top pigment dealer supplemented his Mummy Brown with the bodies of executed criminals and recently deceased slaves, and at least one nineteenth-century painter sourced his Mummy Brown from the disinterred corpses of decomposing French kings. You'd think artists would have sworn off Mummy Brown after learning it really *was*, in some cases, brown mummy. But London's C. Roberson art-supply store, which stocked the pigment through the 1920s, only declared its stockpile of mummy remains depleted in 1964. "We might have a few odd limbs lying around somewhere," its managing director told *Time*, "but not enough to make any more paint."

For much of human civilization, our color palette was limited to what we could chisel from rocks: white from chalks, green from celadonite, red from ochres, maybe some black from charred bones. But we had urges! We craved more colors than nature alone could provide, and human history is also the story of our ongoing quest to control color. Blue, a so-called "latecomer in paint," was especially elusive. The very first synthetic pigment ever developed was a zippy blue the color of a cloudless sky that the Egyptians discovered how to make five thousand years ago by heating sand, limestone, and copper minerals. The Egyptians were after a pigment that would imitate the brilliant blue of lapis lazuli, a metamorphic rock that's used to make ultramarine paint and, in Renaissance Europe, cost as much as gold. (It nearly bankrupted Vermeer: His *Girl with a Pearl Earring* is also "Girl with an Ultramarine Headscarf.") According to a fifteenth-century Italian painting manual, artists who coveted

ultramarine paint had to make it through a laborious process that included pounding the lapis lazuli, sifting it, pounding it again, mixing it
with three different pastes, then kneading it daily for at least three days
in preparation for a series of lye baths and more massages. (And that's
only *after* the lapis lazuli traveled via donkeys, camels, and boats to get to
Europe from mines in Afghanistan.) The nineteenth century delivered a
revolution in organic chemistry, which made it a boom time for domesti-
cating color. Driven by demand for snazzier fabrics, chemists synthesized
new pigments like cadmium yellow (a banana-peel shade discovered in
1817) and viridian (a mossy green introduced in 1838). That and the
invention of the metal paint tube allowed us to use more colors, more easily. "I have got new ideas and I have new means of expressing what I
want, because better brushes will help me, and I am crazy about those
two colors, carmine and cobalt," Van Gogh wrote in 1885, a few decades
after an industrially produced version of sapphire-like cobalt blue became
commercially available. Since then, new pigments have just kept coming: traffic-cone cadmium orange, emoji-eggplant cobalt violet, Palm
Springs–motel cobalt teal. Savor your neon-pink sneakers and the cow-
pee yellow of taxis: There's never been a more colorful time to be alive.

That's certainly how I felt. Being around Julie forced me to wrap
my head around new sides of color's personality—namely, its hue,
value, and saturation. What Julie called "hue" is what I'd always referred to as plain old *color*: pale violet, Persian rose. "Value" refers to
the lightness or darkness of a color, meaning its proximity to white or
black. (Value sits on a scale with white on one end, black at the other.)
"Saturation" is variously defined as the intensity or purity of a color's
hue, with "strong," "vivid" colors at one end of the spectrum and "weak,"
"washed-out" colors at the other. (The red of a Coca-Cola label is more
saturated than is the scarlet of brick apartment buildings, which is

more saturated than the "gray" of Julie's studio door.) Around Julie, color practically felt three-dimensional.

She talked about the greens, pinks, and peaches of her paintings as if they were finicky coworkers prone to violent mood swings. When painting with Flashe, she had to deal with colors that were fickle and turned cooler as they dried. Nothing rivaled the concentrated snap of color you got with gouache. Adding black was a quick way to darken colors but gave you a hue that was "dead," while juxtaposing complementary colors—think yellow and purple, or red and green—made a painting dance. (Complementary color pairs, which are opposite each other on a color wheel, are generally made up of one cool color and one warm color.) Julie pointed out that she used lots of complementary color pairs in her paintings: "It helps to balance the composition," she told me. She'd figured out that paintings clicked better when she mixed a little bit of the complementary colors she used in the foreground to create whatever color she was planning for the background. "It just homogenizes everything," Julie said. "It's like yin-yang. It's *so* infinitesimal, but it's like, the eye kind of picks up on it." She stepped back to consider the bathroom painting and looked pleased. The gray she'd ended up using for the stalls—which had traces of the orange and turquoise she'd used to paint the feet—would "stimulate or vibrate the green of the shoe."

Letting my eyes wander around her studio, I spotted complementary-color pairings all over. She'd painted a woman at a hair salon sitting on a bright green chair facing a magenta-pink wall. There was a painting of a woman straddling a motorcycle, whose bronze orange tailpipe glowed against a turquoise background. The color pairs jostled each other with their own gravitational force and jiggled my brain and eyeballs simultaneously. Staring at the paintings practically tickled.

Around this time, I got obsessed with staring at walls. Dirty tiles by subway platforms, green panels around construction sites—any wall would do, the blander the better. Jack had also stoked my passion for staring at walls, but back then I analyzed them for nicks and sub-par spackling jobs. Now I stared, slack-jawed and eyes slightly blurred, trying to switch color constancy on and off while I challenged myself to name which of Julie's colors I'd mix together to get the precise hue of the ceiling at the dentist's office. I kept pushing myself to question color, not just accept it. To go deeper.

For weeks, not much changed. But then, as I was stepping off the sidewalk on an otherwise unremarkable afternoon, a wall across the street stopped me in my tracks. The drab limestone facade of an apart-ment building I'd passed every day for nearly ten years had shattered into a dazzling puzzle of orange highlights, lavender nooks, and blue shadows.

And that wasn't the last time it happened. I can't believe I'm saying this, but there's an apartment building on East Eighty-First Street whose radiant stone blocks nearly moved me to tears. I made a new hobby of watching my apartment's "white" walls glow pink as the sun rose. I be-came a broken record on walks around the park with my husband. "The COLOR!" I'd squeal, tugging him over to see some green leaves that were massaging my eyeballs. The pleasure of spotting a Fanta-orange coat on the subway felt hedonistic, like heavy bass vibrating my guts at a concert or fat melting on my tongue as I bit into a pork bun. There were colors that caressed and colors that made the hairs on the back of my neck stand up. My experience of color had taken on a fourth dimension be-sides hue, value, and saturation: pure, unadulterated joy.

CHAPTER FIFTEEN

While I was off staring at walls, Julie seemed increasingly concerned with the question of whether her career was about to implode.

The trouble was the auctions. As the *Artnet* article had reported, a small painting of Julie's called *Princess*—a portrait of a woman with dark hair knotted into Princess Leia buns—had sold the prior spring at the auction house Phillips for $106,000, which was 8,000 percent more than Julie had sold it for two years earlier. Seeing the piece sell for so much "was really a bit unsettling," Julie told me. "But it's worse now." A few months after *Princess* sold, another painting of hers was auctioned off for $250,000. Then two more—each for more than $400,000. "So it's getting worse and worse."

If you aren't up on the art market, you might think that, for Julie, discovering she can charge a few thousand times more for a painting is terrific, life-changing news. Say she paints an average of three

paintings a month, times twelve months, times $400,000 a painting—
by golly, she'll make millions!

Short answer: no. Julie made most of her money by selling art via
her gallery (also known as the primary market, in contrast to the secondary market, which includes auctions). She'd made $600 when she
sold *Princess* initially, zilch when it sold for six figures at auction. And
while Anton Kern Gallery had raised prices on Julie's paintings, her
pieces were nowhere near the $400,000 apiece they'd fetched at auc-
tion and probably wouldn't be for a while. Artists who'd had big museum shows and won major awards sold work for that much; that wasn't
yet Julie. Even small paintings by Gauguin and Renoir had recently
sold for less. Frankly, everyone seemed stunned by the auction prices,
Julie included. "Who *are* these people?" she wondered. "It seems kind of
like a lot of money for a nobody like me, you know what I mean?"

Pursuant to the upside-down "logic" of the art market, Julie was
now praying for her auction prices to go down. Big prices meant big
temptation for collectors to flip their Julie Curtiss paintings for a nice
profit, and the more of her paintings went to auction, the more whispered doubts there'd be about Julie's longevity as an artist. The Heads
considered it awfully early in Julie's career for people to be reselling
her paintings, and buyers' willingness to part with her work suggested
they didn't trust her pieces to be worth more in the future—which
risked setting off the artsy equivalent of dumping a stock. Collectors—
as gallerists loved reminding me—are sheep. Gallerists' version of telling scary stories around a campfire was repeating cautionary tales
about too-big-too-fast artists like Anselm Reyle, who showed with
powerhouse galleries like Gagosian before his work started getting
flipped at auction. Reyle's prices grew more than 1,000 percent in a
year—then demand cratered. Lots of Reyle pieces went to auction and

failed to sell, and in 2014 Reyle announced at the ripe old age of forty-four that he was retiring. He was unable to keep funding his studio practice. One gallerist called it a "wipeout."

There was also the issue that the pure consider high prices to be in bad taste. "An artist who experiences too much popularity or commercial success, it's like, a certain type of curatorial set doesn't want to deal with that because it's kind of, like, *gross*," the gallerist Bridget Donahue had told me. There was a delicate dance between building the work's artistic value (in the minds of those who mete out cultural capital) and its financial value (in the minds of the privately banked who wire capital capital). "The market can really damage me, where they're inflating me so much," Julie fretted, as she sat on a stool repainting the black high heels on one of her figures. "It's like a soufflé. It can really inflate and—*PLUTZ!*—collapse because there wasn't a sustainable growth." As the *Artnet* article showed, the vultures were already circling.

I began to notice that Julie was singing less and glancing more at her phone, often picking it up to read a text and then sigh. As we dragged in a box of art supplies one Friday morning, Julie mumbled that someone had just messaged her to say he'd be auctioning off a painting of hers that he'd bought two years before—"*I really need the money*," Julie paraphrased, rolling her eyes. "I mean, *everybody* can say they have money problems." (The painting, for which the guy had paid $1,400, would eventually sell for $209,000.) We were walking back to the studio after lunch a few days later when Julie mentioned that a gallery she used to work with had contacted her on behalf of a collector: The collector was threatening to auction off their Julie Curtiss work but would *consider* holding on to it if Julie could prove that she had a big career coup in the works. Julie was determined to purge the auctions from her brain, but they kept wriggling in. She'd just picked up a paintbrush to work on the painting of the woman with her legs spread that I'd sat for when her phone buzzed. Julie scanned the text, then dropped the phone roughly. "It makes me *so* angry, people," Julie announced, the edges of her voice curling with frustration. The text was about a collector couple. Julie wouldn't name them, but a little digging revealed them to be self-styled benefactors who ran an artists' residency in Italy and did softball interviews touting their "efforts to establish long-term relationships with their artists." They'd decided to flip their Julie Curtiss painting, ostensibly because they were peeved that her gallery was making them wait to buy another one. The cruel irony of the situation was that Julie's auction prices were going nuts precisely because people didn't want to wait to buy her art. The demand for Julie's work was greater than the supply, and the alternative to currying favor with a gallery and putting your name on their waitlist was just to hold up your auction paddle the longest. Money, as any Miami VIP will tell you, doesn't wait.

Julie didn't expect you to keep her pieces till you croaked. She just thought it'd be more considerate if you resold them via her gallery. True, you'd probably earn less than if you sold at auction—"Buy yourself, I don't know, a sauna or whatever," Julie grumbled. "Like, something stupid that no one really needs in real life." But that way it wouldn't be public, the gallery could keep track of where her work went, and Julie, who you'll recall made the art in the first place, could earn a few bucks—potentially 10 percent of the sale.

But Julie is not a victim, which I feel obligated to say because she said it so often to me. Julie saw her peers forced into tired stereotypes: the sellout, the starving artist, the innocent lamb slaughtered by the market. She rejected them all.

Over the weeks, my responsibilities had gradually migrated away from Julie's canvases and onto her laptop, and I'd gotten used to showing up in the morning to find one to-do list for Julie—"*Moi*"—taped up beside a second to-do list for me—"Bianca." The "*Moi*" list Julie left for herself one Tuesday was typical: two pages long, a mix of the administrative ("Answer to Linda"), artistic ("Glaze resin japanese sculpture"), financial ("*faire budget*"), and annoying ("Look for new health insurance"), plus a cry for help (Julie had written "Answer to Linda" twice). The to-do lists appeared to be spawning, and they crawled the walls like outbreaks of black mold. "Yoga. It's only 15 minutes" appeared on a Post-it above Julie's minifridge. "I don't take time to do stuff. *Important* stuff, like exercising, feeling healthy," Julie explained. Scraps of torn paper materialized beside several paintings, where Julie scrawled notes to herself for how to improve each piece. For example, the to-do list hung beside the painting of the woman riding the motorcycle read:

* Fur Coat
* grey Flexible tube
* toes?
* Spikes/Fins?

Having it there helped her stay focused: "I've been really distracted lately, and I've been having a hard time getting started."

While Julie worked on adding three silver spikes to the motorcycle's muffler and a seam to the rider's black bodysuit, I attacked each day's to-do list. I scheduled DHL pickups, updated Julie's CV, drafted an artist statement, inquired after her 401(k), got her $200 she was owed for talking to a class of undergrads, told a gallery in Japan that Julie unfortunately couldn't do a show with them ("Just write a nice message... I'm booked for the next coming year and a half, your space is so nice, thank you so much for thinking of me..."), and informed a college student she unfortunately couldn't do a print with him ("Be really kind and THANK him and say, 'Oh, that's lovely'"). I declined an interview request from British *GQ* ("I don't quite understand the context"), sent a maybe to *Playboy* ("It's edgy, it's visually compelling"), and said yes to *Gourmand* ("Better context"). We weighed certain decisions together, like how to assemble her archive, and I emailed Julie's gallerists, in Julie's voice. "That sounds like me but like, a better me," Julie beamed, after I read aloud the message I'd drafted. She got mock-serious: "The *professional* me!" In the one email I signed as Bianca, Julie told me to identify myself as her studio manager—"You've been upgraded."

These tasks felt even more intimate than gessoing, and as Julie shared medical documents and tax returns, I took pride in being inaugurated into the business of being Julie Curtiss. To be clear, Julie Curtiss was an artist. Julie Curtiss was also a business. I don't mean that she churned out paintings like Hostess Twinkies, but I'd had such a starry-eyed focus on the creative process that I'd barely considered all the administrative crap Julie had to wade through to get to her paintings. Julie was head of production at Julie Curtiss. She was also its finance chief, supply-chain manager, PR team, and HR department, which was currently weighing various health-insurance options, none of them halfway decent. Julie's doctor wanted her to get a surgery, but she was putting it off in part because she couldn't get a straight answer on how much it would cost with her current insurance. "You look online and it's like, 'Oh yeah, this is between $3,000 and $15,000.' It's like—*Hold on*. Hold. A. Minute." Julie's gallery pitched in—being represented by Anton Kern meant Julie could lean on them for career support, from booking travel to photographing her pieces. But the nitty-gritty of Julie's practice—and future—was still in Julie's hands.

I prided myself on plowing through my "Bianca" list and then asking Julie to pass off her most annoying paperwork, anything to give her a few more minutes making art. Also selfishly, I felt like the minutiae of Julie's humdrum tasks held the secret to the persistent, elusive question of how exactly an artist got to the point that she could be an artist—not a caterer–bartender–art handler–artist but *just* an artist, who worked on her own art full time and could still afford the gas bill.

Here's how it happened for Julie, I learned: She'd been part of the New York art scene for the better part of a decade—working, waiting, networking, not giving up. She regularly exchanged studio visits with other artists around the city, and during one of them, a painter told Julie to check out Hein Koh, a fellow emerging artist who made spandex sculptures of crying sunflowers and cyclops watermelons. Julie followed Koh on Instagram. They started exchanging compliments on each other's photos, which turned into swapping studio visits. Koh decided to apply to show Julie's work at Spring/Break—a scrappy, emerging-art fair that's slightly more organized than is a bake sale and my personal favorite fair. (Most of the exhibitors are artists, advisors, or independent curators who apply to show underrecognized artists whose work they love.) The booth at Spring/Break was Julie's first solo show in New York City and—Julie couldn't believe it—sold out immediately. After that, two different galleries offered Julie shows. Then a gallerist Julie had known for years through the mosh pit of the city's openings—"She was the friend of my husband and she was curating *his* work and she was not interested in my work at all"—joined Anton Kern Gallery and started to take an interest in Julie's art. Soon Anton Kern Gallery was representing Julie—who, only a few months before, had begun being represented by a gallery in Los Angeles.

Why the sudden interest after—Julie's words—"nothingness for so long"? "It was the right work for the right time," she said. "I don't think my work would be popular if there hadn't been all of these political events recently." Thanks to Trump's election and the #MeToo movement, galleries in the United States had just made the groundbreaking discovery that women make art and had started making a concerted effort to show their work. At the same time, after years of collectors losing their minds over misty silver abstract paintings, figurative art was having a comeback. It also helped that figurative art did superbly well on Instagram—"factor number one in my career," said Julie— because, well, I don't need to tell you that a painting of a woman in a skintight black bodysuit straddling a motorcycle will grab your eyes more than a green squiggle on a field of beige. Julie occasionally posted photos of her work, which collectors noticed, and they began asking to buy her paintings. But why *then* and not before? Julie shrugged. "It's so hard for artists," she told me. "The career, all of that. It's *so* not only up to you and the work. It's such a weird combo of different factors. No one knows really sometimes *why.*"

If you ask me, Julie's account sold herself short. No, the machine didn't solely evaluate art on its merits, and yes, luck and timing absolutely played a role. But Julie was savvy and worked hard. She typically stayed at the studio until eight or nine at night and considered Saturday and Sunday part of the workweek. She'd been picky from early on about where she showed: She consistently put context over making a buck, and when faced with dueling show offers from two different galleries, she chose the one that was closer with artists over the one that was closer to collectors. She was also a good citizen of the New York art world. She was constantly heading out to friends' openings, helping to curate this or that group show, urging me to do studio visits with artists she admired, and devoted most of her Instagram to cheerleading other emerging artists ("Really digging this new body of works by @maria_calandra... keep it up Maria!"). She'd just applied to show her former studio assistant's paintings at Spring/Break—a way of paying forward what Koh did for her.

It was disheartening to hear how diligently Julie had built her career over the years just as collectors seemed poised to undermine it with their flipping. The whole ritual of galleries' vetting buyers had always made my skin crawl, but now I felt a very unwelcome kindling of sympathy for the idea of selling art to Good Persons who wouldn't turn around and resell artists' paintings for a quick buck.

Julie was better than I was at wadding up the auctions and tossing them into a forgotten corner of her brain.

"How do you do that?" I asked one evening, awed by her ability to get carried away by her process.

Julie, who was standing at a painting, didn't bother to turn around. "I know how to work," she said. "I really *love* making art. I get absorbed. I get into my own head." Her voice grew small, quiet, as she repainted, for the umpteenth time, the brown strands of hair on the woman's spread legs. "All that matters is when I go to studio, and I'm listening to music that I love, and then I'm starting to dance a little bit and get in the zone—that's when I'm really the happiest.

"That's why I get a little frustrated when I'm just doing meetings and I'm taking care of all that stuff with business." Her face hovered just above the surface of the canvas, and she whispered to it softly. "I don't want the work to suffer too much." I couldn't tell if she was trying to reassure herself or the painting.

CHAPTER SIXTEEN

I passed a smug dachshund waddling down the sidewalk in a fur coat and the vision of an animal dressed in another animal's fur was so surreal, so uncanny, I had the distinct sense I'd seen a Julie Curtiss painting come to life.

Every day I got closer to solving the mystery of why her art lodged itself in my brain. A big clue arrived while we were working from Julie's apartment one afternoon. (The Wi-Fi in her studio took a lot of sick days.) As I was organizing photos to send to her gallery, Julie stepped into her bedroom to take a phone call.

She stormed back in breathing fire. "*HAUGHHHHHHHH!* So ANNOYING all that stuff."

Barely a week had passed since she'd learned about the collector couple that'd be selling their Julie Curtiss painting, and now *another* painting was going to auction. Julie didn't want to talk about it. She changed the subject. She needed to prep for a talk she'd be giving to a class at the School of Visual Arts.

"I'm going to start preparing my lecture by selecting images of my influences," she announced, hunching defensively over her laptop.

I watched out of the corner of my eye as Julie lost herself on Google. Within a few minutes, she was grinning at her screen. "I have way too many references!" she said happily. "Man, people are going to think I'm dark." She laughed at her computer. "Okay, my art references: *Psycho*." She pulled up a still of a backlit Norman Bates holding a cleaver over a motel shower. "Pretty cool, right? The shadow work in Hitchcock was very, very—LOOK at that one!" she burbled, clicking ahead to a still from Hitchcock's *Notorious*—a shadowy hand curled menacingly over three teacups. "Sooooo creepy." She sounded delighted. Next was Marcel Duchamp's *Étant donnés*, an installation, visible only through peepholes, of a naked woman lying spread-eagle on a bed of branches. "It's about voyeurism and being seen and the danger of looking at art. I could talk about it for a long time." She scrolled past more images: René Magritte, Bruno Gironcoli, Ray Yoshida, Charles Burns, Christina Ramberg, a Robert Gober sculpture of sickly legs in a bathtub. Julie giggled to herself. "Oh my God, *everything's* dark." She filled a scrap of notepaper with more names to add: the graphic novelist Chris Ware, the filmmaker Luis Buñuel, the painter Jean-Auguste-Dominique Ingres.

"That's one of my favorite painters," Julie said, googling Ingres, a French artist from the nineteenth century. Pale, unsmiling nobility in lace and frilly collars stared back at me from Julie's screen—the sort of stiff portraits that I'd probably glance at in a museum and pass right by. She clicked on a painting of the Countess d'Haussonville, who smirked slightly as she leaned against a fireplace in a poufy satin dress. "Isn't that fantastic?" Julie was silent a moment. *"Yeah,"* she said finally, exhaling. "It's so beautiful, this one… He's so good with the textures…"

Julie got distracted by a thumbnail of Ingres's portrait of a Madame Moitessier regally arranged on a pink chaise lounge in a flowery gown accessorized with rubies the size of eyeballs. Julie clicked on it. I'd seen the painting with Jack, who'd extemporized on how Madame looks beautiful from the front, but from the mirror behind her—"someone else's perspective"—her slightly flattened profile made her quite the troll. He'd speculated that Ingres probably didn't want to paint her portrait, so worked in this little jab. And yet where Jack saw social critique, Julie saw *"Pfoooot, it's fucking amazing."* She appreciated the work in a way that was intuitive, effortless, as innate as taking a gulp of water. Either your eye caught on to something or it didn't. I remembered Julie's description of the feeling she was after in her own paintings: "You need to be able to bite it."

Julie jabbed a finger at Madame Moitessier. "Look at that hand!" she shrieked. "It looks like an octopus. It's like a star fish!" As she spoke, I watched the splayed fingers at Madame's temple transform into tentacles, fanned out, exploring their environment. Once again, I felt Julie pulling my attention toward an artist's decisions and away from Madame Moitessier as "the embodiment of luxury and style during the Second Empire, which saw the restoration of the French imperial throne and the extravagant display of wealth." That sentence comes from a museum's description of the piece, which says nothing about the delightful sea-creaturey shape of the hands, or the velvety warmth of Madame's hair. ("The *HAIR*," Julie was saying. "I mean, look at these *luscious* hairs!") As with O'Keefe's photographs, there was an almost physical delight in letting my brain linger on Ingres's brushstrokes and savor each of the choices he'd made. It was a moment that confirmed for me that all the information you need to appreciate an artwork is in front of you.

You don't *need* to know that Ingres was a neoclassical painter who tried to undermine the rise of Romanticism. Sometimes it's better not to know. Julie told me something that echoed what I'd heard from lots of artists who aren't white men: that gallerists and curators tended to shoehorn their work into narrow interpretations, expecting them to grapple with race or gender, while white male artists got free reign to explore an all-of-the-above cornucopia of themes—form, truth, beauty, the nature of existence. Julie didn't feel she'd experienced sexism but did feel she'd been treated differently as a female artist because her work was invariably "seen in the context of your gender," she said. "Personally, I can't be thinking of politics if I'm going to make art," she told me. "Art that feels like they want to convey a very clear message— I think that can be called propaganda."

Julie couldn't tear her eyes away from her computer screen. She treated her favorite images like they were nestled in between her vital organs. "These images that I have inside of me" was how she described them. "Don't you have that? Like, images that you can't get out of your mind? They live with you? I really like how some artworks live with me." These images that lived with her were not quiet, passive cohabitants. Some nudged her, demanding to be let out. Every piece she made was "an image I have in my head, and I need to get out of my system." Others haunted her for years. She traced her fascination with hair back to her discovery, years ago, of a dusty old suitcase in her parents' attic. She'd opened it and found two coils of brown human hair—her mother's and her aunt's—nestled like napping kittens.

I began to see Julie's insatiable appetite for culture as her way of adding ever-more images to her internal stockpile. "They're kind of like stepping stones or blocks that construct my understanding of the world a little bit," she said of images. "It's beautiful to have it in your head."

One of the questions Julie was supposed to answer during her School of Visual Arts talk was *Why do you paint?*, and Julie told me she'd discussed it with Clinton. "He was like, 'I want people to come to my painting and just be *in* the moment when I was making that painting.'" To have an experience, looking at the work, that connected them back to his experience of making the work. Not Julie. She hoped to make an image that crept deep into peoples' innermost thoughts and participated in their lives. "I want them to have an image that sticks in their head. And they can't help it. And this image stays. And they live with it. And it becomes a part of their collective imagination."

That completely changed my understanding of the decisions she made in the studio. The feet under the bathroom stalls, for instance: They had impossibly rubbery toes, no ankle bones, and skin that looked ironed flat. It's not that Julie *couldn't* draw a lifelike foot; she didn't want to. She wanted to strip away the details until she got to an iconic foot that we recognized from someplace deep in our imaginations— essentially, a stock image from our subconscious, or what Carl Jung, a major influence of Julie's, called an archetype. ("Just as everybody possesses instincts, so he also possesses a stock of archetypal images," wrote Jung, who argued that these archetypes shape our view of reality.) I grasped now why she tried to hide her brushstrokes as she painted and why she'd ultimately varnish each painting. She wanted to flatten the surface, even out the glossiness of different kinds of paint, and leave nothing but an image. An image, she hoped, that would slip into your mind and bury itself there like a benevolent parasite—for a month, for a year, for forever, for so long you forgot what the world looked like before.

Months after getting back from Belgium, I was sorting through studies I'd collected at the conference, when one made me straighten

up suddenly in my chair. It was coauthored by the conference's orga-
nizer, an experimental psychologist named Johan Wagemans, and offered a scientific rationale for precisely what Julie was trying to do
with her images. In the paper, Wagemans posed the question of why
we persist in looking at art, even though it can involve difficult, dis-
agreeable, and downright ugly interactions that "hurt our sense of
beauty."

To understand why we engage with art in spite of this, you have
to consider the architecture of our visual system, writes Wagemans.
Our perception of the world is only a prediction—a hallucination,
you might say, shaped by our filters of expectation. And art, Wagemans
contends, deliberately messes with those predictions. Artists create
images that introduce incongruities, such as a plate of sushi made
with eyes instead of fish. Artists defy our expectations, such as by
sticking a pearl-clad woman in wrestling helmet inside a padded
room. Artists introduce "unfamiliar experiences in an otherwise completely familiar setting," writes Wagemans, sounding exactly like the
typical gallery press release applauding an artist who makes the familiar unfamiliar. We're drawn to artwork that subtly deviates from our
predictions of the world—"Too much prediction error is unpleasant or
even disturbing; none or too little is boring"—and new art movements
may emerge as our predictions adjust to (and get bored with) the new
images around us. (We initially reject cutting-edge art because it's too
far afield from our current predictions, according to Wagemans, but
eventually we get used to it, then *too* used to it, and then our brains
start hungering for new surprises.) Over and over, for tens of thousands of years, we have been drawn to the confounding, "unsolvable"
images that artists create, because our brains relish the prediction er-
rors these artworks offer up. "A stimulus has to play hard to get before

it can be pleasing," writes Wagemans, summarizing years of brain research. The glitch that art introduces our brains to is a gift, one that
may nudge us to adjust our filters of expectation—with, the paper
states, "possible existential ramifications."

"EXISTENTIAL RAMIFICATIONS"—those were the perfect
words to describe Julie's effect on me, I thought as I read Wagemans's
study.

At first I thought the changes were confined to how I interacted
with art. At a museum, I got hypnotized by an abstract painting by
Joan Mitchell and lost myself imagining how she'd created her shivery
constellation of blue and brown drips. Mandy AllFIRE looked different too. I'd continued following her butt's adventures around the
tristate area, and I'd gotten even more intrigued by Amanda's work
after listening to Julie celebrate the benefits of giving your tastes a
workout. *Why couldn't ass influencers' butt portraits be art?* I found
myself wondering, *again*, as I stared at the mousetrap Julie displayed on her studio shelf. My time with Julie had convinced me that
Amanda's work needed to be seen. Who knows, maybe I could help—
possibly even organize a show, like Julie was doing for her former studio assistant.

But Julie's effect on me went way beyond art. She was constantly
plucking things from the backdrop of life and making me take a closer
look at them. Inspiration for her painting of the woman riding the motorcycle had come to her while she was walking home one night and
passed a parked motorcycle. "And I just had that vision. It doesn't
make much sense, but it's like, '*Yes!* I'm going to paint that.'" I didn't

see anything in a parked motorcycle except . . . a parked motorcycle. But to Julie—"I just felt like it was such a beautiful object. *Very* sexy." Or take the cavernous marble lobbies in Brooklyn's gleaming new high-rises: "To me they're very unpleasant and depressing. But I think they'd make great paintings."

One morning, Julie came in and announced that the most important thing on my to-do list was researching the Newtown Creek Wastewater Treatment Plant in Greenpoint, Brooklyn.

I'd seen the wastewater plant from the safe, scentless distance of the road, and while I truly appreciated its honorable service on behalf of the city's bowels, it wouldn't have made my list of beloved New York landmarks. Julie apparently felt otherwise. My friends have introduced their firstborns with less enthusiasm than Julie had for the sewage plant. "I just love everything about it, conceptually," she gushed, stepping back from her painting, to look at me, her eyes wide, her brush dancing slightly in the air. "Isn't it a surreal building? . . . It looks like eggs or breasts. It's a very feminine kind of architecture. . . It's a bit utopian, almost. . . I want to visit it. Have you ever visited it?" I got the sense I'd be welcome in her studio for the rest of my life if the answer was yes. She was thinking of including it in a painting, or maybe a whole series of paintings, and wanted me to email the sewage plant to see if she could schedule a tour. "I want to just *see* it closer. And if I'm going to represent it—yeah, I want to know a little more about it." I pulled up the treatment plant's website, and Julie wandered over to stare at it over my shoulder, unable to resist even a photo of the magnificent poop processor. "It's like *such* a beautiful thing—and it treats sewage!"

Like "sexy" and "halitosis," I never expected to hear "beautiful" and "sewage" in the same sentence. But I obediently followed Julie's instructions to email the plant and request a visit, then compiled a long list of bullet points on wastewater purification for Julie's reading pleasure. For example: The Newtown Creek Wastewater Treatment Plant serves about one million rectums and ingests about 170 million gallons of waste daily. The silver breasts that Julie admired, which process sewage sludge into fertilizer, are officially called digester eggs. Unofficially, they're called "shit tits." To my knowledge, only Julie Curtiss calls them "beautiful."

Without fully realizing what I was doing, I began to seek out the shit tits on the skyline. At night, descending into the Midtown Tunnel, I turned in my seat to stare at their iridescent orbs, glowing like alien eggs about to hatch. During the day, I gawked at the way they shimmered beside the flat expanse of brick rectangles behind them. I wanted to know everything about them. I kept refreshing Julie's inbox to see if we'd heard back. I talked my husband's ear off about them. I pitched my editor a story about sewage.

I began to realize that beauty had come to mean something different, more expansive, since I'd begun working with Julie. Her painting of the three feet on the bathroom floor was beautiful. So was her painting of the woman flashing her hairy undercarriage. They weren't beautiful in the way that Erin O'Keefe's photos were beautiful. They certainly weren't beautiful in any way I'd have recognized before. Julie's pieces were beautiful in the way they caught your eye, drew you toward them, and made you want to be in their presence—then stare, probe, pry, and bask in their company.

Beauty, I now understood, pulls you close. Rejecting beauty, which so many Heads had told me to do, suddenly seemed depressingly nihilistic. Julie had made me see that embracing beauty was nothing if not a vote for life—an act of optimism, an excited *Hell yes!* to whatever the world would bring. Beauty, wrote Stendhal, is "only the promise of happiness." Beauty isn't guaranteed to do right by you or stick around. But it will draw you deeper into our existence. I saw it now when I scanned the skyline and felt my eyes drawn toward them: The shit tits are beautiful.

CHAPTER SEVENTEEN

Outside, the world was a mess—new pieces of Julie's kept going to auction, the trolls were getting louder—but at least in the studio, we'd settled into a nice groove. Then Julie ran into Jack.

A few days after Julie's effusive lecture about Ingres, I arrived at the studio and was peeling off my coat to get to work when Julie mentioned that she'd bumped into Jack at an opening the night before.

"How's he doing?" I said with deliberate nonchalance. Inside, my heart skipped a beat. Jack wouldn't badmouth me to Julie—would he? We were all grown-ups. I'd just been paranoid before. I had nothing to worry about.

But clearly, I did. Julie being Julie, she didn't want to gossip, but she conceded that I'd come up in conversation. As the morning went on, her glum mood and monosyllabic answers made it clear she hadn't heard good things.

I went about my tasks with silent, anxious efficiency, instantly reverting to the insecure me I'd been at Jack's gallery. Deep down, I'd been expecting something like this. But my lack of surprise didn't stop me from panicking that Jack's words would torpedo my relationship with Julie. Hoping to get a better handle on the situation, I reached out to a few people who knew both me and Jack. The text messages people showed me confirmed Jack had been airing his doubts about me.

What he was saying was nothing, though, compared to the abuse being hurled Julie's way on Instagram. The trolls, never pleasant to begin with, had gotten louder, crueler, cruder as more of Julie's art trickled into auctions, and they'd crawled out to declare her overhyped and undeserving, albeit rarely with enough conviction to include their real names. One anonymous account sneered that Julie's gallery had turned "shit into gold" and credited her success to her tenure working with KAWS, implying she'd gotten to know KAWS's "Balenciaga/Off-White wearing dealers," his "cosmetic empire collector fanboys," and his "rich Asian ramen empire." (This same account reserved rare words of praise for none other than Jack Barrett Gallery, run by "one of the most hard-working and diligent young gallerists in New York.")

There was an unapologetic snobbery to the trolling, not to mention a strong whiff of misogyny and racism. So Julie couldn't be talented in her own right? Her success had to be due to a man's? The trolls sneered at "dumb rich/middle-class newbie collectors," and with their blustering about "ramen delivery bosses" in the "wild East," seemed to reserve extra scorn for collectors in Asia. Even *The New Yorker* joined in on that one. The magazine's review of KAWS's show at the Brooklyn Museum, which sold out of tickets for weeks on end, argued that KAWS's success was emblematic of a "cheeky, infectious dumbing-down of taste." And precisely who was dumbing down taste? *The New Yorker*'s critic offered his diagnosis in the very next sentence: "KAWS has an immense following in East Asia." If puritanism, as it has been said, is the haunting fear that someone, somewhere may be happy, art criticism seemed to have evolved into the haunting fear that someone, somewhere, was enjoying something they shouldn't.

A couple weeks later, Julie and I were rumbling along the subway to get to a talk she'd be giving at the New York Studio School when she braved opening Instagram to show me the other painters who'd be on the panel with her. Her face sagged into a defeated frown as she realized she was the only one who hadn't posted about the night's talk. She alluded to a "super horrible meme" someone posted a few days before. "That's why I've been like, 'ARGH! Got to protect—got to just not put myself out there as much.'" She slouched in her seat and wrapped her arms across her chest defensively. "I shouldn't care as much. But sometimes, it's just, you know..." She trailed off, seemingly willing herself not to care. "It's like bullying. I was bullied a bit in junior high school. It's familiar."

The bullies on Instagram espoused a view of the art world I recognized all too well from my time at galleries: that contemporary art is a zero-sum game, where opportunities are finite because attention is finite because the audience for art is finite. (And if anything, should be smaller—kick out the Schmos, who are only dumbing down culture, anyhow.) If figuration was in, then abstraction was out. If one artist was succeeding, then another must be failing. Julie treated art as an ever-expanding universe, and in a perverse way, it almost seemed like she was being punished for it. "I don't like my work to be only speaking with a few people," she'd told me once. "I want it to be speaking to anybody, even when people don't have any cultural references."

One afternoon, my to-do list included photographing a painting of Julie's and sending it to a reporter at *Vogue* who was working on a story. The painting depicted a naked woman with dark hair curled up in a human-sized birdhouse. She wore earplugs and a blindfold, and had her arms crossed defensively over her bare breasts. I snapped a photo of the piece and started to draft an email to the *Vogue* writer. But I paused at the painting's title. Which was...?

"*Self-Portrait in Autarky*," Julie called from across the room. She turned to consider her piece. "I thought there was something really, like, self-portrait about it. Like, me. Right now." Julie's gaze lingered on the masked, huddled figure. "Sometimes I want to hide."

Soon thereafter, Julie emailed me to say nicely but in no uncertain terms that she wanted me out. She needed the studio back to herself. "I am realizing now that I need to carve some time alone in the studio, to re-center and reflect. When I say I need it, I mean I am craving it," she wrote. "There has been more press and public attention than I am used to."

I was crushed, but not shocked. The worse the trolling got, the braver I saw Julie was for letting me into her studio for months on end with a tape recorder running. Already one of the trolls had posted screenshots of Julie's quotes from the *Artnet* article mocking what she'd said, and it freaked me out to think one day that might happen with something I'd written. I sensed she was retreating to her fortress of solitude to look after her art, and I completely understood. I admired her, and I took pride in having been useful around the studio. "I'm definitely going to need another Bianca," Julie told me before my last day.

At the same time, there was a less magnanimous thought floating around my head: Namely, *screw those jerks*. The jeering from the cheap seats reinforced the idea, which seemed to pervade the art world, that it was safer to be against something than to be for it. But Julie wasn't like that. She wasn't jaded and cynical and over it.

There is an image of Julie that has inserted itself into my head. It was from an evening earlier that winter. Julie had invited me to an opening at Anton Kern, and we took the subway over together, then circled the show before heading out to the after-party—dinner at a Brazilian restaurant, which I assumed would be the highlight of my evening, given how few after-parties I'd been to.

But it's our walk to the restaurant that sticks out in my mind. We headed west across Manhattan toward Times Square—past the limestone facades of fancy hotels, past various nondescript apartment buildings I'd seen enough times to ignore, past some scaffolding. It was Midtown. It was blah. We passed MoMA's gleaming shell and took a left to head downtown when Julie jerked backward like she'd smacked her forehead into a pane of glass: "*WOW.*"

Julie stopped dead center in the crosswalk and stared straight ahead. "I like this," she murmured, a sly smile spreading across her face.

I followed her gaze across the street to a grid of high-rises bathed in the green glow of traffic lights. A wall of office buildings reared up in front of us, their windows locked together to form a continuous expanse of black-and-gray rectangles that blotted out the sky, as if giant sheets of graph paper had declared war on the city.

"In-saaaaaaaannnnnnneeeeeeeeee," Julie marveled, grinning up at the buildings. "This. Is. *Crazy.*"

We had another ten blocks to go, and as we turned onto Seventh Avenue and into the video-game mania of Times Square, Julie suddenly picked up the pace. A solid column of steam chugged out of a manhole, and a thick, soupy fog had settled over the flashing billboards, blurring them to flashes of red and blue. "I want to walk to that!" Julie said, pointing toward the manhole, and I doubled my stride to keep up with her. I hadn't seen her nearly this excited in the gallery.

We were on one of the most iconic streets in the world, except we weren't any longer: We were caught in a misty, mysterious haze, in a swirl of pulsing, disembodied color. It was as if the city had thrown on a costume to put on a show, just for us, just in this moment.

I'll just come right out and say it: Being around Julie was like being on drugs. I thought of her when I read Aldous Huxley's ecstatic description of tripping on peyote. The details that make it through the "reducing valve" of our sober brains are only a "measly trickle" of consciousness, Huxley argued. But on drugs: Have you ever really looked at pants, man? "The folds of my gray flannel trousers were charged with 'is-ness,'" wrote Huxley, who got mystical meditating on the "allness and infinity of folded cloth."

Forget the hard stuff, Huxley. Try art. Following Julie's lead, I'd started viewing the everyday the way I looked at art—with an extra beat, with an inquisitive eye, with a willingness to linger on form and ask *why*. I'd gone into her studio hoping to see art differently. Bit by bit, I saw everything differently. Have you contemplated the forlorn beauty of a stripped-down storefront glowing white on a dark street? Or watched tarps draped on construction sites shiver with the wind? Like nibbling on a magic mushroom, turning an art eye on reality makes you feel as if the world is performing just for you.

Art knocks us off our well-worn pathways. Other things can do that, too, but art, to Wagemans's point, is arguably designed specifically for that purpose. The writer and neuroscientist Erik Hoel hypothesizes that art, whether it's *Anna Karenina* or *Alien* or *Starry Night*, keeps our brains nimble. Hoel argues that humans evolved the ability to dream as a way to prevent our brains from overfitting our perceptual model of the world so they don't fritz out when we come across something we've never seen before. We can't flap our arms and fly, but dreams suggest we shouldn't rule it out. Works of art, Hoel contends, are artificial dreams that serve the same function: "Just like dreams, fictions and art keep us from overfitting our perception, models, and understanding of the world." There's a reason why gallerists joke that every press release is a variation on "makes the familiar unfamiliar," or vice versa. We assume so much is fixed. Art reminds us that's an illusion. The way things are is not the way they have to be, and art helps us yank off our filters of expectation. I understood now what Julie had said about going to see art: She went to galleries and museums "when I need to clean my eyes."

Our brains evolved into engines for compressing reality and turning it into a trickle. We had to conserve our mental energy so we could spot the predator jumping out of the bushes to eat us. But what happens when we evolve beyond being prey? I'd come to think our brains needed help transforming from trash compactors into microscopes, and that's where art comes in: a way to fight our instincts to truncate and elide, and, in so doing, to notice more, appreciate more, empathize more. Which is all to say, to experience more. If our lives are the set of experiences that we collect, then art can enable us to literally live more in the same amount of time by uncompressing those experiences. Art is practice for appreciating life, but also practice for creating a life worth appreciating.

Each of us creates our own realities, so we might as well do so purposefully. I felt as if I was starting to become more like Julie, someone who took charge in questioning and shaping my hallucinated reality.

I wondered if I could help other people do it too.

Part IV

The Vacuum

CHAPTER EIGHTEEN

As one of the Guggenheim Museum's new security guards, my job was to protect the people, the art, and the tiny film of dust on some furniture by Ramp 5. Ramp 5 was a locked post, which meant we couldn't stray more than a few feet from Joseph Beuys's *Virgin*—an artwork consisting of a lightbulb dangling over a wooden table and chair covered with the aforementioned layer of dust. We needed to be ready to hurl ourselves between the dust and outstretched hands: The curators consider the dust a key part of the art, and it wasn't to be disturbed.

These and other instructions were imparted during day one of training. The Guggenheim's other new guards and I met in the security office off Ramp 2—a windowless room wallpapered with video feeds of exits, elevators, and visitors' bald spots. From there we trailed one of our numerous supervisors around the museum as he recited all the things that could go wrong. Slips, trips, spills, falls, fires, bombs, touches, thefts, bulky backpacks—all of which were now in our

purview. This being the art world, our supervisor offered posh synonyms that made "emergency" sound refined. A fire should be radioed
in as a "smoke situation." Better to call barf a "biological incident."
Bathrooms were not low on toilet paper but "paper products," *please*,
and there were no bombs, only "suspicious packages."

If anyone bothered the dust, I'd need to grab my walkie-talkie
("Supervisor, pick up"), wait for a supervisor to say "Go ahead," then
say, "Incident report, Ramp 5," which would trigger a whole series of
events, including someone sending a report on the dust disruption to, I
don't know, say, thirty people at the museum, and a registrar filing
paperwork noting the layer of dust had been perturbed. A conservator
might be dispatched to Ramp 5 with a little blower to rearrange the
remaining particles and mask the disturbance. The whispered word
among the guards was that an unattended four-year-old had recently
run up and sat on Beuys's dusty chair, which some guards would really
like to be able to sit on themselves, only the Guggenheim required us
to stand on pretty much every post. One exception was the entrance to
the café, where we were to remind visitors that they couldn't eat or
drink in the galleries, then gesture invitingly at a trash can.

A different supervisor, who took over day two of training, rattled
off more occasions when we'd be called on to save the day: riots, strikes,
floods, protests, explosions, natural disasters, medical emergencies,
hazardous-material screwups, and bioterrorism. Not everyone was up
to the job. "One girl, I think she wanted to quit the same day," he said,
eyeing us to see if anyone might run screaming out of the room.

We wouldn't be armed. We couldn't touch visitors or arrest them.
We couldn't kill people, the supervisor reminded. We couldn't eat,
drink, lean, write, draw, check our phones, or chat with other guards
during our shifts. We should stand in each gallery so we could see

what's going on, and we should appear alert. "If you look like you're zoning out, they're going to think it's okay to touch a painting." He snapped his fingers: *That's* how long it takes for someone to touch a painting. We should expect to work every Saturday, because Saturdays are nuts—the sort of days that made older guards look down at the floor and shake their heads. We should be licensed security guards with the state of New York and able to stand for hours on end. Most importantly, we should be prepared to be extremely, mind-numbingly, skin-crawlingly, sanity-endangeringly bored. "You're going to be staring into space for hours. Just a body standing, waiting for someone to talk to," our supervisor warned us on our next-to-last day of training. "You'll be in the vacuum. You have to embrace it."

I COULDN'T HAVE BEEN more excited to begin. I'd applied to be a gallery guide because the job description made it out to be a chatty security guard: I'd need to tell people that flash photography wasn't permitted, but I was also expected to make conversation about the art and invite people to share their questions. There were tourists out there in the vacuum, plus snotty third graders and antsy teenagers and boyfriends who'd been dragged to the museum. I loved the idea that I'd get to discuss paintings with members of the general public who, like me, might have spent a lot of time wandering through exhibitions feeling befuddled. I wanted to see if I could be a warm welcome to the art world for, among others, the individuals the Heads referred to as "Schmos," and I was curious what I might learn from watching thousands of strangers engage with art.

On top of which, I'd become fascinated by museums. Jack, Elizabeth, and Julie were different in so many ways, but each of them said "museum" like it was a prayer, and each jockeyed to get their art in these institutions' hallowed halls. I never saw Jack friendlier than when he was chatting with curators, Elizabeth had me spend a week sleuthing out curators' email addresses so she could pitch them on her shows, and Julie's gallery had lined her up a studio visit with a MoMA trustee. I'd only ever known museums as a ticketed visitor—never as someone who badged in and out of locked doors—and I thrilled at the prospect of being on the inside of what was widely considered the uppermost echelon and desired endpoint of the world I'd thrust myself into. I also wondered how being around art for hours each day, with no ability to escape, would affect me. Julie had showed me that making art helped you read it differently than other people did, but I'd heard being a museum security guard could do that too. Guards spent more time staring at art than basically anyone. More than collectors. "More than the curators. More than anybody," said Armando Garcia, who patrolled galleries at the Whitney. "You notice things that even the curators haven't." Bonding with an artwork for hours, even months, at a time— what's lately been called "slow looking"—was supposed to change you. One of Julie's art-school assignments had been to draw the same Peter Paul Rubens painting every week for a semester, and the psychologist Rebecca Chamberlain, who'd led a slow-looking tour at the Tate Modern the spring before we met in Belgium, reported that after a mere five minutes with a piece, "visitors report really strange things happening." "I really thought I understood art and how to look at it," Armando told me. "Here, I'm realizing that it's duration that gives you a fuller understanding of art." But *how* exactly?

I showed up for my first day on the ramps, smushed myself into the employee bathroom between women tucking in their shirts, then

followed the parade of guards to the morning huddle. The Guggenheim needed around thirty of us to open its doors, and we all formed a
semicircle in the museum's lobby, the mood relaxed and the joints stiff.
The average age was around fifty, pulled up by some elder statesmen in
the security team who'd been around long enough to perfect the art of
dozing standing up, with an equal split of men and women and sizable
portion of people born overseas. The head supervisor led with the
day's announcements: Saint David's second graders were coming in for
a field trip, the public tour topic for the day was something I didn't
catch, and the museum was closing early, so we'd need to "be extra kind
during the sweep"—guardspeak for when, at closing time, we'd start
marching downstairs from the top floor of the museum and continue
till we'd herded out the last stragglers. Our supervisor also wanted at
least one person each morning to share an idea for how to make visitors' experiences better, and he waited for one of us to volunteer. I'd
joined the guard profession at a moment when museums were making
a concerted effort to improve their customer service. This involved
trying to ditch the stereotype of guards as humorless scolds (hence my
mandate to chat with visitors) and replacing our militaristic uniforms
for chiller outfits. ("Suited and booted" for us gallery guides just meant
wearing all black.) A guard who'd been singing old Russian songs in
the locker room raised her hand: She said she liked telling visitors that
the Marc Chagall portrait of a soldier in Monitor 2 had one blue eye
and one green eye. Another guard, who'd been at the Guggenheim
since before the rise of disco, suggested the museum should always
show a Van Gogh, and everyone laughed knowingly. "People come and
always ask for the Van Gogh," he said.

My journey into the vacuum began on Ramp 6, near the top of
the museum, just under its huge domed skylight. Our schedule: forty

minutes per post, nine posts a day, breaks every two hours. For the first moments on post, I stared down at the tiny humans scurrying inside with a feeling of benevolent generosity, like I was welcoming them into my palatial home. The magnanimous mood didn't last. Forty minutes, it turns out, is forever. I checked my watch. It'd been five minutes. I vowed to let at least five minutes pass before checking it again. I peeked down: It'd been three minutes. I stretched my head left, then right, then left again. Thirty seconds.

By the third post, I was so bored that I prayed someone would touch the art. *Do it*, I urged silently from my spot by the wall. *Do it so I can tell you not to.* I fantasized about visitors trying to take a sip of water so I could dash over and stop them. I counted security cameras. I radioed the supervisors to alert them to a stray leaf in Tower 2—not exactly a suspicious package, but I needed *something* to interrupt the tedium.

The more experienced guards tossed out snippets of advice as we passed each other on the ramps. Always report everything, because the video cameras will tattle if you don't. Be sure to share your side of the story before a visitor squeals to a supervisor. Memorize titles and painters' names, because people are constantly requesting specific works. (On cue, a young woman in a silk blouse approached me and another guard to ask whether we knew where to find the portrait of Karl Marx and we both froze—Ramp 4, I discovered later.) Everyone— *everyone*—is a Toucher, my colleagues warned. "They're enthralled with whatever they're looking at, so they want to get close to it. They want to sniff it," cautioned one longtime guard. Oh, and get ready for your body to scream bloody murder. The architect Frank Lloyd Wright designed the Guggenheim to be a "temple of spirit," but his ramps, which wind up the museum in an ascending spiral, have a slight incline that makes his building a butcher of bodies. "The slant is very bad," counseled the guard who'd volunteered the idea about Van Gogh. "Your body realigns." Boredom is just phase one, veteran guards assured me. But you push past it. "After the first week on the ramp, I was like, 'No *way* can I do this,'" one guard confessed. She'd been at the Guggenheim for five years.

I tried to focus on getting to know my new home. From the outside, the Guggenheim—"Gugg" to the guards (pronounced *goog*)—looks like a swirl of vanilla soft serve plopped on a plate. From the inside, it feels like the world's most transcendent parking-garage exit ramp. A few of the galleries are white cubes, but mostly the art swirls up the building along the ramps' outer walls, which are curved, lean back slightly, and require elaborate wood prostheses to hold up the paintings, which are purposefully hung at a slight angle on account of the slant. I liked the ramps: I could look out across the open expanse of the rotunda and watch a man in a suit two floors away dig a wedgie out of his butt, and the skylight bathed the ramps in daylight that shifted moodily, so the white walls glowered one hour and beamed the next. (Wright thought art should be viewed in natural light: "Isn't a picture [like sculpture and like a building] a circumstance in nature; sharing light and dark—warm and cold—changing with every subtle change: seen now in one light; now in another?") There were three shows up at that moment: an exhibit of the greatest hits from the Guggenheim's permanent collection (your Picassos, Monets); a photo show about Robert Mapplethorpe featuring a cornucopia of bare chests; and—in the place of honor in the rotunda—the show *Artistic License*, which was really six minishows curated by six artists who'd picked artworks from the museum's permanent collection that usually sat in storage.

There were almost four hundred works on view, ranging from a

postcard-sized painting of a sailboat to a photographic study of an artist tucking his penis between his legs, and it seemed impossible I'd
ever be able to keep tabs on so much art. The Guggenheim had a reputation for pulling ambitious stunts like dangling nine white Chevys
from its skylight, and in the current shows, there was lots of fuck-you
art to go around. Ramp 4, for instance, had a Richard Serra sculpture,
Tearing Lead, which consisted of a wrinkled rectangle of lead surrounded by four piles of squiggly lead strips. It got confused for trash
so often that Ramp 4 came with a Touch Tally—a clipboard with a
photo of the sculpture and the very *Law & Order: SVU*-ish instructions to "Please indicate where the piece was touched with an X." "This
is *art*?" asked a middle-aged woman incredulously, her eyes bugging at
the Serra. "If this is art, I need to rethink my whole life." Boy, did I
know *that* feeling.

Visitors got nice and chatty around the museum's fuck-you pieces,
which not only broke up the monotony on post but solidified my conviction that I wanted to help get Amanda a show. It was exciting to
witness an object trip the circuit breaker in peoples' minds, and if
a pile of lead strips by a world-famous artist could do that, I couldn't
wait to see their reaction to AllFIRE. It had been months since Amanda's last show, the one where she sat on me, and she didn't have another lined up. She sensed her work was too sexual, too objectifying,
too ambiguous for her colleagues to touch. "I think women always
have a hard time with my work, and then I think if a male gallery
owner or whatever would want to show my work, maybe they would
get shit for it," she told me, during one of our coffee dates. "If a male
artist was doing what I'm doing—like showing off his body, his package or whatever, in whatever way that a man could do it—maybe people would be more accepting in a way. Cause I feel like the female body

right now is still very much taboo and censored. And I feel like in the MeToo era, everyone's just being very cautious." Everyone but me, that is—and I can't underemphasize how out of character that was. I get nauseous just thinking about conflict, and yet some mysterious well-spring of courage had convinced me that what I absolutely had to do, consequences be damned, was get an ass influencer an art show, even though most people I consulted weren't sold on the fact that Amanda's work deserved to be called "art." I was all-in on Julie's philosophy that new cultural experiences are good for the soul, and I convinced Amanda we should apply to the Spring/Break art fair. We sketched out a booth: It'd look like a sleazy nightclub, complete with velvet ropes, and would include framed portraits of AllFIRE's ass as well as two cast sculptures of her butt and a performance by AllFIRE doing a meet and greet with fans. I tried to work on our application during my forty-minute breaks.

Forty minutes, I quickly learned, is an eternity on the ramps but barely enough time to sprint downstairs, through the basement's hall-ways, and over to my locker to get lunch, heat lunch, eat lunch, pee, and stare blankly at my phone for a few moments. Our break room was an underground chamber with several microwaves and zero art. "My room-mate left me at a bad time. So now I'm stuck with this half of the rent. It just... comes at a bad time," I overheard one of my colleagues say at the table next to mine. Lots of the gallery guides, who skewed whiter and younger than the straight-up security guards, identified as "dormant artists" and joked conspiratorially about fighting class oppression by sneezing on rich peoples' coats in coat check. The other security guards— subcontractors employed by an outside company—hailed from Haiti, Ghana, India, Belarus, and the United Arab Emirates and had prior ex-perience as photographers, painters, musicians, engineers, and bankers.

They'd have to work about two hours to pay for one full-price ticket to the museum and didn't flinch at sixty-hour workweeks. A few had second jobs guarding other places. A cheery guard from Trinidad and Tobago told me she worked at a branch of the public library in the Bronx where she'd had to barge in on a blow job and carried naloxone in case of an overdose. "It's nice here," she told me.

On the ramps, my attention kept shifting between the art and the visitors. It was fascinating to study how such a wide variety of strangers approached the works. Besides Touchers, there were Breathers: visitors who got so close to paintings, they exhaled on them. (Good rule of thumb: Give art the same personal space you'd give a human stranger, a courtesy also worth extending to guards.) Completers, who paused dutifully in front of every work like a politician working a room, were rare, while Grazers—who bypassed many works to linger in front of others—were extremely common. Flirters glanced slyly at the work from a safe distance, as if scared of being too forward. Readers searched anxiously for the wall labels mounted beside a piece, then studied the artist's name and moved on with only a passing glance at the art. Encyclopediacs joylessly photographed every piece as though preparing to file an insurance claim, Wrighters came for the architecture, and Hunters, many of whom had *Time Out New York*'s guide to the "five best paintings at the Guggenheim" up on their phones, came frantically searching for a specific famous Picasso.

Totally normal behavior starts to look pretty bizarre out there in the vacuum. When you think about it—and I had nothing *but* time to think about it—it's weird that practically everyone behaves the exact same way around art, no? Sure, there are superficial differences between your Touchers and Grazers, but with each new shift, I found it

increasingly striking that visitors adopted the same stock mannerisms when they cruised through a museum. How did everyone know to
keep their voices low, faces expressionless, and arms clasped at their
crotches? To hush their children for raising their voices? Had I missed
out on some Emily Post guide to art-museum etiquette?

During my shifts in the Guggenheim's library, a little room off
Ramp 2 where we were allowed to read on post, I started to chip away
at the answer. When America's first museums started opening in the
late 1700s, they aimed to attract as wide an audience as possible by
showing off as many strange marvels as they could pack under one
roof. A day touring Peale's Museum in Philadelphia, which opened in
1786, could involve seeing oil paintings but also shells, plants, stuffed
birds, mounted insects, mastodon bones, a perpetual-motion machine, and a cow with five legs nursing a calf with two heads. The
whole idea of "highbrow" and "lowbrow" culture had yet to be invented
(remember "fine art" was in its infancy then, too), and museum collections featured a "wilderness of wonders," as P. T. Barnum described
the museum he took over in 1841 (and aggressively promoted by deliberately hiring the worst band he could find to play outside—in order to
attract customers with the promise of free music, then drive them inside his museum to escape its din). After the Civil War, America's elite
grew competitive with Europeans, who had been busy setting up
grand new art institutions like the Louvre, and the United States threw
itself into a museum-building spree. Gradually, museums like Peale's
and Barnum's were elbowed aside by fine-arts institutions like the Met
and the Museum of Fine Arts in Boston—which went from picky to
pickier about the treasures they'd show. Bit by bit, their collections of
photographs, curiosities, chromolithography prints, mechanical models,

and plaster reproductions of famous sculptures got shoved into storage to make way for what one director of the Museum of Fine Arts called "higher things."

Back then, America's art museums were run by the same kind of people who run them now—rich, educated, influential—and they did *not* like where they saw the country headed. Urban elites were wealthy but insecure—in Boston, they'd lost their grip over local politics in the years following the Civil War—and as immigrants and others flooded into cities during the Industrial Revolution, the upper and middle classes were appalled by what they witnessed on their jaunts around town: riots, drunkenness, theft, poverty, and disease, plus howling Irish widows, the vulgar nouveau riche, and the general tastelessness of the "unwashed Democracy," as one New York lawyer wrote in his diary in 1857. Something had to be done to civilize the masses, and art was a promising cure. After all, intellectuals had been touting art as a colonic for the soul since the 1700s—a moral and spiritual remedy that could deliver religious-type salvation through the thoughtful contemplation of lovely paintings. Urbanites, from art critics to Methodist ministers, rallied around art as an antidote to the country's mayhem. In theory, the people who ran the art museums were all for it. In practice, they really didn't want to let *that* sort of person in. Patrons of Boston's Museum of Fine Arts complained about "loquacious Italians" and families that trekked to the museum with picnics and babies, and the Met fought for twenty years to keep the museum closed on Sundays—the one day of the week the so-called working millions could conveniently come. When the Met finally *did* open on a Sunday, in 1891, it battened down the hatches as if it were bracing for a hurricane: There were eighteen guards instead of the typical eleven, and paintings were quickly covered in glass like windows boarded up before a storm. Even then, its president was scandalized to witness so many Touchers who, he told his board, displayed "peculiar habits which were repulsive and unclean." In response, every employee, including the museum's director, began descending on the museum each Sunday to enforce what they deemed proper etiquette. Like that of gallery guides, their role was to "answer questions, keep order, and protect the collections." (Similar efforts were already underway in Europe, where museums had served as indoor public parks where families gathered to escape the winter's cold. In 1832, *The Penny Magazine of the Society for the Diffusion of Useful Knowledge* published a how-to guide to museums that instructed the "working man" to wear clean clothes, touch nothing, keep quiet, and not be obtrusive, which meant refraining from asking questions.) By 1897, the Met congratulated itself on having instilled "respectable" and "intelligent" behavior among the unwashed Democracy: "You do not see any more persons in the picture galleries blowing their nose with their fingers, no more dogs brought into the museum openly or concealed in baskets . . . no more spitting tobacco juice on the gallery floors . . . no more nurses taking children to some corner to defile the Museum . . . no more whistling, singing or calling aloud to people from one gallery to another."

Dodging snot rockets while trying to enjoy the Mapplethorpe photos in Tower 4 doesn't sound like my dream day either, but something was also lost, I was beginning to realize, when we stopped letting people holler in galleries. We lost our voice as an audience. Policing visitors' behavior turned viewers into "mute receptors" who were expected to passively accept the culture handed down to them from on high and enjoy whatever the intelligentsia told them to, argues historian Lawrence Levine in *Highbrow/Lowbrow.* Levine chronicles how symphonies and theaters joined art museums in enforcing new rules of decorum

that turned art into "a one-way process" and taught Americans to de-
fer to the experts. (Apparently a night at the orchestra in the 1800s
was like going to a football game today: The crowd cut across class
lines, cheered for the songs they wanted to hear, booed the ones they
hated, and would demand instant replays of their favorite moments.)
By narrowing their definition of *fine art* and forcing visitors to adopt
quiet whispers, museums reinforced the idea that there was "low" culture and "high" culture and that high culture belonged in hushed temples where it was safe from the public's grubby mannerisms. This
hierarchy of tastes, which to this day puts Beuys's *Virgin* at the top and
my beloved *Ren & Stimpy Show* at the bottom, was and still is decided
by the tiny group of VIPs who manage these arts institutions. And
what a perk that is: Getting to make what I'd learned were rather arbitrary decisions about which objects are sacrosanct (and how to behave
around them) gives white-collar aesthetes a shared culture they can
use to recognize each other and exclude Schmos. So argues the sociologist Paul DiMaggio in a paper on the rise of Boston's Museum of Fine
Arts: "The creation of a network of private institutions that could define and monopolize high art was an essential part of this process of
building cultural boundaries," writes DiMaggio, noting that the ambiguity about what counts as "high" art is essential to the "ideology of
connoisseurship." The sociologist Pierre Bourdieu, in his typical downer
fashion, contends that museums are *still* guilty of "false generosity":
Though they're *technically* open to all, the "tiniest details" of their
structure and form "betray their true function, which is to reinforce
for some the feeling of belonging and for others the feeling of exclusion," he writes. (A study by the National Endowment for the Arts
found that individuals who consider themselves "upper class" are sig-
nificantly more likely to attend art exhibits than are those who self-

identify as "working class.") I couldn't help but notice that—except for
one night per week when it closed at 8:00 p.m.—the Guggenheim shut
its doors each evening at 6:00 p.m., just as the working millions got off
work.

YOU FIGURED OUT your favorite posts quickly. "I love coat check.
Coat check forever," gushed one guard. Coat check was fast-paced and
could pay more. (A coat-check horror story in twelve words: "I was
here by myself on Labor Day and it was raining.") Directions—at the
base of the ramps, just inside the front door—was beloved by bossy
guards, who got to bark "Tickets, please" and refuse non-ticket-holders
access to bathrooms. A few guards talked wistfully about Ramp 2. It
was carpeted, so more comfortable to stand on.

My favorite post kept changing. One week it was Tower 5, where I
got to watch a curator in high heels command a herd of art handlers,
who slowly, slooooowly—"Whoa! Move it back in!"—eased art out of
sarcophagal wooden crates. I relished getting to watch the grown-up
version of the install process I'd done with Jack, and the little snippets
of conversation I overheard put the final daggers in my fantasy that
the art displayed in museums meets any objective definition of "best."
The registrars and conservators bustling around the gallery kept whispering that that painting over *there* had only been included in the show
because the museum's director insisted it had to go in—"forced" was
the word used. The director himself strolled in one afternoon, while I
was alone in the gallery. "Oh, they've hung some pictures," he said non-
chalantly.

For a time, my favorite posts were the ones that offered me glimpses of the behind-the-scenes life of the museum. In Monitor 2, I got to watch a conservator, magnifying glass protruding from his head like a cricket's antenna, fuss over the heavy wood frame around Picasso's *Woman Ironing*—a very conservative, traditional frame that the work's original owner had picked to give the then-weird Picasso some credibility, I overheard a docent say. On Ramp 2, I chatted covertly with a guy from "ExCon" (Exhibitions Construction) while he touched up the Gugg's white walls. "Every museum has its own white. They *want* their own white," he told me. The Guggenheim's white was Benjamin Moore's "Dove Wing," which is beiger than is MoMA's Janovic-brand "Super White." Some part of the museum was always getting repainted, and yet in most galleries, you could find a shadow of black scuffs somewhere on the wall about four feet up from the floor—a smear of darkness from where the guards, in dark suit jackets, liked to lean. Conservators were especially a delight to be around because they had a nose for disaster. This sculpture broke its head off when someone climbed on it; that sculpture was supposed to be clear, but the plastic had yellowed over the years; and this painting took a foot to the face—the outline of an art handler's shoe was clearly visible if you looked at it from the side, said a Gugg staffer as he and a gaggle of conservators unpacked paintings for a new show.

And then, more than a month into my guarding, I picked up the day's schedule and found myself giving an inward hoot of glee because Tower 2 was on my rotation, and Tower 2 had the Constantin Brancusi, which made it my favorite post.

Never mind the sculpture's title. I don't want to tell it to you because it'll instantly change how you see the piece, and besides, artworks didn't start regularly getting titles until the eighteenth century. I'll describe the piece: There's a circular pedestal, knee-high, made out of a limestone the warm beige of a sandy beach at sunset. On the pedestal, one end resting on the limestone and the other rising gently toward the ceiling, is a swoop of the softest white marble you've ever seen—marble so irresistibly smooth and round you want to bite it, like a new eraser, or stroke it, like a breast. The piece isn't obviously representative of any one thing, but the way its graceful white body flumps on the pedestal and then sweeps up toward the sky brings to mind a squirt of toothpaste getting squeezed out of a tube.

My first impression of the sculpture hadn't been great. I'd found the piece pleasant but slightly dull—the harmless stranger you sit next to at a wedding and are fine with never seeing again.

But that had been a couple weeks earlier, before I'd started giving myself little assignments in order to break up the routine in the vacuum. Count how many people stop at the Louise Nevelson sculpture, I instructed myself one morning on Ramp 6. See if you can find something new in the Zanele Muholi photos. One Thursday, I decided to force myself to look at just one piece per post, for a full forty minutes. I was inspired by an art-history professor I'd read about who forbade her students from writing about an artwork until they'd spent a full three hours in its presence.

That day, I rotated into Tower 2 and stared down Brancusi's sculpture. Some curator had positioned the piece so the flat oval face at the top of the toothpaste squirt pointed toward you as you walked into the gallery. From that angle, the sculpture looked like a trained seal balancing an invisible ball on its nose.

I rummaged around my brain for advice I'd gotten on befriending sculptures. "You can't possess a sculpture all at once, you have to walk around it," a gallerist told me once (and from Jack: "Never, *ever* step over a sculpture, even if it's on the floor—it's disrespectful").

I moved a few inches to my right. The seal morphed into a foot squeezed into a high heel. After a few minutes, I moved right again. Now the sculpture was a semihard penis. Then it was a slug, a fat boomerang, a sullen woman in a hijab, a finger. The marble glowed. My eyeballs slid around sculpture's sleek curves and felt as if they were handling silk. When the forty minutes were up, I didn't want to leave.

I started going out of my way to say hi to the sculpture after that, even if it cut into my breaks. The sculpture's mood changed constantly. One afternoon it was out for blood and its flank looked unusually swollen, as if it'd hoovered up some poor French tourist. Another day it was stretching toward the window overlooking Fifth Avenue as if to make its escape. "It's quiet today," a middle-aged man said to me one Tuesday, staring at the sculpture. *Of course, it was*, I thought. *Look at it, it's been in a fight.* It'd taken me a few hours of staring at the piece to register the subtle gray dappling of the marble, which made the poor thing look bruised. After even more time, I discovered that the base of the marble sculpture rested on a small foot the shape of a duck bill. I just kept following my interest around the piece, as I had watched Julie do with the Ingres, and I keep noticing five new things, then five more.

What did the sculpture mean? I didn't look for meaning. Or rather, to me, its meaning wasn't a punch line, a definitive answer to be learned, like, *This is a commentary on Hitler's rise to power.* (Brancusi, who was born in Romania, finished the sculpture around 1932.) Its meaning was in the richness of its company. The piece felt more like a companion than an object, and it had a different story to tell each day, depending on whether it was a bird, a wave, a vase, a sex toy, or a string of poop about to hit the ground.

As I continued my experiment of focusing on a single work for the full forty minutes at each post, I struck up more relationships with the art on the ramps, not all of them friendly. I picked petty fights with a few abstract expressionist paintings next to my locked post on Ramp 3—those smug jerks were so pleased with themselves—and I got sucked into an intense affair with the Francis Bacon triptych on Ramp 4. Bacon's *Three Studies for a Crucifixion* showed three figures—one flayed, one shot, one strung up and butchered—contorted in grotesque, blood-spattered postures of pain. I went through a phase where my favorite post was whichever got me close to the Bacon, until one day it turned my stomach to even look at it. I kept my distance for a few weeks. Eventually, we reconciled.

I'd never had these sorts of feelings for an artwork before. Being around the Guggenheim's collection filled me with a comfortable familiarity I associate with friends I've known since preschool. And then there was a feeling I recognized from being in love: that I could be around these pieces for as far as I could see into the future and I wouldn't get sick of their company. Not every piece, mind you. Not the same pieces as you, maybe. But some. And knowing that it could happen with a few pieces, that I was capable of love for a hunk of marble, made me excited to keep looking for new art to fall in love with.

I cringe as I write this, because it's so painfully obvious to say that the more time we spend looking at an artwork, the better we understand it. But then why don't more of us do it? A study conducted at the Metropolitan Museum of Art found that the median time visitors spent with a work of art—including reading its wall label—was seventeen seconds, which almost certainly skews high, since it only included people who bothered to stop at the painting. (Another study found visitors spent four times longer reading the description of the art than they did looking at the art itself—an average of eight seconds versus a

measly two.) And let me say I'm no better. Before joining the Guggenheim, the only time I'd stared at an artwork for forty minutes straight
was never. It took fifteen security cameras and the threat of getting
fired to stop me from wandering away or pulling out my phone.

But when we do force ourselves to bond with artworks, the pieces
change and so do we. In 1998, Irwin Braverman, a now-retired professor of dermatology at the Yale School of Medicine, started supple-
menting his students' lectures on skin lesions with field trips to the
university's museum of British art. Braverman had noticed some worrying trends in his field: Physicians, who are often rushed to see as
many patients as possible in a limited period of time, were overrelying
on tests and zeroing in on details that fit a known pattern instead of
observing their patients holistically—in essence, letting their filters of
expectation guide the diagnosis. What physicians needed, he decided,
was to learn how to look. And so, as part of a course that's since become mandatory at Yale and is now part of the curriculum in more
than two dozen medical schools, Braverman had his students spend
fifteen minutes studying various paintings, like a J. M. W. Turner view
of a sailboat in Dordrecht Harbor, then asked them to describe what
they saw. (The goal, he explained in a presentation, was to "lower the
threshold of observation so that the normal becomes as important
as the abnormal"—so that the familiar becomes unfamiliar, you might
say.) The visits to the museum provided students with much more than
just a break from reviewing plaques and pustules. Studies by Braverman and others found that after going through this art-based visual
literacy course, medical students who then examined a patient observed more, offered more sophisticated descriptions of what they saw,
were better at reading human facial expressions, and tended to make
fewer mistakes than did control groups who, say, went to an anatomy

lecture or sat through a tutorial on physically examining a patient. NYPD detectives, FBI agents, and Navy SEALs have all since made their own treks to museums to relearn looking by spending time with paintings.

Fifteen minutes is nothing compared to the more than fifteen years Imani Lane has spent guarding art at Yale University's art museum. The art seeps into your psyche, she and other guards agreed. After five years patrolling galleries, Imani, whom I met through one of her former colleagues, told me she'd felt compelled to start making her own art. She'd started with a twenty-dollar watercolor kit from an outlet store and lately had been making black-and-white drawings inspired by works in the museum's collection, from Picasso paintings to George Grosz's satirical sketches of Weimar German society. Imani hoped to show her work in an upcoming exhibition of art made by museum employees. Museums tend to boast about their commitment to education—or, as the Guggenheim laid out in its original 1937 charter, the "mental or moral improvement of men and women." But Imani had even more expansive ideas. Art museums were "a way that the average person can get to see beautiful things on a regular basis." And being around beauty—"it enlightens you, it makes you feel—you know what? It gives you that feeling of being rich." In her experience, beauty begat beauty. "Now, I see it everywhere," she said.

I'd always thought that the Completers had the right idea: The way to see a museum was to look at every single thing, top to bottom. Exhaustion and scorched-earth viewing—*that's* how you get your money's worth.

Now, I thought that was insane, maybe even unhealthy, the visual equivalent of going to a Las Vegas–casino buffet and gorging on pizza, tuna rolls, waffles, clam chowder, and mimosas, then wondering why you feel sick. There were several hundred works of art up in the Guggenheim at that moment. It felt almost punishing how much we put out for you to see. I bristled when one of the gallery guides climbed onto his high horse to berate visitors for ignoring certain pieces: "The things people walk by—it's *insane*," he said, with a whiff of condescension. *But it's self-preservation!* I wanted to protest. How else do you stay sane? I wanted to pull visitors aside and tell them to try my method: Pick one piece per room, and see what happens. *I've been staring at this sculpture an hour a day for weeks, and I'm still discovering things.* A museum does not have to be read like a book, from beginning to end. I began to think of it more like ordering off a menu. You try a few things. You don't have to choke down the whole shebang.

Every afternoon, the Guggenheim hosted a free tour for visitors, and every morning, our supervisors gathered us in the lobby to review the theme for that day's tour. I snapped to attention one morning when a supervisor announced that Wednesday's tour would be "One Hour, One Object." *Lightweights*, I scoffed silently. What were these speed demons thinking? An hour with one work—you'd barely scratch the surface.

CHAPTER NINETEEN

Even after so many hours in the vacuum, I craved art when I left the museum each night. On my walks home, I peered up into the lit windows of apartment buildings and snuck glimpses at the art that hung in strangers' living rooms. A Richard Prince painting of a nurse winked at me from somewhere near East Eighty-Fifth Street. An Ed Ruscha gas station flashed me from above Fifth Avenue. It seemed so magical that you could take home an artwork, then bond with this treasure while you brushed your teeth. I was enchanted by the idea of living with something I found as endlessly fascinating as the Brancusi sculpture.

It's not as if I lived surrounded by empty white walls or anything. But the things up in my apartment—mostly a mix of photographs and prints—were largely pieces that my husband had picked out over the years and I'd gone along with, not feeling confident enough to either agree or disagree. But I had opinions now. *Strong* opinions. As I rotated through my posts in the Guggenheim—a museum that grew out

of one man's art collection—I couldn't stop fantasizing about what I'd
take home with me. I'd toss out my sofa in a heartbeat and stick the
Brancusi there instead, only I couldn't very well sneak it out of the museum. And yet despite my experience selling art in Miami and beyond,
I still couldn't picture myself taking the plunge and buying a piece.

I liked the idea that filling your home with art should be simple—
you just buy what you love (or, in Julie and Clinton's case, rescue it
from the trash). Only I'd lost some of my innocence along the way. I'd
seen collectors back-channeling with museums, and I'd picked up that
there were certain protocols to buying art from the most pedigreed
galleries. Lots of VIPs treated art buying less as a hobby than a profession. I wondered how it worked for those of us who, say, filed W-2s, weren't
descended from the world's foremost American art collectors, or didn't
live in New York City. Which is why I was so intrigued by the Icy Gays.

I initially heard about the Icy Gays at an opening, from two artists
who'd sold them work, and with a name like that, I had to look them
up. The Icy Gays turned out to be Rob and Eric Thomas-Sewall, a couple
in their forties who live in Minot, North Dakota—home to the Minot
Air Force Base and a population of forty-eight thousand, one-quarter
the size of Manhattan's Upper East Side.

The Icy Gays and I started Skyping in the evenings, after work,
and I learned that Rob and Eric's interest in contemporary art had
taken root just three years before in an accidental sort of way. Rob, a
cherubic ear-nose-and-throat surgeon, had grown up in a conservative
Christian family in Alabama whose taste in art was "white Jesus." He
went to a conservative Christian college, George Bush's inauguration,
a pro-life march at the Capitol, and then medical school, where he
started to question everything he'd been taught growing up. He came
out. During his residency, Rob met Eric, who grew up in Virginia,

obsessively collecting space LEGOs and Transformers, then became a political-theory instructor with a penchant for Grateful Dead shirts. (Also a "pot-smoking Communist," per Rob.) After Rob's job took them to Minot, they filled their home with family heirlooms and flea-market finds: a Gustav Klimt poster, various Kool-Aid-colored vases, a framed napkin of wide-eyed donkeys. "It was my impression that that was the only kind of art that we could possibly buy," Rob said. "Because everything else cost $5 million, and they won't sell it to us."

Rob and Eric got married and, while waiting for a table for brunch one morning during their honeymoon in San Francisco, wandered over to a park to check out art by local artists. One of the artists suggested they go to the De Young museum to see the show by David Hockney (a British artist famous for his vibey Southern California pool paintings). David *who*? "Honestly, none of those words made any sense to me at all," said Rob, but they went to the museum anyway and were blown away. Three years later, they were shopping for an anniversary gift when Eric suggested that instead of spending $5,000 on the limited-edition Hockney book they were coveting, maybe they could get an original work of contemporary art instead. Yeah, right: Rob doubted they could find a piece for that cheap, but a little research led them to the *Artnet* article "10 Emerging Artists to Keep on Your Radar," then to a painting by Corydon Cowansage. It was a vaguely cartoony portrait of brick steps covered with a few tentacles of green grass. "We were both just like, 'Oh my God, this is the coolest thing I have ever seen,'" said Rob. They emailed the gallery. It was $5,000. Sold.

That kicked off a curiosity that snowballed into an obsession. By the time we started Skyping, Rob and Eric had joined the board of their local art museum and were spending over a hundred thousand dollars a year buying dozens of new artworks. Eric had sold his

Transformers collection so they could buy a painting of a hairy naked man asleep in bed, and Rob was thinking about off-loading a car so they could buy more art. Practically every time we Skyped, Rob and Eric would hijack the conversation to introduce me to a new piece. "We were *not* supposed to buy anything in Miami," said Eric sheepishly, as Rob commandeered the computer to show off three artworks they'd picked up during the Miami fairs. Next time, hot off their trip to art fairs in LA, there were two more works—"We said we weren't going to buy anything, and then we did," Rob confessed. They gravitated toward art by emerging artists who were female or queer, with a special fondness, I noticed, for bare thighs, flaccid leaves, and breasts that looked capable of bombing civilization back to the stone age. Near the Icy Gays' front door was a broad-brimmed sun hat covered in spidery links of braided hair—the work of a certain Julie Curtiss. "One of the first artists that we really liked was Julie Curtiss, and this was before she had any of her big shows and things," Eric gushed, unaware that I'd worked for her. I felt a jolt of excitement at seeing her work so beloved and a dash of pride that I'd lent her a hand.

Rob and Eric's default vacation was now traveling to art fairs, which meant they were coming to New York for Armory Week's traveling circus of fairs and hobnobbing. I asked if I could tag along. I found their passion magnetic, and I was eager to see what I might pick up from them about the mechanics of buying art. Sure, they told me: Join us.

Two weeks before we were supposed to meet, Rob was already a geyser of adrenaline. They'd be in the city six days and had scheduled six studio visits, three art fairs, three artist dinners, three gallerist drink dates, two Broadway shows, and one Michelin-starred meal, as well as to meet me as early as possible on VIP day of the Spring/Break art fair. "You're always hoping, '*Wow*, maybe we'll find the next Julie

Curtiss this Spring/Break,'" Eric said excitedly. That being said, they swore they didn't want to buy anything and were just coming to see as much art as possible. Uh-huh, I said, forcing myself to keep a straight face. We made plans to meet at Spring/Break as soon as they'd landed.

ROB HAD SLEPT max four hours, I learned as he and Eric speed-walked through a lobby in Midtown to get to the fair. He and Eric had had to leave for the airport at 4:00 a.m. to catch their two flights to New York, but Rob had been up till past midnight shopping for art. He'd been desperately refreshing the Spring/Break website trying to buy a painting by Julie's former studio assistant Margaux Valengin, the artist whose work Julie had curated into a solo show at the fair. "So I'm sitting there pressing refresh. Eric is like, 'You *need* to go to bed'... I'm like, 'NO! I *have* to buy art!'" chattered Rob, whose energy was hummingbird on speed. "I'm sitting there pressing refresh-refresh-refresh and then I'm like, 'THE WEBSITE'S CRASHED! I CAN'T GET IN!'... He's, like, 'It's fine, I'm sure you'll get it.' I'm like, 'NO!' And now it's gone." Rob sounded deflated. "It's *fine*," he added, in a tone that indicated it definitely wasn't. "I should have you pressing refresh, too," he told Eric.

Rob chatted excitedly in the elevator, oblivious to the icy stares from New Yorkers, and we exited onto a maze of white cubicles that rioted with sequined soda cans and rainbow-sprinkled paintings. Spring/Break, true to its reputation as the scrappy art fair, had set up shop in Ralph Lauren's former headquarters, and Rob and Eric bee-lined to Valengin's booth, where a painting of a woman's face juxtaposed with sneakers and German shepherds hung over a converted cubicle. I spotted Julie, and we hugged hello. (We were still in close touch, and Julie had asked me to gallery-sit for her husband's Spring/Break booth later in the fair.) The Icy Gays made no effort to conceal how thrilled they were to discover Julie herself in the booth, and after chirping hellos, they told her all about the refresh-refresh-refresh website ordeal, confirmed their plans to all get dinner in a few days, and were out the door to see the next booth when Rob spotted a prominent collector he knew from Instagram. "What do you think about Jon Key's work?" Rob asked shyly, sidling up to the man. Key, one of the artists Elizabeth and I had included in our Hong Kong show, was showing at Armory this year, and the Icy Gays had asked Key's gallery to put a piece of his on hold until they could see it in person the first day of the fair.

Rob barreled through the booths, high on caffeine and art, and as I scurried behind him, he tossed out footnotes to explain his methodology for working a fair. "You have to remember, if someone invited you to the fair, you better go see them," he said, hunting for someone named Lauren. Also, you have to press the flesh. "Nowadays, as collectors, it helps for people to know who you are to get access to certain works and that kind of thing," Rob said, shortly before calling Eric over to hand out one of their freshly minted Icy Gays business cards. Also, you need to see as much art as you can because art orgies like this don't come around every day in Minot.

We eventually found Lauren, and as they spoke with her and other art sellers, I started to pick up on a pattern to the Icy Gays' patter. Rob and Eric listened to each gallerist pitch them on the art, then pitched themselves right back: They introduced themselves as collectors from North Dakota, name-dropped Julie and a few other artists whose work they owned, then introduced me as a best-selling writer who was following them around. I'd figured Rob was just being friendly, but he set me straight. "You're obviously aware that we're kind of using being with you to say, 'Look at us as collectors! We have this author with us, and *she* wants to know what we're doing, don't *you*?'" he told me. "I LOVE it." Like the artists in their collection, I was context.

"Oh! Is that Todd Kramer?" Rob asked suddenly, gazing over Lauren's shoulder at a gallerist he recognized. "Oh! I was just going to say hi. Oh! He's gone. He's got a *huge* Instagram presence, oh my God." Rob had prepped for this trip by googling "everyone we're supposed to know but don't really" and trying to memorize their faces, and he kept dashing away to introduce himself to some obscure art-world celebrity. By contrast Eric, who'd so far doled out a handful of two-word sentences, paled and stopped breathing anytime he thought someone he didn't recognize was about to say hi.

As we weaved in and out of booths, I pumped the Icy Gays for details about how they'd put together their art education. Rob's compulsive streak had come in handy. "I love a complicated hobby, and this is a *very* complicated hobby," said Rob, who'd completed every single *New York Times* crossword the year before. After buying the Cowansage piece, Rob had assigned himself a graduate seminar's worth of homework. He watched art documentaries, scoured art publications, listened to art podcasts, and devoured art books, including art-history tomes like *Art Since 1900*, which was brutal. "I'm like, if I can take your thyroid out, I can read this book. But that's not true. The key fact is—that's *definitely* not true." Rob flung himself down a social-media rabbit hole and followed galleries, gallerists, artists, the artists those artists follow, the collectors that follow those artists. "Honestly, the fine-art world is basically a giant social network—it just is—and Instagram works perfectly with that. So, I'm like, 'Well, Brigitte'"—a director at Anton Kern who worked closely with Julie—"'is following this person, so we need to pay attention to this person,'" Rob said. Lying in bed at night in Minot, Rob toured New York studios and galleries through other peoples' posts. "These people go on gallery walks. They'll just have a wonderful Friday evening where they see the best art basically in the universe, because they're in New York City and they can just go do that. And we can't do that," he told me. "We would not be the collectors that we are without Instagram."

None of that was Eric's speed. Lately, he'd tried to improve his Eye by teaching himself to paint. He didn't read Rob's books, scrutinize Instagram, or put much stock in context. "Art as peer pressure? No thank you," he said. "It's almost like you can know too much." Eric still combed thrift stores for paintings, while Rob thought, "There's a reason they're in this trash bin." Rob summarized his collecting philosophy as "I want to buy the art that's on the list" and said Eric's was "Why don't we buy the thing that's *going* to be on the list." It was Eric's opinion that good context let bad artists get away with murder. Like *that* person: We passed a painting by an artist who was a darling of the downtown arts scene, and Eric shared his suspicion that the artist was only popular because, early on, someone influential had proclaimed her very bad work to be good. Rob overheard this and promptly lost his mind.

"STOP TALKING!" Rob whirled around, his eyes wide with horror. "Jesus Christ, what the FUCK." I thought he'd clamp his hands over Eric's mouth. "Oh no. Nuh-uh. Not okay with that quote. Not okay with anything you just said AT ALL."

They squabbled for a few minutes about what Eric could and couldn't say, and Eric agreed to change the subject. "The art world is built around your reputation," said Rob once he'd calmed down. "Once that reputation is gone, you have nothing, and so everyone here is doing this dance where they're desperately trying to show that they're excited about what's exciting. And it is a huge risk to say anything negative because if you *do*, and you say the negative thing to the wrong person, it's *over*."

Rob's warning about reputation was the same one, practically verbatim, I'd gotten months and months before, and as much as I wanted to reassure him, I sympathized with Rob's fears.

Art had enriched my life in so many ways, but the cloud of mutual suspicion that hung over the New York art world had enveloped me too. It didn't help that I'd been privy to so much gossip, from which the Icy Gays themselves were not immune. A collector I knew, who'd scoffed when I mentioned the Icy Gays, had waved away their enthusiasm and openness as merely a ploy to boost their profile. And I mean, *maybe*. But to me they seemed more like people who hadn't yet learned to look at art with reptilian detachment. "*Super* cool!" Rob crowed, as we made our way around Spring/Break. "*Love* it!" Their bubbly delight forced me to acknowledge how much of my overly enthusiastic personality I still tamped down out of concern for what the Heads might think. But being around the Icy Gays also made me resolve to just let loose my inner overexcited cheerleader, no matter what it might do to my reputation.

AS WE MEANDERED through Spring/Break, we passed a shoulder-high pile of pancakes, a man in underwear being used as a plate, and a six-screen installation of *The Most Beautiful Dick Pics of All Time*, featuring penises ejaculating glitter and blowing bubbles. We did not, alas, pass my and Amanda's booth. We'd been rejected. Evidently the judges thought pirouetting penises were more thought-provoking than Amanda's four-year-running immersion as AllFIRE—though I couldn't help thinking, competitively, that our pitch was better than what I spied in certain corners of the fair. It could be my delusions of grandeur talking, but Elizabeth, who'd reviewed our proposal, did say she was "frankly shocked" we weren't accepted, which seemed more strongly worded than it needed to be if she were just trying to be nice.

Rob and Eric sprinkled compliments and questions behind them as they perused the shows. "Very upsetting," Rob said approvingly to an artist who painted sad ghostly faces nestled underground like rocks. Rob described the unifying theme of their collection as art that exposes "greater truths about the world" and used words like "shocking" and "gross," as synonyms for "good." Rob was drawn to Key's painting of a shirtless Black man, in part because Rob had showed Key's work to his nurses in Minot, and they hated it. "Cause it's scary," they'd told Rob. "I'm like, 'Or—it could be powerful and queer,'" Rob countered. Because of their budget, the Icy Gays focused more on emerging artists: $15,000 was on the high side of what they'd pay for an artwork, and they mentioned wanting to stop by a pop-up show where they could find pieces for $30 each. "We want to support artists that are maybe being overlooked and promote them," Eric told me.

I followed the Icy Gays into a booth of paintings depicting dystopian Martian landscapes filled with creatures that had kale for skin and sickly corncobs for feet.

Their mood changed instantly. They both got extremely quiet, riveted by the gross alien worlds. Rob immediately turned to a pale thirtysomething guy who stood guard over the price list. "Are any of these available?" Rob asked, a hard edge of panic in his voice. A nod confirmed they were.

He and Eric stopped at a painting, *the accelerationists,* of five humanoid lizards draped over hairy couches while taking hits off something that looked like the love child of a urinal and sleep apnea machine. "It's sweet and kinda weird and gross, I love it," Rob said quickly in a quiet, no-nonsense monotone.

Eric's eyes were glued to the humanoid lizards. "I'd be down with it," he said with a firm intensity I hadn't heard before.

They had to fight off a few other people to get their hands on the price list and in so doing learned that the pale guy in the booth was in fact the artist, Jeremy Olson, and that one piece had sold but *the accelerationists* could be theirs for $6,400. Eric and Rob got very quiet again, then asked Olson a series of questions that I recognized from Miami as the standard collector pickup lines: "Do you have an MFA?" Yes. "Have you had a lot of shows?" Well, group shows. "Who are some of your inspirations?" Brueghel, Bosch, David Altmejd. ("You know David Altmejd," Rob cued Eric. "The crystals in the head and the smoking. Four eyes. Anton Kern.")

They spent eight minutes in the booth and then stepped outside, hovering next to the door as if unconvinced they should leave.

"That's crazy good. That's amazing," Eric bubbled with uncharacteristic animation. He looked a little flushed.

Rob, clearly on the fence, pulled up pictures of Olson's work on his phone and examined them. "Is it terrible that I want to ask him if he's gay?" Rob mused. "No!" he decided. "I'm *not* going to go in and be like, 'Hey! By the way, are you gay? Because that matters—you can't be in our collection if you're not gay.' Like, it's *crazy,* right? It's stupid."

Rob kept glancing at Olson's paintings on his phone as he paced ahead into a booth of ceramic takeout containers covered in sculpted cockroaches. Eric, who reluctantly tore himself away from Olson's booth, had lost his quiet composure. Olson's paintings seemed to have jimmied something loose in him, and now he rattled around the fair repeating Olson's name.

First, he tried gathering intelligence. "Have you seen Jeremy Olson?" he asked a painter we went to see on the fair's second floor. Next, he tried stoking Rob's FOMO. "We won't make *that* mistake with Jeremy Olson," he said, when Rob mentioned an artist whose work they didn't buy when they could have and was now prohibitively expensive. There was positive visualization: "I am *super* excited about our new painting!" There was bullying. "He's gotta wait for Jerry Saltz"—*New York* magazine's art critic—"to tweet about it. And *then* he'll want to buy it," Eric said, staring at Rob.

I asked Rob what else he'd want to know about Olson.

"I'd probably just buy it," Eric said, as if anyone had any doubt.

Rob ignored that and ticked off questions: "Who else has bought him? Who else is excited about him? What group shows has he been in?"

"It doesn't matter, because everyone's going to be excited about him in like two years," Eric protested.

We stayed at Spring/Break for more than four hours, probably a record for anyone who wasn't actively working the fair, and I think the only way I got Rob out the door was by promising I'd take him to see even more art at a collector's open house in Tribeca. "Oh my *God*, that was so great," Rob chattered as we stepped out of Spring/Break into the cool night air. "Loved it. *LOVED* it."

Later that night, back at their hotel, Rob lay awake in bed scrolling through photos of art he and Eric already owned. He was up before dawn the next morning to Instagram highlights of art he'd seen at Spring/Break.

I found the Icy Gays a few hours later in the antsy crush of the Armory Show's VIP line. Eric was one big smile. Just before going to sleep, they'd bought Olson's painting, Rob announced. "And since then, the whole show sold out," Eric said proudly.

I asked Rob what had changed his mind. He told me he'd looked up Olson's Instagram and noticed that a few artists whom the Icy Gays admired had "liked" Olson's posts, on top of which Rob had posted Olson's painting on the Icy Gays' Instagram and gotten a good response. It certainly didn't hurt that *The New York Times* had featured one of Olson's paintings in their article on Spring/Break. But context wasn't the deciding vote. "Eric was *so* excited about the painting. Just could not stop talking about it. He was like, 'It's going to be in a museum, come on, have you ever seen anything so beautiful?' And so we came to the decision that it dialogues well with the rest of our collection, we love it, so—*fuck* everyone else," Rob declared. "We have all these factors that I'm trying to bat around in my head to make a scientific decision. Ultimately it came down to: It makes my husband super happy."

We spent eight hours at Armory. A novel coronavirus—I'd just learned the term—was hopping continents like New Yorkers jump turnstiles, and there had been cases reported in the city, but most people at Armory seemed convinced there was no way it could have procured VIP passes. The Independent Art Fair was the next day—followed by a forced march through galleries downtown—and while I dragged myself home each night to face-plant into reheated pad Thai, the Icy Gays zipped around the city doing studio visits, dining with artists, going back to Spring/Break to buy another piece and back to Independent three more times.

One afternoon, I joined Rob and Eric for a tour of Lower East Side galleries. To my surprise, the tour started at the cool Chinatown gallery run by the woman who'd first mentioned me to Jack. It ended at Jack Barrett Gallery. In between, I listened as collectors bragged about who'd been the earliest to buy Julie Curtiss's work, raved about the painter Jack and I had dined with during our trip to Yale, and chatted up a gallerist who worked closely with the artist who'd invited me to Hudson for Labor Day. After the tour, the Icy Gays wanted to get a bite before heading to the theater, and we ended up at Dimes, the kale-forward restaurant where I'd had breakfast with the gallerist Bridget Donahue. As the Icy Gays and I settled into a booth with a painter they'd invited to join us, I spotted the small table where, many months before, Bridget had rattled off unfamiliar names faster than I could write them down.

All week, I'd had the peculiar sense that I kept running into myself. The Icy Gays collected Julie's art; I'd worked for her. They liked Key's work; I'd put it in a show. They'd debated buying a piece by Haley Josephs; I'd helped install her first exhibition with Jack. As we toured the fairs, I kept bumping into artists I knew or breaking away from the Icy Gays to catch up with gallerists I hadn't seen since the last fair cycle. (Hello, Beth Rudin DeWoody; hello, Elizabeth, Rob, Jack—all of whom, in a major milestone, were showing at Armory for the first time.) Over the past few days, it had begun to dawn on me just how far I'd come. Of course—say it with me—the art world is *so* small, and there are so many art worlds. But I'd immersed myself in this one more than I'd ever dreamed.

While the four of us waited for our food, Rob and Eric's thoughts strayed to North Dakota and the work they'd be bringing back with them—for themselves and for their friends. Rob's sister had spotted *the accelerationists* on Rob's Instagram and written to tell him she thought it was gross, awful, and upsetting, which delighted Rob. "I want people to walk into our house and be like, 'Oh my fucking GOD.' Like, 'WHAT the FUCK,'" he said, grinning mischievously.

The conversation wandered—Eric rapped about Heidegger, the painter confessed how hard it'd been fitting into the New York art scene after she moved here from Florida ("Like, oh *God*, I gotta tone it down with these pastel shorts and crop tops"). But within a few moments, Rob was back to discussing his art.

"What we try to do with our collection," Rob was explaining to the painter as I refilled our water glasses, "is bring in artists that open your mind and open your horizons and say, 'You may not have this experience as a gay man, or you may not have had this experience as a woman, but this is what we feel. And here we are. And you can feel it through our work.'"

I glanced up at Rob. His eyes were glassy with tears.

"And these straight white men and women that live in North Dakota who come into our house—" Rob's voice cracked. "Like, this is *us*. This is fucking what we feel every goddamn day, and you can feel it by looking at this weird shit on the wall." Rob sniffed. "I'm crying—but it's like really *neat* that this can happen through art, and we can be a part of it. And that as a collector—I have the money, and I don't have the talent—I can say, 'This is *special*, and you're doing something cool. You're making me feel something awesome or sad or awful or like I want to cry or I want to laugh or I want to hug.' And I can say, 'That's special, and I want to help you show that to the world.' That's something we can do. And I said, 'If we can do that, let's fucking *do* it.'"

As a doctor, Rob helped people for a living. He removed cancerous thyroids, eased suffering, and gave parents more hours with their children. And yet while he clearly cared for his work, that didn't seem to be what gave him purpose. "*My* identity? I would rather be someone that is an art collector than a surgeon, honestly," he said. He credited art with teaching him to be true to who he is as a person. "I've never had anything like this. Where I was like, 'Oh my God, this is special. Something special is happening.'"

But their collection wasn't only about them. Rob and Eric seemed to share their art more widely than many of the VIPs I'd met. They regularly posted their latest acquisitions to Instagram, and they kept a browsable inventory of their collection on a website called Collecteurs—all of which other buyers seemed loath to do lest they tip off the competition to hot artists or risk getting outed when they flipped a piece. The Icy Gays also participated in various local fundraisers where they opened up their home for tours, and their art collection had brought hundreds of Minotians to gawk at Julie's hair hat and a Sophie Larrimore painting of a woman being fondled by a poodle. "I think we're kind of blowing people's minds here in North Dakota," Rob told me. "But to be honest, I kind of love that. That's part of what I like about our art too: is that it challenges people in a lot of different ways." I'd heard collectors say that art was like a religion to them—a spiritual balm that gave their lives meaning and shaped how they see the world. For the Icy Gays, art seemed to be all that and more: a belief system, one they wanted to evangelize on behalf of.

As I rode home on the subway that evening, I felt as if I'd misunderstood art collecting. It didn't have to be a bloodless act of trophy hunting and mounting rare, dead species on the wall. What the Icy Gays described sounded more like a collaboration. Yes, the umbilical cord of gold ran between them and the artists, but in this case it seemed to be keeping both parties alive. The Icy Gays were supporting artists, and the artists were supporting the Icy Gays—through their randy poodles, their hair hats, their tapestries of pubic hair. And together, they were trying to bring new experiences to more people.

Even though I couldn't fathom acquiring art on the scale they did, watching the Icy Gays in action made living with art feel vital, even urgent. Putting art on your walls wasn't the same as decorating. Buying art also meant helping artists thrive and enlivening your hours on this planet by surrounding yourself with objects that could tweak your humanity. And to state the obvious: You don't have to be in New York to buy great art. (There are some *wild* things being shown by Minot's galleries, let me tell you.) You certainly don't have to spend a ton of money. *Why would anyone buy anything except the work of emerging artists?* I'd started to wonder. The big galleries supported a winner-take-all model and the fantasy that talent was in short supply. But you could buy a print for $150 at Denny Dimin or spend $10 and get a small sculpture of candy from Spring/Break, where the work jarred loose my filter of expectation more than did anything I saw at the week's more prestigious fairs. You could take chances for prices like that. You could back a different way of seeing the world—and potentially change your own while you're at it. Or you could spend nothing: My conversations with artists and gallerists left me with the sense that you could support art just by seeing it and letting it work its magic on you.

CHAPTER TWENTY

There was so much I wanted to tell you out there in the vacuum. I hovered at each post like a coiled jack-in-the-box ready to spring and I'd seize on the flimsiest excuse to draw you into conversation, which was part of my job description, after all. You there trying to use our library as a love nest—have you seen this Hilla Rebay collage just to the left of the library's door, and did you know Rebay is the reason we're standing here in the Solomon R. Guggenheim Museum, because she was Guggenheim's art advisor and the one who got him excited about collecting abstract art—which back then they called non-objective painting and is the cornerstone of our collection? If you took a photo with flash, I'd be on you faster than the speed of light to say, "Please don't," then ask you what drew you to that piece.

Some of my questions were selfish. I had spent weeks locked in a bitter feud with Beuys's *Virgin*. Even after contemplating its dust-covered furniture and dangling bare lightbulb for numerous forty-minute shifts, I still found the piece incomprehensible (or "ungenerous," as an art critic might say). I started asking visitors what *they* got from it. They stopped and gamely struggled with *Virgin*, even though they didn't necessarily know the artist and I was putting them on the spot. "It reminds me of one of those Soviet investigation rooms," said a mop-haired chemistry student from Hungary. "They'd sit you down in a very simple room and ask you questions and—*wham!*—hit your head on the table." A gangly Russian woman noticed the bar of soap on the dusty table and thought of a parent washing his kid's mouth out with soap. An eighteen-year-old girl from Colombia saw the piece as a message to reject brainwashing. As we careened between interpretations, Ramp 5 began to feel like a portal to other places. I'd take myself to post, ask visitors questions, and, as they spoke, travel to a rickety church, a Soviet prison camp, a classroom.

I loved hearing what people saw in the work. Their responses moved me way more than did anything I read in the wall labels. "Looking at art is like looking into the future," said a visitor who couldn't tear himself away from an Agnes Martin painting of a gray grid on a white expanse. I delighted in watching a couple in their forties go around the museum laughing uproariously at each piece they passed— they pointed at the Serra and burst into guffaws. A man stood in front of a Wojciech Fangor painting of a brilliant olive-green circle surrounded by a halo of sky blue, and I watched as his face broke into a huge smile. "Wow. Wow. *Wow* ... It's pulling you into another dimension. It's an opening to another world."

On the ramps, I got to witness different iterations of what it meant to have an Eye. There were visitors who treated art as a portal to history. Visitors who, like Jack, stared at a piece and saw its potential to change the world. Some were like Julie and used the art to uncover a more dynamic reality. Still others were like Elizabeth and sought beauty. All of them provided flashes of insight into the value of art in our lives.

I was guarding my beloved Brancusi sculpture one afternoon when a guide, dressed like a comp-lit professor in round glasses and a tight blue blazer with elbow patches, walked in escorting a tour behind him. He spoke in the vaguely continental accent of the doctoral class, drawing out… every… statement… with… exaggerated… *grah*vitas… He lectured in front of Brancusi's *Flying Turtle* and then—HOW COULD HE—moved on without so much as a glance at my favorite piece.

This was inexcusable. I paced up and down along the wall behind my sculpture, hoping to catch the visitors' attention and tempt them over. But after just a few moments, I was alone again.

I started to imagine how I'd lead my own tour. You'd meet me in the rotunda, just outside the ticket desk, and we'd begin by settling on some ground rules.

One: You don't have to look at everything.

Two: You do have to look at something for at least five minutes.

Three: Don't you dare lay eyes on the wall text—that is, the paragraph-long explanation pasted on the wall beside many of the artworks.

Lots of guards agree with me on this. (Artists, too: Looking at a painting while reading the wall text "is like trying to have a conversation with the work and someone keeps interrupting," Julie told me once.) And trust me, I know it's hard to resist. I read the wall text too. I will break my own rule and continue reading the wall text even after I write this. Occasionally it's helpful, and for years I thought it was downright rude when museums and galleries didn't offer an explanation of each work. But now, more often than not, I wanted to tear the labels all down.

The wall text hovers just to the side of art, like the answer key at the bottom of a word search, its definitive tone sending the message that there's only one right answer to the art. I don't think museums *mean* to do that—I think they just want to offer up a helpful interpretation or highlight the thesis of a particular show. But I'd experienced the way that wall text could turn us into "mute receptors," who'd bypass our own observations about the art in favor of skipping to the expert-approved answer.

Who says you have listen to those experts anyhow? Guarding at the Guggenheim had made me see that art historians could be unreliable narrators. One day I called up a conservator to ask why we had to stand in one place for forty minutes guarding the dust on *Virgin*, and his answer was: You don't. Some influential curator at MoMA had apparently decided the layer of dust mattered to Beuys—even though Beuys, his assistants, and the conservators who worked with him never said it did. And thus *Virgin* now needed to gather dust, and we couldn't move for forty minutes on Ramp 6. Or consider the Serra sculpture: All day, every day, we carefully noted on our Touch Tallies whether the tangled strips of lead had accidentally been nudged a few centimeters to the right so a conservator could come out in the middle of the day, get down on her hands and knees with white gloves, and reposition the little tangles of lead *just so* so that they matched the picture on our sheet. Yeah, *actually*, said the conservator I talked with, that piece was made to have the metal pieces thrown haphazardly. Those lead ribbons would get tossed into a big box when the current show came down, and whoever installed the piece next time would just randomly pick out pieces and throw them on the ground. The work looks different every time it's shown, not that you'd know it from the wall text.

Paintings are constantly shape-shifting too. The blue splotch that an art critic obsessed over in the 1970s might look green to you, and not only because the light is different in the gallery or because you've suspended color constancy (congratulations, by the way). Van Gogh, for instance, painted his famous sunflowers with a yellow paint made from then-brand-new lead chromate pigments, which too late were discovered to be "fugitive colors" that caused his bright yellow petals to fade to brown, just like real flowers rotting in a vase. In the 1960s, Frank Stella painted geometric abstract canvases featuring jittery stripes of fluorescent colors, like Day-Glo orange and caution-tape yellow, which are already starting to fade. Left unrestored, one conservator warns, they'll wind up "milky-colored ruins."

That's tragic. And magnificent. It's another reminder to have faith in your own eyes. These works are not immutable. They spoil, rot, and sag. The wall text, I couldn't help thinking, is a little outdated. You know the work best because you're looking at it right now, in this moment, in this light, in this day and age, on this tour.

Which isn't to say your eyes don't need work. As you follow me up the ramp and into the gallery, I just want you to keep in mind that we're less-than-objective judges. You're likely to prefer an artwork if you think it was hard to make, and to value it more highly too. ("I just went to the Frick museum with my wife to see Vermeer. The skill involved! The beauty! How can you compare this?" demanded a white-haired lawyer offended by Beuys's *Virgin*.) Research shows that we like a painting less when it's hung below eye level, prefer the bigger version of two identical paintings, and have a weird fetish for originals, to the degree that one study, which asked subjects to imagine that the *Mona Lisa* was destroyed in a fire, found 80 percent of them would rather see the painting's ashes than a perfect replica. On this tour, you'll probably see artworks you've never seen before, and I want you to prepare yourself: You might not like them. Try viewing them again. Then again. Research has found that our fondness for certain Monet, Manet, and Degas works can be explained by the mere "exposure effect"—a scientific term for our tendency to like things for the arbitrary reason that we've interacted with them more. In other words, we may celebrate pieces—and raise them into the annals of art history—not necessarily because of their appearance but because we've seen these works over and over and thus are now convinced they're good.

For all these reasons and more, I'm also going to insist—rule number four—that you don't look at the little label beside each artwork. That label—officially called a "tombstone"—lists the artist's name, the work's title, the date the piece was made, what materials it was made with, and who gave it to the museum. It lists context, in other words. For now, please ignore it.

We're entering the gallery now—Tower 2, a white cube with a sliver of window at the back. There are towering carved wood sculptures, pieces in white marble, photographs of the artist in his studio. Go ahead and pick whichever piece you want, but I won't dissuade you from looking at the Brancusi sculpture I love so much. If I've learned one thing in the vacuum, it's that sometimes being forced to look at an artwork, even when you don't want to, is life-changing.

You've got five minutes. I'm going to leave you alone with the piece. No, wait—one more thing: Stay in the work. Five things. What do you see?

If you get stuck, move. Get closer, walk backward, or go around it.

You can be bored. Go ahead and ask yourself why you agreed to go on this stupid tour to begin with. Feel sorry for yourself that you're stuck with this mute hunk of rock. Just keep looking, and not at your phone.

Notice. Notice the most obvious things, the most surprising things, the things that grab your eyeballs despite you. Fight the urge to see what you expect to be there; focus instead on what *is* there. Maybe ask yourself how you'd describe the piece. Or let yourself wonder what it was made with. I don't need to know what it's about. I'm not concerned with whether you think it's good. Just watch the thing in front of you.

You have my permission to yell at the sculpture. You can laugh at it. You can cry, you can take notes, you can draw something, you can sing. An Italian psychiatrist who treated more than a hundred tourists stricken with dizziness, fainting, nausea, exhaustion, euphoria, panic, paranoia, depression, and hallucination after visits to art museums and churches in Florence coined the term "Stendhal syndrome" to describe the experience of people who go to pieces while looking at pieces of art. Skeptics attribute Stendhal syndrome to jet lag, dehydration, or underlying psychiatric issues. But the fact remains that merely being in the presence of art can cause us to do strange things. A guard in Houston who watched over a gigantic Cy Twombly painting—composed of scattered scribbles and vivid pom-poms of paint—once stumbled onto a woman standing naked in front of the work, her clothes in a pile. Another woman was arrested for kissing a different Twombly. My Brancusi sculpture has a hairline fracture near its head where one visitor, a guard told me, was possessed to mount it.

After five minutes you may, if you must, glance at the wall label. I only say that because in my experience, seeing what materials a piece was made with can kick off a whole new exciting avenue of looking. (It took me weeks with Lee Bontecou's *Untitled* on Ramp 6 to realize the disembodied gnashing teeth were made of saws, not zippers, and longer still to figure out where she'd used the black velvet.) You could check what year it was made: Touring the Guggenheim with Julie made me see dates as another layer of data about process and decisions. If you want some good art gossip, skip down to the label's bottom line to see which muckety-muck gave the piece to the museum—a bit of data that, to context hounds, is like studying the bloodlines of a thoroughbred.

Or you can keep ignoring the wall label. Keep staring at the piece. When I guarded the Brancusi sculpture, I tried to stand in front of the wall label so people couldn't see it, and when I did, their interpretations went wild. They saw a middle finger, a woman giving birth, a graph, a Kurasawa character, a cannon, a dolphin, a nose, a fish. But when their eyes darted to the wall label and scanned the title—I'll come clean: the piece is called *Miracle (Seal [I])*—they gave up. "Yes! I KNEW it was a seal!" one visitor said, then walked on.

WE'RE LEAVING the museum now, but the tour isn't over. You're going to follow me back down the ramps, out the front door, and down Fifth Avenue. We're going to head into Central Park to see the art exhibits there: the hyperrealistic pencil portraits of tourists laid out on card tables. The caricatures of doe-eyed lovers sketched by a guy squatting on a plastic stool. The break-dancing performers near Bethesda Fountain (*"Tiiiiiiit's showtime!"*). There's an installation I want you to see: Look at this hot-dog cart wrapped head to toe in the most eyeball-jittering, borderline pornographic drawings of chili cheese dogs you've ever seen. Go ahead and tell your filter of expectation to take a hike. Fight the reducing tendences of your mind. Look at the cart the way you stared at Brancusi's *Miracle*. Stop. Notice. Wonder.

The jostle we get from art can be found nearly anywhere. There is an artist in each of us to the extent that we struggle to keep our brains from compressing our experience. Art is a choice. It is a fight against complacency. It is a decision to forge a life that's richer, more uncomfortable, more mind-blowing, more uncertain. And ultimately, more beautiful.

The Opening

A Beginning

I quit art cold turkey. To some extent, we all did. In early March, just a few days after Spring/Break ended, I started getting text messages that New York City was shutting its bridges, so get all the cash you can *now*. On March 12 the mayor tweeted there was "NO TRUTH to rumors about Manhattan being quarantined," which of course got us all wondering if Manhattan was about to be quarantined. On March 13 the Guggenheim closed its doors until further notice, as did the Met, MoMA, and Whitney. More museums and galleries (along with practically everything else) followed. Soon, the art you could see was limited to what you had when you sheltered in place, what you could make, or what you could scroll through.

At first, I was too concerned that the world was ending to think about anything except about how to get toilet paper and why, of all things, toilet paper stood between me and the apocalypse.

Gradually, though, the panic subsided, or more likely I just got used to it. I was fortunate: fed, housed, healthy, able to work from home. As the weeks elapsed and the hours within the same four walls dragged on, though, there came a turning point: I didn't just miss art. I craved it. While other people obsessively checked for paper towels to be back in stock, I compulsively checked galleries' websites to see when they'd reopen. Today? Soon? When? My hunger to see art felt physical, less a desire than a need.

Initially I tried feeding my art craving through the thin gruel of Zoom calls. If I couldn't see it, at least I could talk about it.

The Icy Gays, who were anxiously waiting for seven new pieces to arrive, agreed I'd unfortunately have to postpone my trip to Minot. Elizabeth assured me Denny Dimin's clients were still buying plenty of art—it didn't take long for them to get new homes outside the city with lots of empty walls to fill. That, plus a break on rent, had kept Denny Dimin from going under. Jack, according to the joyless eternity I spent on Instagram, was planning a summer pop-up show in the Hamptons, and I got grade-A gossip that he'd apparently just placed one of Guadalupe Maravilla's pieces with MoMA—the ultimate Good Person. Even though we had no idea when galleries would reopen, Amanda and I kept strategizing to get her a show. We pitched our exhibit to various open calls held by galleries and nonprofit arts spaces, then waited, fingers crossed. The unprecedentedness of these Unprecedented Times had shaken up the status quo and given people "permission slips," one artist told me, to try their hands at things they'd never done before—online-only shows, NFTs, virtual art fairs—and I hoped something would come through for Amanda. She told me Mandy AllFIRE had recently expanded beyond Instagram to the website OnlyFans, where paying subscribers could see *all* of AllFIRE. Her NSFW business was booming during the lockdown—AllFIRE's fans were homebound and

horny—and Amanda had decided to get breast implants. "I just wanted
to take my project to the next level," Amanda told me a few days after
she had her surgery. "Hopefully this goes well and I heal and everything's fine and then I would consider the next surgery." Amanda was
hardly the first artist to incorporate plastic surgery or nudity into her
practice—Julie's former boss, Jeff Koons, did a whole series of himself
having sex with his then-wife, the porn star Cicciolina—but AllFIRE's
new direction kicked off a whole new set of questions around *what is
art* and how an ass influencer fits in.

I video-chatted with Julie. She was thriving. You might even say
thrilled. Time alone? In her studio? With nowhere to be and no one
around? Um, *heaven*. She felt almost as if she'd willed it into existence.
I didn't mention the auctions. The pace of resales had slowed somewhat, and after a lot of reading, I'd come to think that the panic over
artists' careers getting destroyed by flippers might be overblown. (I
saw that even Anselm Reyle, the artist who'd suffered the career "wipeout," was actively making art while being represented by six galleries
around the world.) Julie worried a little about her upcoming solo show
at FIAC, the one she'd been prepping for during our time together, but
the fair wasn't for another few months and the lockdowns couldn't
possibly still be in place come the fall—right? Julie crumpled imagining people only getting to experience her paintings online—the laborious gray of the bathroom with its three feet, the meticulously painted
strands of hair on the exposed sliver of crotch. There were, of course,
the online art fairs, but Julie fretted that putting her work in a virtual
show "would kill it." Listening to her made "seeing" art seem like a
misnomer. "In a sense, all your senses are engaged," Julie said, casting
a protective glance at the paintings in her studio. "It's kind of beautiful

to realize how important it is for people to experience anything—people, shows, art—in person."

One day, some day indistinguishable from the blur of all the others, I concluded I couldn't go any longer without art. I'd just have to make my own. As she did with everything she loved, Julie had talked so persuasively about the seductive texture and color of gouache that I felt like I *had* to try it. I was able to order a pack of gouache, rustle up some paintbrushes, and get ahold of some unlined paper. The artist Liz Ainslie and I had planned on going to a figure-drawing class in late March that they didn't have to bother telling us was canceled, and now we started meeting on FaceTime to paint. Once a week, we propped up our phones and challenged each other with small assignments: Make a portrait of your foot. Draw your self-portrait without looking in the mirror. Draw someone you know without looking at them. Paint your teeth, your breakfast, the sky, and—most maddening of all—paint something abstract. (Do not underestimate the difficulty of abstraction until you've tried it.)

The point, Liz coached me when we began, was not to make a finished product or a lovely piece to hang on the wall. The point was to get lost and not know where you'd end up.

I basked in the uncertainty. Liz's instructions helped me quit fussing over my mistakes. Following my hand around the page reminded me of getting lost on long walks in a new city. I thought of Julie's credo that travel can lead to new experiences that can lead to a new understanding of yourself. Sitting at a blank piece of paper with a pencil in hand could do it too.

My favorite prompt was this one, which was Liz's idea: Pick an object, describe it to your drawing partner as though you're an alien who's never seen this thing before, and have them draw the mysterious thing you describe.

It offers a crash course in seeing for both parties, I realized as I listened to Liz describe a teardrop shape with wavy parts coming out of it and two ovals pointing inward toward each other at the center. (A small brooch of a lion's head, it turned out.) Like becoming aware of the fact that the misshapen fuzzy lump at the bottom of your field of vision is your very own nose, the exercise forced me to look critically at the process of seeing. It made me aware of the assumptions my brain makes when my eyes graze something I think I already know, and I felt like I was glimpsing the outlines of my filter of expectation. "There's something magical about learning how to look at the world without identifying what you're looking at. You see so, so, so much more," Liz told me. "When I first saw the New York City subways, I was just blown away. I was like, 'Oh my God, all the color, all these weird little machines, all these little tiny buttons and things.'" I loved the idea of something as pedestrian as the subway dissolving into a million little miracles—the gleaming poles, the improbability of the underground tunnels, the rather philosophical disembodied voice barking, *Whoever is holding the doors, make a decision, are you in or are you out?* The trick was to see things by unseeing them.

If I couldn't get to art, I'd bring art to me, I decided. Inspired by my walk through Times Square with Julie and Amanda's broad idea of art, I tried to yank off my filter of expectation and see art everywhere. It was a lot of the same in those days: the same walks down the same streets; the same people in the same rooms. I kept looking. I tried to examine my toothbrush as if it were a Brancusi sculpture or study a chair as if it were an object I needed to describe to Liz. And then, in the shower one morning, time suddenly slowed: In the warm glow of the early sun, I caught sight of individual droplets of water glittering with tiny rainbows. My breath caught in my throat. Why had I never noticed that before? Could I ever again?

At the supermarket a few days later, I turned into the frozen-food aisle and just stared. Get a load of *this*: My eyes felt like they were quivering in their sockets as they gorged on the surreal, hyper-rainbow BUY ME absurdity of the scene. The dancing nuggets and erupting popsicles, the canoodling apple blintzes. I drew closer. What an endless expanse of fabulous nonsense words: HUNGRY-MAN, WYNGZ, BUBBA BURGER, FIRE GRILLED CHUNKS. A grin spread across my face. Anyone pushing their cart down the aisle would have taken one look at this strange woman, standing bug-eyed and unblinking in front of the bouncy Popcorn Chicken, and picked up their pace. But could Andy Warhol—or any pop artist, or any artist period—have crafted something so utterly strange and disorienting? I can't imagine how. But then, I can't imagine I'd have seen what I did without looking at art. I know for certain I wouldn't have recognized the beauty.

I still knew lots of artists who'd gag at that bourgeois profanity "beauty," but my time with Julie had got me thinking: What if beauty was just our name for experiences that push us out of our mental ruts and burst open our reducing valves of consciousness? A cave painting of a warty pig could do that, maybe more so in its time. Bacon's triptych of flayed, shot, and butchered figures on Ramp 4 could do that. ("Oh, honey," a turtlenecked visitor said when I told her it was one of my favorite pieces at the Gugg. "You're sick.") A supermarket aisle full of JUICY JUICE could do it too. What's beautiful depends on who we are, what we've encountered, where we live, and when. Likewise, the art that opens us to the chaotic stream of reality—the art we find beautiful—changes with time and with us, as we evolve. Beauty, I'd come to think, doesn't have to have a physical form, and it certainly doesn't have to be something we agree on. Beauty is that moment your mind jumps the curb. Beauty is the instant you sit up and start paying attention. Whatever makes that happen for you can be beautiful. Math equations. Gymnastics. Planes landing. But you have to be open to seeing it. Beauty doesn't find you. You create beauty by looking for it, and the moment you *do* find it, stop and pay attention. Beauty is infinite, if you decide it can be, but you may never see it the same way twice.

I got frustrated thinking about those in the art world pitching the artificial scarcity of great art. Beauty was not expensive or a luxury or hard to come by. It was attention that was in short supply.

I thought of my grandmother a lot during this time. Her stories about the war always made my guts clench and my heart beat faster, and the only reassurance I took from them was that, having heard her stories, I'd know what to do, I'd be prepared, I'd see the writing on the wall. Things couldn't change too fast for *me*. But having seen Times Square empty and a field hospital in Central Park, I didn't believe that anymore. I thought of my grandmother while I hid from the news. And I thought of her while I painted and learned to reexamine reality with a new expansiveness. Lifting your filter of expectation felt like a way to get your bearings in a new world. You observed. Examined. Noticed. I imagined her trying to make sense of what life looked like after she left the camps—without a home or a homeland, adrift from her family, staring into the yawning abyss of life in a country she didn't know, in a place she couldn't picture. I wondered if art had also helped her relearn a new world. And find the beauty in it.

INTROSPECTION is maddeningly unavoidable when you're trapped inside with only your husband and houseplants, and I started taking stock of whether I'd changed since giving my life over to art. On the surface, it seemed as if the answer was no: I didn't move cities. I didn't join an ashram. I didn't even dye my hair or get a tattoo.

I still asked the question "Is that art?" But I asked it less accusatorily and more out of genuine curiosity, and I asked less in galleries and more while out in the world—while watching a music video, say, or lingering in front of the crystalline lines of a bridge. I still thought a lot of art criticism was frustratingly dense, but now I had an alternative to offer: The best art-history education I ever got was staring at art while guarding at the Guggenheim. I got to know the artworks as intimate acquaintances, with their own personalities, instead of as a string of memorized words attached to someone else's judgments. Now, whenever I saw new pieces by Beuys or Brancusi, they fit into a context I'd created myself.

I still had flashes of paranoia about my reputation among the Heads, but the art world's popularity contest felt less relevant in isolation and puny compared to bigger concerns about life and the people I love. And gradually, the reality sunk in that I trusted myself around art and didn't need anyone to sign off on my choices. Disliking a work was my prerogative. Feeling nothing for it was too. But not engaging with art at all was, to me, no longer an option.

There were growing pains that went along with all this too. My taste, for instance, was unrecognizable. If there was one piece I could have taken home from Spring/Break—a piece by an artist named Colin Radcliffe that I *still* obsess over—it would have been a palm-sized ceramic of a naked bald man with protruding ribs, an enormous schlong, and one hand in a bag of Cheetos. The sculpture would not have gone famously with the serene black-and-white photos of a tree my husband and I picked up on our honeymoon. Leaving the reliability of my known preferences was scary, like stepping over a threshold without knowing if there's a floor to support you. It was also—to put it mildly—totally inconvenient. I can't say I was *thrilled* to realize that I couldn't stand to be around various objects and clothes I'd shelled out good money for in years' past. But I didn't feel as if I could have reversed my evolving tastes even if I'd wanted to, which I didn't.

Other parts of my life no longer fit me the way they had. Most awkwardly, my relationship to my own work had been thrown into disarray. I envied artists' freedom to experiment, the way they followed their interests and curiosities, then incorporated them into their pieces, without having to justify a news peg to an editor or scrunch their work to fit a prescribed word count. (Julie had stared at me with a look of abject horror when I described how an editor got to go over my work and make suggestions—"*Wow*, that must be annoying," she said, accustomed to gallerists who did no such thing.) In the Notes app on my phone, the list of story ideas I wanted to pursue began to veer off in strange and unfamiliar directions: WWE wrestling, jellyfish, beauty pageants, Dolly Parton. I wanted to find a way to dive into the world's odd treasures and make something out of that encounter using language, only I struggled to figure out how I could do with writing what Julie had done with, say, the plastic sushi *sampuru*. My life felt more expansive than it had, but in the process, I pushed up against limits I hadn't even noticed before and yearned to move beyond.

Being cooped up, aching to get to galleries, made me appreciate what a crucial part of my life art had become and—growing pains be damned—I wanted to make it part of *your* life too. As I drummed my fingernails, waiting for shows to open, my thoughts began to crystalize into what would become a manifesto I'd deliver to my friends whenever they innocently inquired about art.

I'd offer them unsolicited advice: *Go see as much as you can.*

People were right when they'd told me, early on, that to develop my Eye, I needed to see as much art as I could. Only I wish I'd learned sooner to stay in the work. To slow down. To demote context and ignore the press release. To let myself focus on the physical creation of the piece and the physical feeling of standing in front of it.

I'd urge people to supplement their museum visits with trips to the local art school or to some gallery based out of a garage. It's not that art in museums can't be hair-raisingly superb. It's just that the work has gone through so many layers of vetting by individuals who, like all of us, are biased, flawed, and operating within certain limitations. I'd seen the way artists got overlooked by the machine. I knew that the people pulling the strings often cared more about context than I did. I knew that New York didn't have a monopoly on good artists, that neither did art schools, and that "good" was a moving target anyway. That summer, as protests erupted and ambulances continued to wail, art's gatekeepers turned a critical eye on whom they'd excluded, for how long, and why. And yet nothing I witnessed magically fixed the flaws in the machine.

The hunger for messiness that I'd experienced after Miami had only intensified. Before the world screeched to a halt—and then after it opened up again—I kept gravitating toward open-studio events or upstart galleries tucked under sidewalks, where the mix of art had gone through fewer filters. (If you want or have suggestions, email me: bianca.bosker@me.com.) It can take some work to find these places, and the art scene's cliquey clubbiness can make you feel like the odd man out. But please don't let that stop you.

Now, I admit the work at these sorts of places can be chaotic. You could end up having your face sat on. But the uncertainty of not knowing what you'll find is part of the thrill. I got an adrenaline rush from the new, the weird, the unvetted, and not entirely figured out. Going to the Guggenheim was like a night at the theater—scripted, planned, impeccably rehearsed. Seeing work by emerging artists was like juggling chainsaws during a roller derby: Anything can happen. I, for one, relished going on that adventure.

I finally knew what Julie meant: New tastes create a new self. I saw that for certain late one August evening. It was the sort of summer night where the city feels like one big living room—warm, bright, people lounging everywhere—and I went to East Williamsburg to see Julie for the first time since March. I marched up the steps of her apartment rehearsing conversation topics, terrified of the degree to which my social skills had atrophied.

As it turns out, I didn't get four feet into the apartment before Julie's husband, Clinton King, threw himself into his rolling desk chair and shot himself over to his computer. He'd been working on a new video piece, he called over his shoulder while hammering at the computer keys. It was going to be a twenty-four-hour-long cycle of viral videos pieced together from memes, hallucinatory fractal patterns, and home-video detritus he'd scrounged up on the internet. He'd already assembled the first eight hours of the piece and didn't wait for me to sit down or put down my bag before hitting play.

Dancing cockatoos cut to swirls of water cut to painful accidents with lawn mowers. Green crystal patterns bled over the screen. Someone drove into a lake. Twitchy images hurled themselves at me one after another after anotherafteranother. An apartment in China. A manic barking Yorkipoo. Maybe I grunted something. Probably I had drool on my chin. My eyes felt like they were melting.

Forty-five minutes later, I still hadn't budged. I didn't want to move. Clinton's video was quenching some primal thirst, and it was like gorging on water after a long run in hundred-degree heat: refreshing, necessary, delicious. I hadn't seen anything, hadn't *imagined* anything like that in a long time. When Julie finally made him hit pause, I felt hyped up and invincible, practically sweaty. I could do anything. The world was limitless. We climbed up to the roof on a white metal ladder that hovered dangerously over the three-story drop of their building's stairwell, then stretched out on the roof's scratchy asphalt, watching Manhattan's skyline perform. Closer by, the shit tits sparkled and lights glowed yellow in low brick buildings as artists worked late into the night.

We drank beers. We talked about hunting for old Greek pottery shards, getting inspired by Coney Island oddities, and Salvador Dalí showing up in New York and attaching bread to a broom handle with the intention of shocking the city (then no one raising an eyebrow). I'm sure I laughed too hard. *Yes,* I thought, *this is what I'm talking about!* Bread and broom handles and trying to jostle our minds loose.

The evening threw into stark relief what I'd lost these last few months: the sense that anything was possible. The rules, as I knew them, did not have to apply. Art had taught me to embrace an improv-like *Yes, and . . .* approach to life. So many paths and possibilities seemed open. There was beauty everywhere, now that I knew how to look for it.

ACKNOWLEDGMENTS

Far more artists, curators, collectors, critics, viewers, dealers, gallerists, scientists, teachers, and friends contributed to this book than are named in its pages, and I thank each and every one of them for shaping my thinking and my journey, which feels in many ways like it's just begun. It's been years since I embarked on the adventure that became this book, and while certain things have changed since then, what hasn't is my profound sense of gratitude for having been welcomed in by so many art lovers who graciously shared their time, expertise, and existence with me (and often my notebook and tape recorder) for hours or months at a time, over a period of many years.

My deepest thanks to Elizabeth Denny and Rob Dimin for throwing me into the deep end and jumping in with me; to Julie Curtiss for her continued inspiration and for shaping much more than my Eye; to Amanda Alfieri for transforming my outlook on everything from art to asses; to Rob and Eric Thomas-Suwall for their infectious passion and stamina; and to Jack Barrett for imparting such invaluable wisdom and being willing to have the difficult conversations. I am extremely grateful to Johan Wagemans, Rebecca Chamberlain, and all of the attendees and organizers of the Visual Science of Art Conference who gave up their coffee breaks and lunches to huddle around my notebook explaining things to me. I am also thankful to—and filled with admiration for—the staff of the Solomon R. Guggenheim Museum. Please go visit them, and while you're at it, swing by Jack Barrett

Gallery, which is now in Tribeca, right around the corner from DIMIN (Rob's new space) and where Denny Dimin once stood. (Elizabeth has moved on to Over/Under Fine Art.) For drawing me deeper into this world, drawing connections I wouldn't have seen otherwise, and simply sitting down to draw with me: Thank you to Alex Adler, Liz Ainslie, Bridget Donahue, Jesse Greenberg, Rujeko Hockley, Jon Huddleson, Clinton King, Bibi Lenček, James and Kriz Wines, and Mitchell Algus, whose shows regularly blow my mind and whose gallery you should also definitely go see.

There'd be no book in your hands if it weren't for my editor, Lindsey Schwoeri, who gets the picture in every sense and is the most incredible (and patient) collaborator a writer could ask for. My enormous thanks to her, as well as to Allie Merola and the entire Penguin Random House team, who has shepherded this book with boundless enthusiasm, talent, and care. Sean Lavery, who didn't flinch when I dumped endless pages of notes on him, rigorously fact-checked this book and for that I thank him. Richard Pine: I'm the luckiest to have you on my side.

To my friends and family: Thank you all for being so supportive even when you wondered whether I'd dropped off the face of the earth. (Cathy, Zung, Lena, Gideon, Tanya: I'm thinking particularly of you.) Thank you especially to Chris Berger, Hannah Goldfield, Anna Harman, Daphne Jovanovic, Alice Lloyd George, Ari Lovelace, Blake Lyon, John McPhee, Christine Miranda, Rashaun Mitchell, Susan Orlean, Silas Riener, Elisabeth Robinson, Ali Sutherland-Brown, and Sophie von Haselberg for asking great questions and offering great answers. AZN, you've inspired me since before the beginning. And Matt. Thank you for believing and being there.

SELECTED BIBLIOGRAPHY

Abbing, Hans. 2002. *Why Are Artists Poor? The Exceptional Economy of the Arts.* Amsterdam: Amsterdam University Press.

Abiodun, Rowland. 1994. "Understanding Yoruba Art and Aesthetics: The Concept of *Ase*." *African Arts* 27 (3): 68–103.

Adam, Georgina. 2014. *Big Bucks: The Explosion of the Art Market in the 21st Century.* Surrey: Lund Humphries.

———. 2017. *Dark Side of the Boom: The Excesses of the Art Market in the 21st Century.* London: Lund Humphries.

Adams, Samuel. 2016. "Installation Views: A Historical Compendium." In *The Artist's Museum*, edited by Dan Byers, 184–244. Boston: Institute of Contemporary Art; Munich: DelMonico Books/Prestel.

Aerts, Anastasia, Lotte Feremans, and Andreas Pauls. 2016. "Do Art Experts Resist the Reward of Beauty?," Master's thesis, KU Leuven.

ahtone, heather. 2019. "Considering Indigenous Aesthetics: A Non-Western Paradigm." *American Society for Aesthetics Newsletter* 39 (3): 3–5.

Ajíbóyè, Olusegun, Stephen Fọlárànmí, and Nanashaitu Umoru-Ọkẹ. 2018. "Orí (Head) as an Expression of Yorùbá Aesthetic Philosophy." *Mediterranean Journal of Social Sciences* 9 (4): 59–70.

Alberro, Alexander, and Blake Stimson, eds. 1999. *Conceptual Art: A Critical Anthology.* Cambridge, MA: MIT Press.

Albers, Josef. (1963) 2013. *Interaction of Color.* New Haven, CT: Yale University Press.

Aleem, Hassan, Ivan Correa-Herran, and Norberto M. Grzywacz. 2020. "A Theoretical Framework for How We Learn Aesthetic Values." *Frontiers in Human Neuroscience* 14 (345): 1–18.

Allman, John Morgan. 1999. *Evolving Brains.* New York: Scientific American Library.

Alper, Neil O., and Gregory H. Wassall. 2006. "Artists' Careers and Their Labor Markets." In *Handbook of the Economics of Art and Culture*, Volume I, edited by Victor A. Ginsburgh and David Throsby, 813–64. London: Elsevier.

Amirshahi, Seyed Ali, Gregor Uwe Hayn-Leichsenring, Joachim Denzler, and Christoph Redies. 2016. "Color: A Crucial Factor for Aesthetic Quality Assessment in a Subjective Dataset of Paintings." Paper presented at the AIC 2013 Congress.

Anon Collective, ed. 2020. "A List of Famous Artists Who Used to Be Invigilators." In *Book of Anonymity*, 142–50. Goleta, CA: Punctum Books.

Archer, Michael. 2015. *Art Since 1960.* London: Thames & Hudson.

Armstrong, Elizabeth, and Joan Rothfuss. 1993. *In the Spirit of Fluxus.* Minneapolis: Walker Art Center.

Arnheim, Rudolf. 1974. *Art and Visual Perception: A Psychology of the Creative Eye.* Berkeley: University of California Press.

ARTnews. 2018–2023. "Top 200 Collectors." ARTnews.com. https://www.artnews.com/art-collectors/top
-200-collectors/top-200-collectors/.

Asher, Tedi. "A Neuroscience-Informed Approach to the Design of Art Experiences in a Museum Setting."
Lecture, Peabody Essex Museum, Salem, MA, April, 2, 2019.

Aston, Stacey, and Anya Hurlbert. 2017. "What #TheDress Reveals about the Role of Illumination Priors in
Color Perception and Color Constancy." *Journal of Vision* 17 (9): 1–18.

Atencio, Tiqui. 2016. *Could Have, Would Have, Should Have: Inside the World of the Art Collector.* London:
Art Books.

Baedeker, Karl. 1888. *Paris and Environs with Routes from London to Paris.* London: Karl Baedeker.

Baines, John. 1985. "Color Terminology and Color Classification: Ancient Egyptian Color Terminology and
Polychromy." *American Anthropologist* 87 (2): 282–97.

———. 1994. "On the Status and Purposes of Ancient Egyptian Art." *Cambridge Archaeological Journal* 4
(1): 67–94.

Ball, Philip. 2013. "Neuroaesthetics Is Killing Your Soul." *Nature* (March 22).

Bankowsky, Jack. 1991. "Slackers." *Artforum* (November): 96–100.

Bannister, Scott. 2019. "Distinct Varieties of Aesthetic Chills in Response to Multimedia." Edited by Ron-
ald Fischer. *PLoS ONE* 14 (11): e0224974.

Bar, Moshe, and Maital Neta. 2006. "Humans Prefer Curved Visual Objects." *Psychological Science* 17 (8):
645–48.

Bardes, C. L., D. Gillers, and A. E. Herman. 2001. "Learning to Look: Developing Clinical Observational
Skills at an Art Museum." *Medical Education* 35 (12): 1157–61.

Barham, Lawrence. 2002. "Backed Tools in Middle Pleistocene Central Africa and Their Evolutionary Significance." *Journal of Human Evolution* 43: 585–603.

Barham, Lawrence S. 2002. "Systematic Pigment Use in the Middle Pleistocene of South-Central Africa."
Current Anthropology 43 (1): 181–90.

Barnes, Julian. 2015. *Keeping an Eye Open: Essays on Art.* New York: Alfred A. Knopf.

Batchelor, David. 2000. *Chromophobia.* London: Reaktion.

Bauck, Whitney. 2022. "The Toxic History of Color." Atmos.com (November 21). https://atmos.earth
/natural-dyes-synthetic-color-toxic/.

Beam, Christopher. 2012. "Kehinde Wiley's Global Reach." *New York Magazine*, April 20. https://nymag
.com/arts/art/rules/kehinde-wiley-2012-4/.

Beck, Graham T. 2008. "A Portrait of the Artist as a Young Assistant." *The Brooklyn Rail*, February.
https://brooklynrail.org/2008/02/artseen/a-portrait-of-the-artist-as-a-young-assistant.

Bednarik, Robert G. 2013. "Pleistocene Palaeoart of Africa." *Arts* 2 (1): 6–34.

Behrman, S. N. (1952) 1972. *Duveen.* Boston: Little, Brown.

Belke, Benno, Helmut Leder, and Claus Christian Carbon. 2015. "When Challenging Art Gets Liked: Evi-
dences for a Dual Preference Formation Process for Fluent and Non-fluent Portraits." *PLoS ONE* 10 (8):
e0131796.

Bell, Lawrence T. O., and Darrell J. R. Evans. 2014. "Art, Anatomy, and Medicine: Is There a Place for Art
in Medical Education?" *Anatomical Sciences Education* 7 (January): 370–78.

Berger, John. 1972. *Ways of Seeing.* London: British Broadcasting Corporation and Penguin Books.

Berger, Maurice. 1990. "Are Art Museums Racist?" *Art in America*, September.

Biederman, Irving, and Edward A. Vessel. 2006. "Perceptual Pleasure and the Brain: A Novel Theory Explains
Why the Brain Craves Information and Seeks It through the Senses." *American Scientist* 94 (3): 247–53.

Bimler, David L., Megan Snellock, and Galina V. Paramei. 2019. "Art Expertise in Construing Meaning of
Representational and Abstract Artworks." *Acta Psychologica* 192 (January): 11–22.

Bitgood, Stephen. 1989. "Deadly Sins Revisited: A Review of the Exhibit Label Literature." *Visitor Behavior* 4 (3): 4–11.

———. 2009. "Museum Fatigue: A Critical Review." *Visitor Studies* 12 (2): 93–111.

Bomford, David, and Ashok Roy. 2009. *A Closer Look: Colour.* London: National Gallery.

Böthig, Antonia M., and Gregor U. Hayn-Leichsenring. 2017. "Taste in Art—Exposure to Histological
Stains Shapes Abstract Art Preferences." *i-Perception* (September–October): 1–6.

Boucher, Brian. 2015. "Mellon Foundation Study Reveals Uncomfortable Lack of Diversity in American
Museums." *Artnet News*, August 4. https://news.artnet.com/art-world/mellon-foundation-museum
-diversity-study-322299.

Bourdieu, Pierre. 1984. *Distinction: A Social Critique of the Judgement of Taste.* Translated by Richard
Nice. Cambridge, MA: Harvard University Press.

Bourdon, David. 1977. "A Critic's Diary: The New York Art Year." *Art in America*, July/August.

Bourriaud, Nicolas. (1998) 2002. *Relational Aesthetics.* Paris: Les Presses du Réel.

Braden, L. E. A. 2016. "Collectors and Collections: Critical Recognition of the World's Top Art Collectors."
Social Forces 94 (4): 1483–1507.

Brieber, David, Marcos Nadal, Helmut Leder, and Raphael Rosenberg. 2014. "Art in Time and Space: Context Modulates the Relation between Art Experience and Viewing Time." *PLoS ONE* 9 (6): e99019.

Brielmann, Aenne A., and Denis G. Pelli. 2017. "Beauty Requires Thought." *Current Biology* 27 (10): 1506–1513.e3.

———. 2018. "Aesthetics." *Current Biology* 28 (August): R847–70.

———. 2019. "Intense Beauty Requires Intense Pleasure." *Frontiers in Psychology* 10 (November): 1–17.

Brielmann, Aenne A., Lauren Vale, and Denis G. Pelli. 2017. "Beauty at a Glance: The Feeling of Beauty and the Amplitude of Pleasure Are Independent of Stimulus Duration." *Journal of Vision* 17 (14): 1–12.

Brimo, René. 2016. *The Evolution of Taste in American Collecting.* Translated by Kenneth Haltman. University Park: Pennsylvania State Press.

Bringley, Patrick. 2023. *All the Beauty in the World.* New York: Simon & Schuster.

Brinkmann, Hanna, Jane Boddy, Beatrice Immelmann, Eva Specker, Matthew Pelowski, Helmut Leder, and Raphael Rosenberg. 2018. "Ferocious Colors and Peaceful Lines. Describing and Measuring Aesthetic Effects." *Wiener Jahrbuch für Kunstgeschichte* 65 (1): 7–26.

Brinkmann, Hanna, Laura Commare, Helmut Leder, and Raphael Rosenberg. 2014. "Abstract Art as a Universal Language?" *Leonardo* 47 (3): 256–57.

Brooks, Alison S., John E. Yellen, Richard Potts, Anna K. Behrensmeyer, Alan L. Deino, David E. Leslie, Stanley H. Ambrose, Jeffrey R. Ferguson, Francesco d'Errico, Andrew M. Zipkin, Scott Whittaker, Jeffrey Post, Elizabeth G. Veatch, Kimberly Foecke, and Jennifer B. Clark. 2018. "Long-Distance Stone Transport and Pigment Use in the Earliest Middle Stone Age." *Science* 360 (6384): 90–94.

Brownlee, Peter John. 2009. "Color Theory and the Perception of Art." *American Art* 23 (2): 21–24.

Brumm, Adam, Adhi Agus Oktaviana, Basran Burhan, Budianto Hakim, Rustan Lebe, Jian-xin Zhao, Priyatno Hadi Sulistyarto, Marlon Ririmasse, Shinatria Adhityatama, Iwan Sumantri, and Maxime Aubert. 2021. "Oldest Cave Art Found in Sulawesi." *Science Advances* 7 (3): eabd4648.

Buchloh, Benjamin H. D., and Judith F. Rodenbeck. 1999. *Experiments in the Everyday: Allan Kaprow and Robert Watts—Events, Objects, Documents.* New York: Wallach Art Gallery.

Burnham, Sophy. 1973. *The Art Crowd.* New York: D. McKay.

Burt, Nathaniel. 1977. *Palaces for the People: A Social History of the American Art Museum.* Boston: Little, Brown.

Cahn, Steven M., and Aaron Meskin, eds. 2008. *Aesthetics: A Comprehensive Anthology.* Malden, MA: Blackwell.

Carbon, Claus-Christian. 2017. "Art Perception in the Museum: How We Spend Time and Space in Art Exhibitions." *i-Perception* (January–February): 1–15.

Carrier, David. 1987. "The Display of Art: An Historical Perspective." *Leonardo* 20 (1): 83–86.

Carroll, Noël. 2004. "Art and Human Nature." *Journal of Aesthetics and Art Criticism* 62 (2): 95–107.

Casson, Dinah. 2020. *Closed on Mondays: Behind the Scenes at the Museum.* London: Lund Humphries.

Cavanagh, Patrick. 2005. "The Artist as Neuroscientist." *Nature* 434 (7031): 301–7.

Cela-Conde, Camilo José, and Francisco J. Ayala. 2018. "Art and Brain Coevolution." *Progress in Brain Research* 237 (April): 41–60.

Celender, Don. 1978. *Observations, Protestations and Lamentations of Museum Guards throughout the World.* New York: O.K. Harris Gallery.

Chamberlain, Rebecca. 2017. "The Development of Expertise in the Visual Arts." In *The Science of Expertise: Behavioral, Neural, and Genetic Approaches to Complex Skill,* edited by David Z. Hambrick, Guillermo Campitelli, and Brooke N. Macnamara, 129–150. New York: Routledge.

———. 2018. "Drawing as a Window onto Expertise." *Current Directions in Psychological Science* 27 (6): 501–7.

Chamberlain, Rebecca, Jennifer E. Drake, Aaron Kozbelt, Rachel Hickman, Joseph Siev, and Johan Wagemans. 2019. "Artists as Experts in Visual Cognition: An Update." *Psychology of Aesthetics, Creativity and the Arts* 13 (1): 58–73.

Chamberlain, Rebecca, I. Chris McManus, Nicola Brunswick, Qona Rankin, Howard Riley, and Ryota Kanai. 2014. "Drawing on the Right Side of the Brain: A Voxel-Based Morphometry Analysis of Observational Drawing." *Neuroimage* 96 (August): 167–73.

Chamberlain, Rebecca, Lena Swinnen, Sarah Heeren, and Johan Wagemans. 2017. "Perceptual Flexibility Is Coupled with Reduced Executive Inhibition in Students of the Visual Arts." *British Journal of Psychology* 109 (2): 244–58.

Chamberlain, Rebecca, and Johan Wagemans. 2015. "Visual Arts Training Is Linked to Flexible Attention to Local and Global Levels of Visual Stimuli." *Acta Psychologica* 161 (October): 185–97.

Chang, EunJung. 2006. "Interactive Experiences and Contextual Learning in Museums." *Studies in Art Education* 47 (2): 170–86.

Charlin, Ventura, and Arturo Cifuentes. 2020. "The Price of Color in Mark Rothko's Paintings." *SSRN,* February.

Charney, Noah. 2017. "Did Jeff Really Paint That Koons? Working at a Modern Studio Isn't Exactly a Renaissance Apprenticeship." Salon.com, June 25. https://www.salon.com/2017/06/25/did-jeff-really
-paint-that-koons-inside-the-studio-system/.

Chatterjee, Anjan. 2014. *The Aesthetic Brain: How We Evolved to Desire Beauty and Enjoy Art*. New York:
Oxford University Press.

Che, Jiajia, Xiaolei Sun, Víctor Gallardo, and Marcus Nadal. 2018. "Cross-Cultural Empirical Aesthetics."
In *Progress in Brain Research*, edited by Julia F. Christensen and Antoni Gomila, 77–103. London: Elsevier.

Cheung, Olivia S., and Moshe Bar. 2012. "Visual Prediction and Perceptual Expertise." *International Journal of Psychophysiology* 83 (2): 156–63.

Christov-Bakargiev, Carolyn, ed. 2005. *Arte Povera*. London: Phaidon.

Chua, Hannah Faye, Julie E. Boland, and Richard E. Nisbett. 2005. "Cultural Variation in Eye Movements
during Scene Perception." *Proceedings of the National Academy of Sciences* 102 (35): 12629–33.

Cifuentes, Arturo. 2019. "Pricing Beauty: Is It Risky to Invest in Art?" Paper presented at the Columbia
Global Center Conference, Santiago, Chile, September.

Cifuentes, Arturo, and Ventura Charlin. 2023. *The Worth of Art*. New York: Columbia Business School.

Coles, David. 2018. *Chromatopia: An Illustrated History of Color*. New York: Thames & Hudson.

Conklin, Harold C. 1986. "Hanunóo Color Categories." *Journal of Anthropological Research* 42 (3):
441–46.

Constable, William George. 1964. *Art Collecting in the United States of America: An Outline of a History*.
London: Nelson.

Corbett, Rachel. 2018. "The End of Exhibitions? As Attendance Plummets, New York Dealers Are Scrambling to Secure the Future of the Art Gallery." *Artnet News*, July 18. https://news.artnet.com/market
/foot-traffic-galleries-new-york-1318769.

Coulson, Sheila, Sigrid Staurset, and Nick Walker. 2011. "Ritualized Behavior in the Middle Stone Age:
Evidence from Rhino Cave, Tsodilo Hills, Botswana." *PaleoAnthropology* 2011: 18–61.

Crane, Diana. 1987. *The Transformation of the Avant-Garde: The New York Art World, 1940–1985*. Chicago: University of Chicago Press.

Cupchik, Gerald C., and Robert J. Gebotys. 1990. "Interest and Pleasure as Dimensions of Aesthetic Response." *Empirical Studies of the Arts* 8 (1): 1–14.

Cupchik, Gerald C., Oshin Vartanian, Adrian Crawley, and David J. Mikulis. 2009. "Viewing Artworks:
Contributions of Cognitive Control and Perceptual Facilitation to Aesthetic Experience." *Brain and
Cognition* 70: 84–91.

Curran, Kathleen. 2016. *The Invention of the American Art Museum: From Craft to Kulturgeschichte,
1870–1930*. Los Angeles: Getty Research Institute.

Cutting, James. 2003. "Gustave Caillebotte, French Impressionism, and Mere Exposure." *Psychonomic
Bulletin & Review* 10 (2): 319–43.

———. 2007. "Mere Exposure, Reproduction, and the Impressionist Canon." In *Partisan Canons*, edited by
Anna Brzyski, 79–94. Durham, NC: Duke University Press.

Danto, Arthur C. 1964. "The Artworld." *Journal of Philosophy* 61 (19): 571–84.

———. 1992. *Beyond the Brillo Box: The Visual Arts in Post-historical Perspective*. New York: Farrar, Straus
and Giroux.

———. 1997. *After the End of Art: Contemporary Art and the Pale of History*. Princeton, NJ: Princeton University Press.

———. 1998. "The End of Art: A Philosophical Defense." *History and Theory* 37 (4): 127–43.

———. 2002. "The Abuse of Beauty." *Daedalus* 131 (4): 35–56.

———. 2003. *The Abuse of Beauty: Aesthetics and the Concept of Art*. Chicago: Open Court.

———. 2013. *What Art Is*. New Haven, CT: Yale University Press.

Dart, Raymond A. 1974. "The Waterworn Australopithecine Pebble of Many Faces from Makapansgat."
South African Journal of Science 70 (June): 167–69.

Davis, Ben. 2013. *9.5 Theses on Art and Class*. Chicago: Haymarket Books.

Davis, Steven, ed. 2000. *Color Perception: Philosophical, Psychological, Artistic, and Computational Perspectives*. New York: Oxford University Press.

De Coppet, Laura, and Alan Jones. 1984. *The Art Dealers: The Powers behind the Scene Tell How the Art
World Really Works*. New York: C.N. Potter.

De Winter, Stefanie, Pieter Moors, Hilde Van Gelder, and Johan Wagemans. 2018. "Illusory Depth Based
on Interactions between Fluorescent and Conventional Colours: A Case Study on Frank Stella's Irregu-
lar Polygons Paintings." *Art & Perception* 6: 116–50.

Diessner, Rhett. 2019. *Understanding the Beauty Appreciation Trait: Empirical Research on Seeking
Beauty in All Things*. Palgrave Macmillan.

DiMaggio, Paul. 1982a. "Cultural Entrepreneurship in Nineteenth-Century Boston: The Creation of an Organizational Base for High Culture in America." *Media, Culture and Society* 4 (1): 33–50.

———. 1982b. "Cultural Entrepreneurship in Nineteenth-Century Boston, Part II: The Classification and Framing of American Art." *Media, Culture and Society* 4 (4): 303–22.

DiMaggio, Paul, and Francie Ostrower. 1990. "Participation in the Arts by Black and White Americans." *Social Forces* 68 (3): 753–78.

DiMaggio, Paul, and Michael Useem. 1978. "Social Class and Arts Consumption: The Origins and Consequences of Class Differences in Exposure to the Arts in America." *Theory and Society* 5 (2): 141–61.

Dissanayake, Ellen. 1995. *Homo Aestheticus: Where Art Comes from and Why.* Seattle: University of Washington Press.

———. 2011. "Doing without the Ideology of Art." *New Literary History* 42 (1): 71–79.

———. 2015. " 'Aesthetic Primitives': Fundamental Biological Elements of a Naturalistic Aesthetics." *Aisthesis* 8 (1): 5–24.

Doering, Zahava D. 1999. "Strangers, Guests, or Clients? Visitor Experiences in Museums." *Curator: The Museum Journal* 42 (2): 74–87.

Dolev, Jacqueline C., Linda Krohner Friedlaender, and Irwin M. Braverman. 2001. "Use of Fine Art to Enhance Visual Diagnostic Skills." *JAMA: Journal of the American Medical Association* 286 (9): 1020–21.

D'Souza, Carin Laura. 2012. "Art and Neuroscience: The Historical Emergence and Conceptual Context of Neuro-art." PhD diss., Jacobs University.

Dutton, Denis. 2009. *The Art Instinct: Beauty, Pleasure, and Human Evolution.* New York: Bloomsbury.

Dyck, John, and Matt Johnson. 2016. "Appreciating Bad Art." *Journal of Value Inquiry* 51 (August): 279–92. https://doi.org/10.1007/s10790-016-9569-2.

Eco, Umberto, ed. 2010. *History of Beauty.* New York: Rizzoli.

Elkins, James. 2004. *Pictures and Tears: A History of People Who Have Cried in Front of Paintings.* New York: Routledge.

Eskine, Kendall J., Natalie A. Kacinik, and Jesse J. Prinz. 2012. "Stirring Images: Fear, Not Happiness or Arousal, Makes Art More Sublime." *Emotion* 12 (5): 1071–74.

Esplund, Lance. 2018. *The Art of Looking: How to Read Modern and Contemporary Art.* New York: Basic Books.

Essel, Osuanyi Quaicoo, and Ebenezer Kwabena Acquah. 2016. "Conceptual Art: The Untold Story of African Art." *Journal of Literature and Art Studies* 6 (10): 1203–20.

Estrada-Gonzalez, Vicente, Scott East, Michael Garbutt, and Branka Spehar. 2020. "Viewing Art in Different Contexts." *Frontiers in Psychology* 11 (569): 1–20.

Etcoff, Nancy. 1999. *Survival of the Prettiest: The Science of Beauty.* New York: Anchor Books.

Everson, Jane E., Denis V. Reidy, and Lisa Sampson, eds. 2016. *The Italian Academies 1525–1700: Networks of Culture, Innovation and Dissent.* New York: Routledge.

Fancourt, Daisy, and Saoirse Finn. 2019. "What Is the Evidence on the Role of the Arts in Improving Health and Well-Being?" Copenhagen: WHO Regional Office for Europe.

Filipovic, Elena. 2014. "The Global White Cube." *OnCurating* 22. https://www.on-curating.org/issue-22-43/the-global-white-cube.html

Fine, Gary Alan. 2018. *Talking Art: The Culture of Practice & the Practice of Culture in MFA Education.* Chicago: University of Chicago Press.

Finlay, Victoria. 2004. *Color: A Natural History of the Palette.* New York: Random House.

Florida, Richard. 2017. "NYC Has More Artists Than Ever." *Bloomberg,* July 25. https://www.bloomberg.com/news/articles/2017-07-25/nyc-is-still-the-us-capital-for-artists.

Fong, Wen. 1962. "The Problem of Forgeries in Chinese Painting. Part One." *Artibus Asiae* 25 (2/3): 95–119.

Forbes, Jack D. 2001. "Indigenous Americans: Spirituality and Ecos." American Academy of Arts and Sciences. https://www.amacad.org/publication/indigenous-americans-spirituality-and-ecos.

Fraiberger, Samuel P., Roberta Sinatra, Magnus Resch, Christoph Riedl, and Albert-László Barabási. 2018. "Quantifying Reputation and Success in Art." *Science* 362 (6416): 825–29.

Fu, Xiaowei, and Yi Wang. 2015. "Confucius on the Relationship of Beauty and Goodness." *Journal of Aesthetic Education* 49 (1): 68–81.

Garber, Marjorie B. 2008. *Patronizing the Arts.* Princeton, NJ: Princeton University Press.

Gartus, Andreas, Mark Völker, and Helmut Leder. 2020. "What Experts Appreciate in Patterns: Art Expertise Modulates Preference for Asymmetric and Face-like Patterns." *Symmetry* 12 (5): 707.

Gilman, Benjamin Ives. 1918. *Museum Ideals of Purpose and Method.* Boston: Museum of Fine Arts.

Girst, Thomas, and Magnus Resch. 2016. *100 Secrets of the Art World.* London: Koenig Books.

Gogosian, Jerry (@JerryGogosian). n.d. Instagram. https://www.instagram.com/jerrygogosian/.

Goldstein, Malcolm. 2000. *Landscape with Figures: A History of Art Dealing in the United States.* Oxford: Oxford University Press.

Gómez-Puerto, Gerardo, Jaume Rosselló, Guido Corradi, Cristina Acedo-Carmona, Enric Munar, and Marcos Nadal. 2017. "Preference for Curved Contours across Cultures." *Psychology of Aesthetics, Creativity, and the Arts* 12 (4): 432–39.

Grasskamp, Walter. 2007. "The White Wall: On the Prehistory of the 'White Cube.'" *OnCurating* 9. https://www.on-curating.org/issue-9-reader/the-white-wall-on-the-prehistory-of-the-white-cube.html.

Greenberg, Clement. 1961. *Art and Culture: Critical Essays*. Boston: Beacon Press.

Gregory, Richard, John Harris, Priscilla Heard, and David Rose, eds. 1995. *The Artful Eye*. New York: Oxford University Press.

Guggenheim, Barbara. 2016. *Art World: The New Rules of the Game*. Beverly Hills: Bobby Woods/Marmont Lane Books.

Guggenheim Museum. 2009. *The Guggenheim: Frank Lloyd Wright and the Making of the Modern Museum*. New York: Guggenheim Museum.

Haden-Guest, Anthony. 1996. *True Colors: The Real Life of the Art World*. New York: Atlantic Monthly Press.

Halperin, Julia, and Charlotte Burns. 2019. "Museums Claim They're Paying More Attention to Female Artists. That's an Illusion." *Artnet News*, September 19. https://news.artnet.com/womens-place-in-the-art-world/womens-place-art-world-museums-1654714#:~:text=the%20Art%20World-.

Halpern, Daniel, ed. 1988. *Writers on Artists*. San Francisco: North Point Press.

Handa, Rumiko. 2013. "Sen No Rikyū and the Japanese Way of Tea: Ethics and Aesthetics of the Everyday." *Interiors* 4 (3): 229–47.

Hannah, Duncan. 2018. *20th Century Boy: Notebooks of the Seventies*. New York: Vintage.

Hardin, C. L., and Luisa Maffi. 1997. *Color Categories in Thought and Language*. Cambridge: Cambridge University Press.

Harris, Neil. 1966. *The Artist in American Society: The Formative Years, 1790–1860*. New York: G. Braziller.

Hass, Nancy. 2018. "Are Fabricators the Most Important People in the Art World?" *The New York Times Style Magazine*, June 22. https://www.nytimes.com/2018/06/22/t-magazine/art-fabricators.html.

Hawley-Dolan, Angelina, and Ellen Winner. 2011. "Seeing the Mind behind the Art: People Can Distinguish Abstract Expressionist Paintings from Highly Similar Paintings by Children, Chimps, Monkeys, and Elephants." *Psychological Science* 22 (4): 435–41.

Hayn-Leichsenring, Gregor U. 2017. "The Ambiguity of Artworks—a Guideline for Empirical Aesthetics Research with Artworks as Stimuli." *Frontiers in Psychology* 8: 1857.

Hayn-Leichsenring, Gregor U., Nadine Kloth, Stefan R. Schweinberger, and Christoph Redies. 2013. "Adaptation Effects to Attractiveness of Face Photographs and Art Portraits Are Domain-Specific." *i-Perception* 4: 303–16.

Heidenreich, Susan M., and Kathleen A. Turano. 2011. "Where Does One Look When Viewing Artwork in a Museum?" *Empirical Studies of the Arts* 29 (1): 51–72.

Herman, Amy E. 2016. *Visual Intelligence: Sharpen Your Perception, Change Your Life*. Boston: Mariner Books/Houghton Mifflin Harcourt.

Hertz, Richard. 2003. *Jack Goldstein and the CalArts Mafia*. Ojai, CA: Minneola Press.

Hoel, Erik. 2021. "The Overfitted Brain: Dreams Evolved to Assist Generalization." *Patterns* 2 (5): 100244. https://www.cell.com/patterns/fulltext/S2666-3899(21)00064-7?_returnURL=https%3A%2F%2Flinkinghub.elsevier.com%2Fretrieve%2Fpii%2FS2666389921000647%3Fshowall%3Dtrue.

———. 2022. "Exit the Supersensorium." *The Intrinsic Perspective*, October 19. https://erikhoel.substack.com/p/exit-the-supersensorium.

Hook, Philip. 2013. *Breakfast at Sotheby's: An A–Z of the Art World*. London: Particular Books.

———. 2017. *Rogues' Gallery: A History of Art and Its Dealers*. London: Profile Books.

Hovers, Erella, Shimon Ilani, Ofer Bar-Yosef, and Bernard Vandermeersch. 2003. "An Early Case of Color Symbolism: Ochre Use by Modern Humans in Qafzeh Cave." *Current Anthropology* 44 (4): 491–522.

Howe, Winifred E. 1913. *A History of the Metropolitan Museum of Art*. New York: Metropolitan Museum of Art.

Huang, He. 2018. "The Route of Lapis Lazuli: Lapis Lazuli Trade from Afghanistan to Egypt during Mid-Late Bronze Age." *Advances in Social Science, Education and Humanities Research* 183: 391–99.

Hurlbert, Anya. 1999. "Colour Vision: Is Colour Constancy Real?" *Current Biology* 9 (15): R558–61.

———. 2019. "Challenges to Color Constancy in a Contemporary Light." *Current Opinion in Behavioral Sciences* 30 (December): 186–93.

Hurlbert, Anya, and Christopher Cuttle. 2019. "New Museum Lighting for People and Paintings." *LEUKOS* 16 (1): 1–5.

Huston, Joseph P., Marcos Nadal, Franciso Mora, Luigi F. Agnati, and Camilo J. Cela-Conde, eds. 2015. *Art, Aesthetics, and the Brain*. Oxford: Oxford University Press.

Huxley, Aldous. (1956) 1963. *The Doors of Perception, and Heaven and Hell.* New York: Harper & Row.

Ibanga, Diana-Abasi. 2017. "The Concept of Beauty in African Philosophy." *Africology: Journal of Pan African Studies* 10 (7).

Ishizu, Tomohiro, and Semir Zeki. 2011. "Toward a Brain-Based Theory of Beauty." *PLoS ONE* 6 (7): e21852.

———. 2014. "A Neurobiological Enquiry into the Origins of Our Experience of the Sublime and Beautiful." *Frontiers in Human Neuroscience* 8 (November): 1–10.

Israel, Matthew. 2020. *A Year in the Art World: An Insider's View.* London: Thames & Hudson.

Itten, Johannes. 1961. *The Art of Color: The Subjective Experience and Objective Rationale of Color.* Translated by Ernst van Haagen. New York: John Wiley & Sons.

Jahoda, Susan, Blair Murphy, Vicky Virgin, and Caroline Woolard. 2014. "Artists Report Back." A report by BFAMFAPhD.

Jameson, Kimberly A., Alissa D. Winkler, Christian Herrera, and Keith Goldfarb. 2015. "The Veridicality of Color: A Case Study of Potential Human Tetrachromacy." *GLIMPSE Journal* 12 (January): 1–36.

Jasani, Sona K., and Norma S. Saks. 2013. "Utilizing Visual Art to Enhance the Clinical Observation Skills of Medical Students." *Medical Teacher* 35: e1327–31.

Jucker, Jean-Luc, Justin L. Barrett, and Rafael Wlodarski. 2014. "'I Just Don't Get It': Perceived Artists' Intentions Affect Art Evaluations." *Empirical Studies of the Arts* 32 (2): 149–82.

Jung, Carl G., M.-L. von Franz, Joseph L. Henderson, Jolande Jacobi, and Aniela Jaffé. (1964) 1968. *Man and His Symbols.* New York: Dell.

Kambaskovic-Sawers, Danijela, and Charles T. Wolfe. 2018. "The Senses in Philosophy and Science: From the Nobility of Sight to the Materialism of Touch." In *A Cultural History of the Senses in the Renaissance,* edited by Herman Roodenburg, 108–25. New York: Bloomsbury.

Kanu, Macaulay A. 2007. "African Art and Its Aesthetic Values in African Philosophy." *Flash* 1 (1).

Kelly, Kenneth L., and Deane B. Judd. 1976. *Color: Universal Language and Dictionary of Names.* Washington, DC: US Department of Commerce National Bureau of Standards.

Kenett, Yoed N., Lyle Ungar, and Anjan Chatterjee. 2021. "Beauty and Wellness in the Semantic Memory of the Beholder." *Frontiers in Psychology* 12 (August).

Kinsella, Eileen. 2021. "Archaeologists Have Uncovered Cave Art That's Way Older Than Any on Record—and It Was Made by Children." *Artnet News,* September 16. https://news.artnet.com/art-world/scientists-discovered-that-hand-prints-made-by-children-are-earliest-prehistoric-art-2009974.

Klonk, Charlotte. 2009. *Spaces of Experience: Art Gallery Interiors from 1800 to 2000.* New Haven, CT: Yale University Press.

———. 2015. "Myth and Reality of the White Cube." In *From Museum Critique to the Critical Museum,* edited by Katarzyna Murawska-Muthesius and Piotr Piotrowski, 67–79. London: Routledge.

Korsmeyer, Carolyn. 1999. *Making Sense of Taste.* Ithaca, NY: Cornell University Press.

Kristeller, Paul Oskar. 1951. "The Modern System of the Arts: A Study in the History of Aesthetics Part I." *Journal of the History of Ideas* 12 (4): 496–527.

Lachapelle, Richard, Deborah Murray, and Sandy Neim. 2003. "Aesthetic Understanding as Informed Experience: The Role of Knowledge in Our Art Viewing Experiences." *Journal of Aesthetic Education* 37 (3): 78–98.

Laing, Olivia. 2020. *Funny Weather: Art in an Emergency.* New York: W. W. Norton.

Lauring, Jon O., Matthew Pelowski, Michael Forster, Matthias Gondan, Maurice Ptito, and Ron Kupers. 2016. "Well, If They Like It… Effects of Social Groups' Ratings and Price Information on the Appreciation of Art." *Psychology of Aesthetics, Creativity, and the Arts* 10 (3): 344–59.

Lauter, Devorah. 2021. "In an Astounding New Book, a Neuroscientist Reveals the Profound Real-World Benefits Art Has on Our Brains." *Artnet News,* March 2. https://news.artnet.com/art-world/art-that-heals-science-1945970.

Leahy, Helen Rees. (2012) 2016. *Museum Bodies: The Politics and Practices of Visiting and Viewing.* London: Routledge.

Learner, Thomas J. S., Patricia Smithen, Jay W. Krueger, and Michael R. Schilling, eds. 2007. *Modern Paints Uncovered: Proceedings from the Modern Paints Uncovered Symposium.* Los Angeles: Getty Conservation Institute.

Leder, Helmut, Gernot Gerger, Stefan G. Dressler, and Alfred Schabmann. 2012. "How Art Is Appreciated." *Psychology of Aesthetics, Creativity, and the Arts* 6 (1): 2–10.

Leder, Helmut, and Marcos Nadal. 2014. "Ten Years of a Model of Aesthetic Appreciation and Aesthetic Judgments: The Aesthetic Episode—Developments and Challenges in Empirical Aesthetics." *British Journal of Psychology* 105: 443–64.

Leder, Helmut, Pablo P. L. Tinio, David Brieber, Tonio Kröner, Thomas Jacobsen, and Raphael Rosenberg. 2019. "Symmetry Is Not a Universal Law of Beauty." *Empirical Studies of the Arts* 37 (1): 104–14.

Lee, Alan. 1981. "A Critical Account of Some of Josef Albers' Concepts of Color." *Leonardo* 14 (2): 99–105.

Lindell, Annukka K., and Julia Mueller. 2011. "Can Science Account for Taste? Psychological Insights into Art Appreciation." *Journal of Cognitive Psychology* 23 (4): 453–75.

L'invitation à la beauté. n.d. "Revue de Presse." Accessed September 24, 2023. http://www.linvitationala beaute.org/revue-de-presse/?fbclid=IwAR2pFxBCyVbGoVMSmBgXtUIHFboZmZGx3WZkxsAVsqgN csGo6hsNSO8LQCU.

Lopes, Dominic McIver. 2008. "Nobody Needs a Theory of Art." *Journal of Philosophy* 105 (3): 109–27. https://doi.org/10.5840/jphil200810531.

Lukach, Joan M. 1984. *Hilla Rebay: In Search of the Spirit in Art*. New York: George Braziller.

Lukehart, Peter M., ed. 2010. *The Accademia Seminars: The Accademia di San Luca in Rome, c. 1590–1635*. Washington DC: National Gallery of Art.

Lyssenko, Nathalie, Christoph Redies, and Gregor U. Hayn-Leichsenring. 2016. "Evaluating Abstract Art: Relation between Term Usage, Subjective Ratings, Image Properties and Personality Traits." *Frontiers in Psychology* 7 (973).

Magsamen, Susan, and Ivy Ross. 2023. *Your Brain on Art: How the Arts Transform Us*. New York: Random House.

Mangla, Ravi. 2015. "True Blue." *The Paris Review*, June 8. https://www.theparisreview.org/blog/2015/06/08/true-blue/.

Marean, Curtis W., Miryam Bar-Matthews, Jocelyn Bernatchez, Erich Fisher, Paul Goldberg, Andy I. R. Herries, Zenobia Jacobs, Antonieta Jerardino, Panagiotis Karkanas, Tom Minichillo, Peter J. Nilssen, Erin Thompson, Ian Watts, and Hope M. Williams. 2007. "Early Human Use of Marine Resources and Pigment in South Africa during the Middle Pleistocene." *Nature* 449 (7164): 905–8.

Mason, David D. M., and Conal McCarthy. 2006. "'The Feeling of Exclusion': Young Peoples' Perceptions of Art Galleries." *Museum Management and Curatorship* 21 (1): 20–31. https://doi.org/10.1080/09644777 0600402101.

McClellan, Andrew. 2008. *The Art Museum from Boullée to Bilbao*. Berkeley: University of California Press.

McCouat, Philip. n.d. "The Life and Death of Mummy Brown." *Journal of Art in Society*. https://www.artinsociety.com/the-life-and-death-of-mummy-brown.html.

Meskin, Aaron, Mark Phelan, Margaret Moore, and Matthew Kieran. 2013. "Mere Exposure to Bad Art." *British Journal of Aesthetics* 53 (2): 139–64.

Miranda, Carolina A. 2020. "Are Art Museums Still Racist? The COVID Reset." *Los Angeles Times*, October 22, 2020.

Mitchell, Michaelyn, ed. 2021. *The Sleeve Should Be Illegal & Other Reflections on Art at the Frick*. New York: DelMonico Books/The Frick Collection.

Mullin, Caitlin, Gregor Hayn-Leichsenring, Christoph Redies, and Johan Wagemans. 2017. "The Gist of Beauty: An Investigation of Aesthetic Perception in Rapidly Presented Images." *Electronic Imaging* 29 (January): 248–56.

Munsell, Albert Henry. 1916. *A Color Notation: An Illustrated System Defining All Colors & Their Relations by Measured Scales of Hue, Value, and Chroma, Made in Solid Paint for the Accompanying Color Atlas*. Boston: G. H. Ellis.

Museum of Modern Art. 2008. *Color Chart: Reinventing Color: 1950 to Today*. New York: Museum of Modern Art. Exhibition catalog.

Nadal, Marcos, Víctor Gallardo, and Gisèle Marty. 2018. "Commentary: But Is It Really Art? The Classification of Images as 'Art'/'Not Art' and Correlation with Appraisal and Viewer Interpersonal Differences." *Frontiers in Psychology* 8 (2328).

Naghshineh, Sheila, Janet P. Hafler, Alexa R. Miller, Maria A. Blanco, Stuart R. Lipsitz, Rachel P. Dubroff, Shahram Khoshbin, and Joel T. Katz. 2008. "Formal Art Observation Training Improves Medical Students' Visual Diagnostic Skills." *Journal of General Internal Medicine* 23 (2008): 991–97.

National Endowment for the Arts. 1996. "Artists in the Work Force: Employment and Earnings, 1970 to 1990." Santa Ana, CA: Seven Locks Press.

———. 2008. "Artists in the Workforce, 1990–2005." Washington, DC: National Endowment for the Arts.

———. 2019. "Artists and Other Cultural Workers: A Statistical Portrait." Washington, DC: National Endowment for the Arts.

National Museum of Women in the Arts. 2022. "Get the Facts about Women in the Arts." NMWA.org. https://nmwa.org/support/advocacy/get-facts/.

Nehamas, Alexander. 2017. *Only a Promise of Happiness: The Place of Beauty in a World of Art*. Princeton, NJ: Princeton University Press.

Nelson, Maggie. 2009. *Bluets*. Seattle: Wave Books.

Neuendorf, Henri. 2016. "Art Demystified: Why Do Contemporary Artists Use So Many Studio Assistants?" *Artnet News*, July 14. https://news.artnet.com/art-world/art-demystified-the-use-of-assistants-549284.

———. 2017. "It's Official, 80% of Artists Represented at NYC's Top Galleries Are White." *Artnet News*,

June 2. https://news.artnet.com/art-world/new-york-galleries-study-979049#:~:text=And%20nearly %2020%25%20are%20Yale%20grads.&text=Courtesy%20of%20James%20Case%2DLeal.

Noë, Alva. 2011. "Art and the Limits of Neuroscience." *The New York Times*, December 4. https://archive .nytimes.com/opinionator.blogs.nytimes.com/2011/12/04/art-and-the-limits-of-neuroscience/.

Nzegwu, Nkiru. 2019. "African Art in Deep Time: De-race-ing Aesthetics and De-racializing Visual Art." *Journal of Aesthetics and Art Criticism* 77 (4): 367–78.

O'Doherty, Brian. 1986. *Inside the White Cube: The Ideology of the Gallery Space*. San Francisco: Lapis Press. https://arts.berkeley.edu/wp-content/uploads/2016/01/arc-of-life-ODoherty_Brian_Inside_the _White_Cube_The_Ideology_of_the_Gallery_Space.pdf.

Office of the New York City Comptroller. 2019. "The Creative Economy: Art, Culture, and Creativity in New York City." Comptroller.nyc.gov (October). https://comptroller.nyc.gov/wp-content/uploads /documents/Creative_Economy_102519.pdf.

Palmer, Stephen E., and Karen B. Schloss. 2010. "An Ecological Valence Theory of Human Color Prefer-ence." *Proceedings of the National Academy of Sciences* 107 (19): 8877–82.

Paper Monument, ed. 2009. *I Like Your Work: Art and Etiquette*. Brooklyn: n+1 Foundation.

———. 2012. *Draw It with Your Eyes Closed: The Art of the Art Assignment*. Brooklyn: n+1 Foundation.

Pelowski, Matthew. 2015. "Tears and Transformation: Feeling Like Crying as an Indicator of Insightful or 'Aesthetic' Experience with Art." *Frontiers in Psychology* 6 (1006).

Pelowski, Matthew, Giulia Cabbai, Hanna Brinkmann, Jan Mikuni, Lisa M. Hegelmaier, Michael Forster, Raphael Rosenberg, and Helmut Leder. 2020. "The Kitsch Switch—or (When) Do Experts Dislike Thomas Kinkade Art? A Study of Time-Based Evaluation Changes in Top-Down versus Bottom-Up Assessment." *Psychology of Aesthetics, Creativity, and the Arts* (March): 1–19.

Pelowski, Matthew, and Rebecca Chamberlain. 2023. "Where Do Artists Come From? A Review of the 'Typical' Visually Creative Life and Artistic Brain as a Basis for Discussing Neurodivergence or Neuro-degenerative Change." In *Art and Neurological Disorders*, edited by Alby Richard, Matthew Pelowski, and Blanca T. M. Spee, 25–63. New York: Humana.

Pelowski, Matthew, Gernot Gerger, Yasmine Chetouani, Patrick S. Markey, and Helmut Leder. 2017. "But Is It Really Art? The Classification of Images as 'Art'/'Not Art' and Correlation with Appraisal and Viewer Interpersonal Differences." *Frontiers in Psychology* 8 (1729).

Pelowski, Matthew, Andrea Graser, Eva Specker, Michael Forster, Josefine von Hinüber, and Helmut Leder. 2019. "Does Gallery Lighting Really Have an Impact on Appreciation of Art? An Ecologically Valid Study of Lighting Changes and the Assessment and Emotional Experience with Representational and Abstract Paintings." *Frontiers in Psychology* 10 (2148). https://www.frontiersin.org/articles/10.3389 /fpsyg.2019.02148/full.

Pelowski, Matthew, Helmut Leder, Vanessa Mitschke, Eva Specker, Gernot Gerger, Pablo P. L. Tinio, Elena Vaporova, Till Bieg, and Agnes Husslein-Arco. 2018. "Capturing Aesthetic Experiences with Installation Art: An Empirical Assessment of Emotion, Evaluations, and Mobile Eye Tracking in Olafur Eliasson's 'Baroque, Baroque!'" *Frontiers in Psychology* 9 (1255). https://doi.org/10.3389/fpsyg.2018.01255.

Pelowski, Matthew, Helmut Leder, and Pablo P. L. Tinio. 2017. "Creativity in the Visual Arts." In *The Cam-bridge Handbook of Creativity across Domains*, edited by James C. Kaufman, Vlad P. Glǎveanu, and John Baer, 80–109. Cambridge: Cambridge University Press.

Pelowski, Matthew, Tao Liu, Victor Palacios, and Fuminori Akiba. 2014. "When a Body Meets a Body: An Exploration of the Negative Impact of Social Interactions on Museum Experiences of Art." *Interna-tional Journal of Education & the Arts* 15 (14): 1–47.

Pelowski, Matthew, Patrick S. Markey, Michael Forster, Gernot Gerger, and Helmut Leder. 2017. "Move Me, Astonish Me… Delight My Eyes and Brain: The Vienna Integrated Model of Top-Down and Bottom-Up Processes in Art Perception (VIMAP) and Corresponding Affective, Evaluative, and Neurophysio-logical Correlates." *Physics of Life Reviews* 21 (2017): 80–125.

Perl, Jed. 2005. *New Art City*. New York: Alfred A. Knopf.

Pihko, Elina, Anne Virtanen, Veli-Matti Saarinen, Sebastian Pannasch, Lotta Hirvenkari, Timo Tos-savainen, Arto Haapala, and Riitta Hari. 2011. "Experiencing Art: The Influence of Expertise and Painting Abstraction Level." *Frontiers in Human Neuroscience* 5 (94): 1–10.

Pogrebin, Robin. 2017. "Art Gallery Closures Grow for Small and Midsize Dealers." Arts, *The New York Times*, June 25. https://www.nytimes.com/2017/06/25/arts/design/art-gallery-closures-grow-for -small-and-midsize-dealers.html.

———. 2020. "Black Gallerists Press Forward despite a Market That Holds Them Back." Arts, *The New York Times*, June 21. https://www.nytimes.com/2020/06/21/arts/design/art-basel-black-owned-galleries.html.

Pollock, Lindsay. 2006. *The Girl with the Gallery: Edith Gregor Halpert and the Making of the New York Art Market*. New York: PublicAffairs.

Porter, Mildred C. B. 1938. *Behavior of the Average Visitor in the Peabody Museum of Natural History, Yale University*. Washington, DC: American Association of Museums.

Potts, Richard, Anna K. Behrensmeyer, J. Tyler Faith, Christian A. Tryon, Alison S. Brooks, John E. Yellen, Alan L. Deino, Rahab Kinyanjui, Jennifer B. Clark, Catherine M. Haradon, Naomi E. Levin, Hanneke J. M. Meijer, Elizabeth G. Veatch, R. Bernhart Owen, and Robin W. Renaut. 2018. "Environmental Dynamics during the Onset of the Middle Stone Age in Eastern Africa." *Science* 360 (6384): 86–90.

Powers, John. 2012. "I Was Jeff Koons's Studio Serf." *The New York Times Magazine*, August 17. https://www.nytimes.com/2012/08/19/magazine/i-was-jeff-koonss-studio-serf.html.

Prinz, Jesse. 2011. "Emotion and Aesthetic Value." In *The Aesthetic Mind: Philosophy and Psychology*, edited by Elisabeth Schellekens and Peter Goldie, 71–88. Oxford: Oxford University Press. https://doi.org/10.1093/acprof:oso/9780199691517.003.0006.

Prum, Richard O. 2013. "Coevolutionary Aesthetics in Human and Biotic Artworlds." *Biology & Philosophy* 28 (2013): 811–32.

——. 2017. *The Evolution of Beauty: How Darwin's Forgotten Theory of Mate Choice Shapes the Animal World—and Us*. New York: Anchor.

Ramachandran, V. S. 2011. *The Tell-Tale Brain: A Neuroscientist's Quest for What Makes Us Human*. New York: W. W. Norton.

Randolph-Quinney, Patrick, and Anthony Sinclair. 2018. "The Revolution That Wasn't: African Tools Push Back the Origins of Human Technological Innovation." *The Conversation*, March 15. https://theconversation.com/the-revolution-that-wasnt-african-tools-push-back-the-origins-of-human-technological-innovation-93231.

Reitstätter, Luise, Hanna Brinkmann, Thiago Santini, Eva Specker, Zoya Dare, Flora Bakondi, Anna Miscená, Enkelejda Kasneci, Helmut Leder, and Raphael Rosenberg. 2020. "The Display Makes a Difference: A Mobile Eye Tracking Study on the Perception of Art before and after a Museum's Rearrangement." *Journal of Eye Movement Research* 13 (2).

Resch, Magnus. 2016. "The Global Art Gallery Report." New York: Phaidon.

——. (2015) 2018. *Management of Art Galleries*. New York: Phaidon.

Restrepo Baena, O. J., Á. Forero Pinilla, and S. Díaz Bello. 2009. "Characterization and Concentration of Specularite as Natural Pigment to Manufacture Anticorrosives Paints." *Revista Mexicana de Física* 55 (1): 123–26.

Robinson, Edward Stevens. 1928. "The Behavior of the Museum Visitor." Washington, DC: American Association of Museums.

Roebroeks, Wil, Mark J. Sier, Trine Kellberg Nielsen, Dimitri De Loecker, Josep Maria Parés, Charles E. S. Arps, and Herman J. Mücher. 2012. "Use of Red Ochre by Early Neandertals." *Proceedings of the National Academy of Sciences* 109 (6): 1889–94.

Rosenthal, Mark. 2003. *Understanding Installation Art: From Duchamp to Holzer*. Munich: Prestel.

Ross, Alison. 2007. *The Aesthetic Paths of Philosophy*. Stanford, CA: Stanford University Press.

Rule, Alix, and David Levine. 2018. "International Art English." *Triple Canopy*, November. https://canopycanopycanopy.com/contents/international_art_english.

Russell, Legacy. 2020. *Glitch Feminism: A Manifesto*. Brooklyn: Verso.

Sagmeister, Stefan, and Jessica Walsh. 2018. *Beauty*. New York: Phaidon.

Salle, David. 2016. *How to See: Looking, Talking, and Thinking about Art*. New York: W. W. Norton.

Saltz, Jerry. 2014. "Zombies on the Walls: Why Does So Much New Abstraction Look the Same?" *New York Magazine*, June 17. https://www.vulture.com/2014/06/why-new-abstract-paintings-look-the-same.html.

——. 2018. "How to Be an Artist." *New York Magazine*, November 27. https://www.vulture.com/2018/11/jerry-saltz-how-to-be-an-artist.html.

Sanchez, Michael. 2013. "2011: Art and Transmission." *Artforum*. https://www.artforum.com/print/201306/2011-art-and-transmission-41241.

Scarry, Elaine. 1998. "On Beauty and Being Just." Presented at the Tanner Lectures on Human Values, March.

Schepman, Astrid, Paul Rodway, Sarah J. Pullen, and Julie Kirkham. 2015. "Shared Liking and Association Valence for Representational Art but Not Abstract Art." *Journal of Vision* 15 (5): 1–10.

Schwabe, Kana, Claudia Menzel, Caitlin Mullin, Johan Wagemans, and Christoph Redies. 2018. "Gist Perception of Image Composition in Abstract Artworks." *i-Perception* 9 (3): 1–25.

Scott, Walter. 2014. *Wendy*. Toronto: Koyama Press.

——. 2016. *Wendy's Revenge*. Toronto: Koyama Press.

——. 2020. *Wendy, Master of Art*. Montreal: Drawn & Quarterly.

Scruton, Roger. 2011. *Beauty: A Very Short Introduction*. Oxford: Oxford University Press.

Seaman, Natasha. 2018. "Looking for Leonardo in Verrocchio's Studio." *Hyperallergic*, September 22,. https://hyperallergic.com/461278/leonardo-discoveries-from-verrocchios-studio-yale-university-art-gallery-leonardo-davinci/.

Semir Zeki. 1999. *Inner Vision: An Exploration of Art and the Brain*. Oxford: Oxford University Press.

Sesser, Stan. 2011. "The Art Assembly Line." Life and Style, *The Wall Street Journal*, June 3. https://www.wsj.com/articles/SB10001424052702303745304576357681741418282.

Sharp, Sonja. 2019. "Day-Glo Masterpieces Are Fading. A Conservator and Her Team Are Racing to Save Them." *Los Angeles Times*, September 5, 2019.

Shepherd, Kathrine, and Moshe Bar. 2011. "Preference for Symmetry: Only on Mars?" *Perception* 40 (10): 1254–56.

Shimamura, Arthur P. 2013. *Experiencing Art: In the Brain of the Beholder*. New York: Oxford University Press.

Shiner, Larry. 2001. *The Invention of Art: A Cultural History*. Chicago: University of Chicago Press.

Shnayerson, Michael. 2019. *BOOM: Mad Money, Mega Dealers, and the Rise of Contemporary Art*. New York: PublicAffairs.

Siddall, Ruth. 2018. "Mineral Pigments in Archaeology: Their Analysis and the Range of Available Materials." *Minerals* 8 (5): 201.

Sidhu, David M., Katrina H. McDougall, Shaela T. Jalava, and Glen E. Bodner. 2018. "Prediction of Beauty and Liking Ratings for Abstract and Representational Paintings Using Subjective and Objective Measures." *PLoS ONE* 13 (7): e0200431.

Simon, Ruth, and Rob Barry. 2013. "Arts-Focused Colleges Rack Up Most Student Debt." US, *The Wall Street Journal*, February 18. https://www.wsj.com/articles/SB10001424127887324432004578306610055834952.

Skov, Martin, and Marcos Nadal. 2017. "Commentary: What Is Art Good For? The Socio-epistemic Value of Art." *Frontiers in Human Neuroscience* 11 (602).

———. 2018. "Art Is Not Special: An Assault on the Last Lines of Defense against the Naturalization of the Human Mind." *Reviews in the Neurosciences* 29 (6): 699–702.

Smith, Jeffrey K., and Lisa F. Smith. 2001. "Spending Time on Art." *Empirical Studies of the Arts* 19 (2): 229–36.

Smith, Lisa F., Jeffrey K. Smith, and Pablo P. L. Tinio. 2017. "Time Spent Viewing Art and Reading Labels." *Psychology of Aesthetics, Creativity, and the Arts* 11 (1): 77–85.

Snapper, Leslie, Cansu Oranç, Angelina Hawley-Dolan, Jenny Nissel, and Ellen Winner. 2015. "Your Kid Could Not Have Done That: Even Untutored Observers Can Discern Intentionality and Structure in Abstract Expressionist Art." *Cognition* 137 (April): 154–65. https://doi.org/10.1016/j.cognition.2014.12.009.

Specker, Eva, Michael Forster, Hanna Brinkmann, Jane Boddy, Beatrice Immelmann, Jürgen Goller, Matthew Pelowski, Raphael Rosenberg, and Helmut Leder. 2020. "Warm, Lively, Rough? Assessing Agreement on Aesthetic Effects of Artworks." *PLoS ONE* 15 (5): e0232083.

Spector, Nancy, ed. 2005. *Guggenheim Museum Collection A to Z*. New York: Guggenheim Museum Publications.

Spehar, Branka, Colin W. G. Clifford, Ben R. Newell, and Richard P. Taylor. 2003. "Universal Aesthetic of Fractals." *Computers & Graphics* 27: 813–20.

Starr, G. Gabrielle. (2013) 2015. *Feeling Beauty: The Neuroscience of Aesthetic Experience*. Cambridge, MA: MIT Press.

St. Clair, Kassia. 2017. *The Secret Lives of Color*. New York: Penguin.

stewart, jude. 2011. "Coking Up Color." *Gastronomica* 11 (3): 53–59.

Syme, Patrick. (1821) 2020. *Werner's Nomenclature of Colours: Adapted to Zoology, Botany, Chemistry, Mineralogy, Anatomy, and the Arts*. Washington, DC: Smithsonian Books.

Tarmy, James. 2015. "The Dangers of Investing in Art." *Bloomberg Businessweek*, February 12. https://www.bloomberg.com/news/articles/2015-02-12/the-dangers-of-investing-in-art-anselm-reyle-s-decline.

Taylor, Richard P., Branka Spehar, Paul Van Donkelaar, and Caroline M. Hagerhall. 2011. "Perceptual and Physiological Responses to Jackson Pollock's Fractals." *Frontiers in Human Neuroscience* 5. https://doi.org/10.3389/fnhum.2011.00060.

"Techniques: The Passing of Mummy Brown." 1964. *Time*, October 2.

Teufel, Christoph, Steven C. Dakin, and Paul C. Fletcher. 2018. "Prior Object-Knowledge Sharpens Properties of Early Visual Feature-Detectors." *Scientific Reports* 8 (10853).

Thompson, Don. 2008. *The $12 Million Stuffed Shark: The Curious Economics of Contemporary Art*. New York: St. Martin's Griffin.

———. 2014. *The Supermodel and the Brillo Box: Back Stories and Peculiar Economics from the World of Contemporary Art*. New York: Palgrave Macmillan.

Thornton, Sarah. 2008. *Seven Days in the Art World*. New York: W. W. Norton.

———. 2014. *33 Artists in 3 Acts*. New York: W. W. Norton.

Tilley, Christopher, Webb Keane, Küchler Susanne, Michael Rowlands, and Patricia Spyer, eds. 2006. *Handbook of Material Culture*. London: SAGE.

Tomkins, Calvin. 2008. *Lives of the Artists*. New York: Henry Holt.

Topaz, Chad M., Bernhard Klingenberg, Daniel Turek, Brianna Heggeseth, Pamela E. Harris, Julie C. Blackwood, C. Ondine Chavoya, Steven Nelson, and Kevin M. Murphy. 2019. "Diversity of Artists in Major U.S. Museums." PLoS ONE 14 (3): e0212852.

Vail, Karole. 2009. *The Museum of Non-objective Painting: Hilla Rebay and the Origins of the Solomon R. Guggenheim Museum*. New York: Guggenheim Museum.

Van de Cruys, Sander, and Johan Wagemans. 2011. "Putting Reward in Art: A Tentative Prediction Error Account of Visual Art." *i-Perception* 2 (2011): 1035–62.

Verhavert, San, Johan Wagemans, and M. Dorothee Augustin. 2018. "Beauty in the Blink of an Eye: The Time Course of Aesthetic Experiences." *British Journal of Psychology* 109 (2018): 63–84. https://doi .org/10.1111/bjop.12258.

Verpooten, Jan, and Siegfried Dewitte. 2016. "The Conundrum of Modern Art: Prestige Driven Coevolutionary Aesthetics Trumps Evolutionary Aesthetics among Art Experts." *Human Nature* 28 (1): 16–38.

Viengkham, Catherine, Zoey Isherwood, and Branka Spehar. 2019. "Fractal-Scaling Properties as Aesthetic Primitives in Vision and Touch." *Axiomathes* 32 (2022): 869–88.

Villani, Daniela, Francesca Morganti, Pietro Cipresso, Simona Ruggi, Giuseppe Riva, and Gabriella Gilli. 2015. "Visual Exploration Patterns of Human Figures in Action: An Eye Tracker Study with Art Paintings." *Frontiers in Psychology* 6 (1636).

Voorsanger, Catherine Hoover, and John K. Howat, eds. 2000. *Art and the Empire City: New York, 1825–1861*. New York: Metropolitan Museum of Art.

Wade, Nicholas J., Josef Brožek, and Jiří Hoskovec. 2001. *Purkinje's Vision: The Dawning of Neuroscience*. Mahwah, NJ: Lawrence Erlbaum.

Wallert, Arie, Erma Hermens, and Marja Peek, eds. 1995. *Historical Painting Techniques, Materials, and Studio Practice: Preprints of a Symposium Held at the University of Leiden, the Netherlands, 26–29 June 1995*. Marina Del Rey, CA: Getty Conservation Institute.

Walsh, David, Elizabeth Pearce, Steven Pinker, Geoffrey Miller, Brian Boyd, and Mark A. Changizi. 2016. *On the Origin of Art*. Hobart, Tasmania: Museum of Old and New Art.

Warburton, Nigel. 2003. *The Art Question*. London: Routledge.

Warr, Tracey, ed. 2007. *The Artist's Body*. London: Phaidon.

Watts, Ian, Michael Chazan, and Jayne Wilkins. 2016. "Early Evidence for Brilliant Ritualized Display: Specularite Use in the Northern Cape (South Africa) between ~500 and ~300 Ka." *Current Anthropology* 57 (3): 287–310.

White, Roger. 2015. *The Contemporaries: Travels in the 21st-Century Art World*. New York: Bloomsbury.

Wiley, Chris. 2018a. "The Toxic Legacy of Zombie Formalism, Part 1: How an Unhinged Economy Spawned a New World of 'Debt Aesthetics.'" *Artnet News*, July 26. https://news.artnet.com/opinion/history -zombie-formalism-1318352.

———. 2018b. "The Toxic Legacy of Zombie Formalism, Part 2: How the Art System's Entropy Is Raising the Political Stakes for Culture." *Artnet News*, July 30. https://news.artnet.com/opinion/the-toxic-legacy -of-zombie-formalism-part-2-1318355.

Wilson, Carl. 2014. *Let's Talk about Love: Why Other People Have Such Bad Taste*. New York: Bloomsbury.

Wilson, Daniel. 2018. "The Japanese Tea Ceremony and Pancultural Definitions of Art." *Journal of Aesthetics and Art Criticism* 76 (1): 33–44.

Winner, Ellen. 2019. *How Art Works: A Psychological Exploration*. New York: Oxford University Press.

Winston, Andrew S., and Gerald C. Cupchik. 1992. "The Evaluation of High Art and Popular Art by Naive and Experienced Viewers." *Visual Arts Research* 18 (1): 1–14.

Wolf, Sibylle, Rimtautas Dapschauskas, Elizabeth Velliky, Harald Floss, Andrew W. Kandel, and Nicholas J. Conard. 2018. "The Use of Ochre and Painting during the Upper Paleolithic of the Swabian Jura in the Context of the Development of Ochre Use in Africa and Europe." *Open Archaeology* 4: 185–205.

Wolfe, Tom. (1975) 2008. *The Painted Word*. New York: Picador.

Woodbury, Charles H. 1925. *The Art of Seeing: Mental Training through Drawing*. New York: Scribner.

Wu, Chin-Tao. 2002. *Privatising Culture: Corporate Art Intervention since the 1980s*. London: Verso.

Zeki, Semir. 1999. "Art and the Brain." *Daedalus* 127 (2): 71–103.

———. 2019. "Notes towards a (Neurobiological) Definition of Beauty." *Gestalt Theory* 41 (2): 107–12.

Zukin, Sharon. (1982) 2014. *Loft Living: Culture and Capital in Urban Change*. New Brunswick, NJ: Rutgers University Press.

INDEX

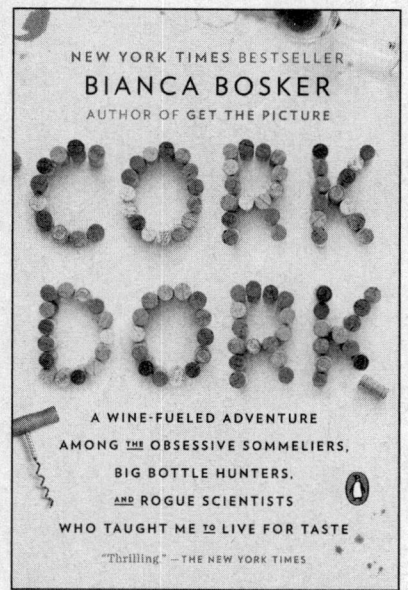